Leading Open Innovation

LEADING OPEN INNOVATION

edited by Anne Sigismund Huff, Kathrin M. Möslein, and Ralf Reichwald

The MIT Press
Cambridge, Massachusetts
London, England

MIT Press books may be purchased at special quantity discounts for business or sales promotional use. For information, please email special_sales@mitpress.mit.edu or write to Special Sales Department, The MIT Press, 55 Hayward Street, Cambridge, MA 02142.

This book was set in Stone Sans and Stone Serif by Toppan Best-set Premedia Limited. Printed and bound in the United States of America.

Library of Congress Cataloging-in-Publication Data

Leading open innovation / edited by Anne Sigismund Huff, Kathrin M. Möslein, and Ralf Reichwald.
p. cm.
Includes bibliographical references and index.
ISBN 978-0-262-01849-4 (hardcover : alk. paper)
1. Technological innovations—Economic aspects. 2. Diffusion of innovations. 3. Open innovation. I. Huff, Anne Sigismund. II. Möslein, Kathrin M. III. Reichwald, Ralf
HD45.L337 2013
658.4'063—dc23
2012020392

10 9 8 7 6 5 4 3 2 1

Contents

Acknowledgments

This book is sponsored by the Peter Pribilla Foundation. The foundations' goal is to promote research and knowledge transfer in the domain of innovation and leadership. Peter and Hannelore Pribilla's personal efforts in this area are described in more detail at the end of the volume. We gratefully dedicate this publication to their memory.

We also acknowledge the many people who have facilitated the annual meetings of the Pribilla network since 2006. Special appreciation goes to Claudia Lehmann, who provides essential organization of the meetings, Ilsa Brink, who designed and produced the booklets that summarized each of the first four meetings, and Vivek Velamui, who organized figures and supported the editors in many other ways as we moved toward publication.

Of course, the most important energy came from network participants. Their interest in and knowledge about open innovation led to wonderful conversations and enduring friendships. A book can only be a static snapshot of our ongoing exchange, but we hope that readers are also engaged by our commitment to understand and advance open innovation.

I WHY AND HOW OPEN INNOVATION WORKS

1 Introduction to Open Innovation

Anne Sigismund Huff, Kathrin M. Möslein, and Ralf Reichwald

Introduction

There are two different types of open innovation. The first is self-organized and self-motivated collaborative activity to achieve a common goal. The second is an organizational strategy to broaden innovation boundaries, often while retaining internal R&D capabilities as well.

An example of open innovation driven by individual contributors is the surprising speed with which publically sourced Wikipedia challenged the niche that the Encyclopedia Britannica had dominated for two centuries. As described in chapter 11 by Andrei Villarroel, in 2000 the Encyclopedia Britannica was employing 4,000 experts to compose a rather expensive 32-volume set of books that contained 65,000 articles written in English. It was widely taken as the best summary of human knowledge available for a general audience. Yet ten years later, Wikipedia was the sixth most frequently consulted site on the Internet. Self-selected contributors from around the world had created a much more encyclopedic *free* resource of over *3.5 million* articles in English, with parallel offerings in 279 other languages. Thirty-six sites in widely used languages went well beyond the Encyclopedia Britannica by each offering at least 100,000 articles.

Several aspects of founder Jimmy Wales's philosophy appear to have been critical in motivating these contributions. Wikipedia was conceived as a free, global site for collecting and dispensing information. Its articles were expected to be written from a neutral point of view and to be accurate, but were not expected to be perfect. Contributors could suggest revisions of current content as long as they followed a code of conduct that assumed good faith and avoided personal attacks (Lakhani and McAffee 2007).

Despite the phenomenal amount of material that quickly accrued and its widespread access, many people were dismissive of this effort. As one junior high school teacher said when she banned student references to Wikipedia, "I am not interested in what someone's Aunt Nancy thinks about your topic." Then in 2005, less than five years after going online, a study published in *Nature* magazine reported that the quality of articles from Wikipedia and Encyclopedia Britannica was basically even, based on a blind review by subject experts (Gilles 2005). After a period of fierce debate, discussion of quality diminished, though it continues.[1] At the same time, Wikipedia keeps growing, along with staff and volunteer efforts to improve input and editing.

Wikipedia is an example of what Eric von Hippel (2006) calls the "democratization" of innovation. In chapter 8 he suggests that organizations as institutions and managers as important drivers of innovation are becoming obsolete. In a groundbreaking empirical study von Hippel and his colleagues support this view with an estimate that UK investment in development and modification of products by *private* individuals is more than two times *corporate* investment in R&D (von Hippel, de Jong, and Flowers 2010). Harnessing this widely dispersed creative energy is the great promise of open innovation.

At the same time organizations are becoming active participants in open innovation by following a somewhat different logic. Relatively small retailers like Threadless, Muji, and Quirky have shown how products can be designed, selected, and marketed by customers (Seybold 2006 provides an early view of customer-led innovation). Other companies are involved in a much broader range of activities. The most-cited example of success is Procter & Gamble. With experience in over 1,000 partnerships, P&G attributed a decade of increasing sales to open innovation.[2] By the end of 2011 other well-known sponsors of OI initiatives included Apple, eBay, Clorox, Cisco, Ericsson, GlaxoSmithKline, General Mills, HP, Johnson & Johnson, Nestlé, Phillips, Royal Dutch Shell, SAP, Whirlpool, Xerox, among many others.

General Mills' G-Win site is particularly well organized. The homepage says:

> At General Mills, we believe that there is a great opportunity for us to enhance and accelerate our innovation efforts by teaming up with world-class innovators from outside of the company. To facilitate this effort, we created the General Mills Worldwide Innovation Network (G-WIN) to actively seek partners who can help us deliver breakthrough innovation in the following categories:
>
> **Products** New products that fit within a General Mills brand or solve a customer need.
>
> **Packaging** Novel packaging technologies or new, consumer-friendly formats.
>
> **Processes** Improvements to quality, efficiency and profitability.
>
> **Ingredients** New ingredients to enhance taste, texture, quality or health benefits.
>
> **Technologies** Enabling food technologies.
>
> **Digital** Emerging digital marketing technologies.[3]

Specific examples of projects in each area are supplemented by stories focused on how customers, suppliers, academics, consumers, employees, and entrepreneurs have made contributions.

Definitions of Open Innovation

To formalize the definition of open innovation it is useful to distinguish invention and innovation. Invention, in patent law as well as in common conversation, is typically defined as the creation of something new, or something that did not previously exist. The word "innovation" can be used the same way, but more accurately is defined as translating an invention into something that people will pay for—it brings something new to market. A few companies have aspired to invent; many more have worked on developing the ability to innovate. Historically, as companies grew in size and complexity, and technologies also became complex, research and development departments grew as well. Over several centuries, secrecy and control were seen as the requirements of success.

While historically there are interesting examples of calls for open invention, current attention to open innovation is the result of the limits of internal, closed development. Henry Chesbrough defined the departure from established practice when he said "open innovation assumes . . . firms can and should use external as well as internal ideas and internal and external paths to market" (2006, p. 1). Five years later Stefan Lindegaard, an author, company advisor, and blogger interested in open innovation elaborated:

> Open innovation should be viewed as a two-way process in which companies have an inbound process in which they bring in ideas, technologies, or other resources needed to develop their own business and an outbound process in which they out-license or sell their own ideas, technologies, and other resources. This should take place during all stages of the innovation process. (2010, p. 4)

Authors of chapters in this volume have been interested in further developing these definitions. Mitchell Tseng, who wrote chapter 15, proposes that the prerequisites of contemporary open innovation projects include:

- a platform (almost always electronic) that promotes information exchange;
- leadership (frequently distributed) that coordinates participation of varied actors and organizes solutions; and
- agreed norms of behavior (often democratic) that specify how resources will be identified, how assets will be exchanged, and how outcomes of interaction will be valued.

The projects he and others describe in this volume point to other details:

1. The ecosystem supporting OI typically is much larger than required by other innovation efforts and is often global in its reach.

2. Complicated problems typically are modularized so that they can be simultaneously addressed by multiple contributors.

3. In contrast to well-established innovation efforts driven by trained professionals, there are lower (often no) a priori qualifications for participation in OI.

4. Participation (especially by solution providers) tends to be voluntary rather than assigned.

5. Intrinsic and/or social motivation is important for many participants.

6. Costs of exchange are relatively low.

7. Transparency both in process and content is valued and used to improve results over time.

8. Control systems tend to be limited and unobtrusive, though they often become more complex in use.

9. Often task-related information is shared freely among participants.

10. Often leaders are selected by those doing the work.

11. Users and customers can be crucial contributors of ideas, inventions, and innovations.

12. The solution set tends to be more varied than solutions produced in other ways.

13. Solution advancing contributions frequently come from people with experience in subject domains unanticipated by problem specifiers.

14. The most successful solutions often improve previously developed ideas.

In aggregate, these characteristics establish a mindset about discovering and developing new ideas that can be used at multiple levels by different kinds of participants to achieve different degrees of openness. As a set, however, they are a startling departure from images of closed innovation that extend from the lonely eccentric working to develop what may become a brilliant new product to the well-run R&D labs of experts found in high-science companies and universities. Closed innovation is carried out by specialists who are employees (think scientists in Bell Labs, Merck, and many other organizations). While a growing number of companies now are broadening their approach, the logic of this kind of closed innovation still has considerable influence on individual actions, organizational investments, and almost all legal systems.[4] This volume examines the limits of that logic.

Why Open Innovation Now?

The growing attraction of open innovation is the result of changes in social organization and markets. Five trends in particular lie behind open innovation as an important strategic option.

First, increasing interactions among individuals and groups around the world are generating new and more varied demands for products, services, and experiences. This is a first important impetus toward OI, made stronger by the growing number of stakeholders who expect to contribute to problem definition and solution.

Luckily, a second development—technological changes that help innovators quickly connect across space and time—facilitates contribution. Collaboration is increasing because of advances in the way goods and services can be produced and distributed. The possibility of cheaply creating prototypes that until recently required expensive equipment and large-scale operations is of particular importance. Individuals and small groups, in varied places and with varied access to resources, have more opportunities to invent and innovate than they have had in the past.

A third contribution to the growth of open innovation is that organizations need more ideas and more varied ideas to face growing global competition and its cost-cutting standards. This pressure faces all organizations—public and private, large and small. Almost all organizational leaders are finding they do not have the intellectual resources they need to meet market demands and opportunities. Opening the innovation process therefore has strong attraction.

Economic uncertainty can be identified as a fourth force that makes leveraging limited innovation resources attractive. As mentioned above, the success of Procter & Gamble's Connect + Develop program has been particularly compelling. P&G's CEO A. G. Lafley followed the lead of pioneers IBM, Eli Lilly, and a few other companies to aggressively channel a major portion of the company's innovation budget to work with outsiders in 2000 (Huston and Sakkab 2006). The strategy is considered a key factor in P&G's renewed sales growth, even during recent economic turmoil.

Finally, an increasingly accessible international labor pool makes open innovation attractive. It is widely recognized that both well-trained workers and low-cost workers can be found in many different locations. The more specific impact of labor on innovation was first expressed by Bill Joy, a founder of Sun Microsystems:

> No matter who you are, most of the smart people work for someone else.[5]

By extension, no matter how insightful the individual, group or organization, an enormous, global pool of people with complementary intelligence and skill is available to help advance innovative ideas.

Purpose of This Volume and Chapter Overviews

This volume describes OI's search for smart people who might expand the space for innovation. It reflects international, cross-sector, and transdisciplinary interests among contributors from the United States, Germany, France, Finland, the United Kingdom, Portugal, Tunisia, Austria, and China working in large multinational organizations, academic institutions, or entrepreneurial projects. They are part of the Peter Pribilla network, which Ralf Reichwald describes at the end of the volume as a point of contact that supports overlapping interests in innovation and leadership.

The objective of the volume is to describe the broad canvas of OI practices, its participants, and future promise. The authors believe the use of open innovation is, in and of itself, a major innovation in the way innovation can be achieved. Since almost all aspects of OI depart from the practices of closed innovation (which include, as noted above, problem definition, participation, control, motivation, cost, information exchange, organizational processes, outputs, and evaluation), it seems obvious that the way OI is managed must involve innovation as well. Yet understanding the demands of open innovation, in our minds and the minds of many observers, is only an interim step. As discussed in the epilogue of this volume, once open innovation becomes established and is understood, it can and should become part of an integrated innovation strategy to successfully bring new offerings to market.

Figure 1.1, based on a graphic used in Siemens and shown in chapter 2, provides an overview. It suggests on the x-axis that the steps of innovation are blurring while the number of potential contributors shown on the y-axis is vastly expanding. We discuss results of these developments under three headings: the way open innovation works, the contributions of primary participants, and promising future developments.

How Open Innovation Works

In chapter 2, Thomas Lackner provides an overview of the OI landscape from the perspective of a large multinational corporation. He emphasizes that all innovation projects must generate money-making products and services—an idea, we observe, that has recently been strongly embraced by many social entrepreneurs interested in the public good as well. Lackner describes the increasing budget devoted to outside innovation by large companies around the world, and then provides illustrative examples from the broad range of OI activities underway in different units of his company. The smart people sought for Siemens's OI projects are sometimes solicited from inside the company. Other projects reach out to targeted groups of outsiders. In

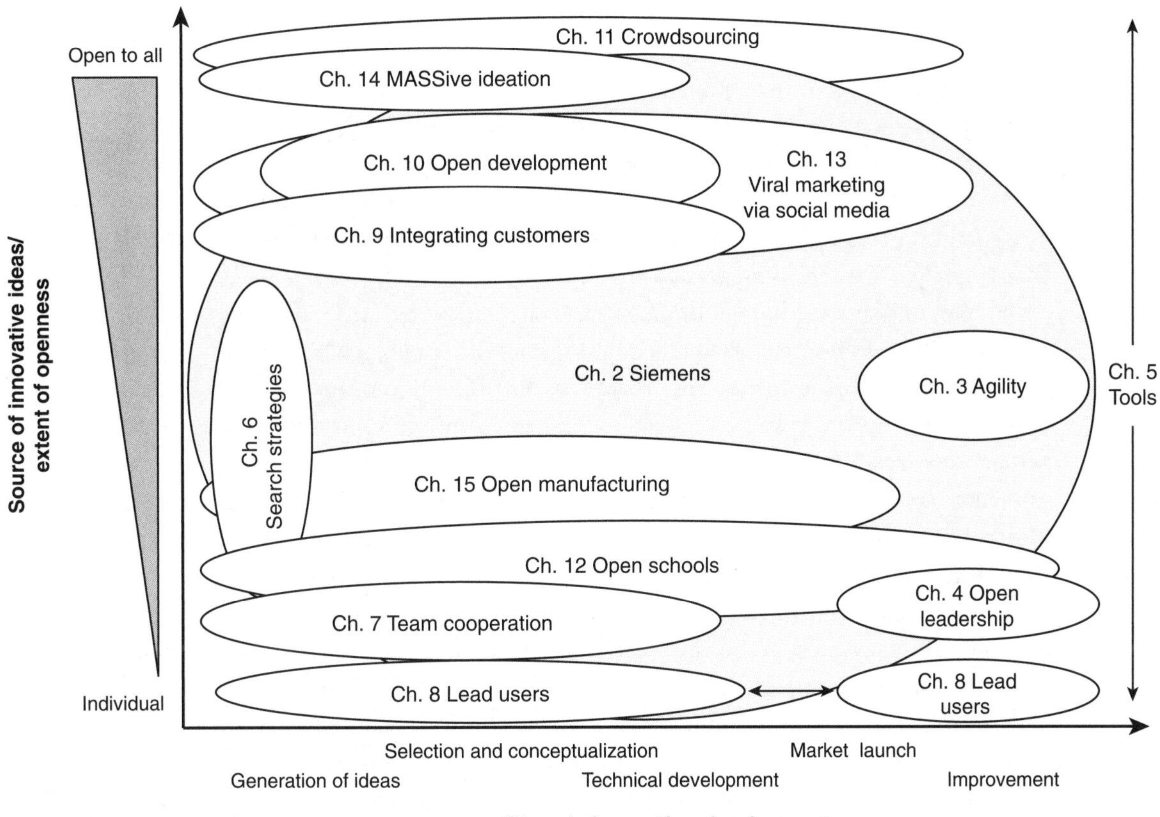

Figure 1.1
Overview of chapters in *Leading Open Innovation*

some cases an open call for contributions is made, often facilitated by independent e-brokers. OI projects vary in their use of these and other possibilities over the course of product and service development. Thus leaders have the very challenging task of defining needed knowledge and bringing knowledge-holders together across complicated organizational structures.

It is interesting that leaders of very successful organizations are taking up this challenge. In chapter 3, Yves Doz reports on a study carried out with Mikko Kosonen, currently head of the Finnish National Fund for Innovation and until recently the chief strategy officer at Nokia. The study focused on six IT companies, including Nokia, an early adopter of OI practices that has nonetheless struggled to maintain its position as an industry innovator. A central conclusion of the study is that actions that sustain growth and high performance of leading information technology firms create rigidities over time that "require strategic processes to be decentralized, distributed, internally participative, and (selectively) open externally."

Doz focuses on an organization's leaders as smart contributors to this process. Rebuilding agility is a process of increasing internal tension via more varied information sources while simultaneously addressing strategic, leadership, and resource issues. The energy for this very challenging task comes from emotional commitment—a topic that is rarely discussed in organizational life.

Companies that have not yet found success also can benefit from open innovation. Rudolf Gröger was responsible for the rapid turnaround of O_2, a mobile phone service in the German market at that time owned by British Telecom. In chapter 4, Gröger describes how open access to performance and other information was a key aspect of achieving profitability, which also focused on rebranding and repositioning services offered. Everyone in the organization is a smart person in charge of change. In Gröger's view, leaders must lead by example and encourage people in the organization to use their emotional energy. The most difficult leadership task, however, is to work on everything at once. In his words, "there is a logical chain of things that must be done, and they all depend on each other." As organizations become more open to inputs, this perennial leadership challenge is exacerbated.

Kathrin Möslein concludes the first part of the volume by laying out five categories of tools available for open innovation in chapter 5. This chapter returns to the idea that open innovation is advancing on two fronts: among individuals who are affiliated by common interests rather than institutional ties, and among organizations that are discovering new ways to blend internal efforts with the contributions of outsiders. She describes innovation contests, innovation markets, communities, toolkits, and technologies that leaders might use to increase smart contributions to their innovation efforts.

Open Innovation Participants

The second section of this volume looks in more detail at various players involved in OI. Chapter 6 focuses on tactics for finding innovative ideas shared among peer organizations. John Bessant has worked with Bettina von Stamm to promote an on-going series of innovation workshops in the United Kingdom, Denmark, Germany, France, and other countries. The smart people for developing innovations who they describe are managers from different organizations with OI experience. Leaders of other organizations are encouraged to try strategies that OI pioneers have used successfully, but also to think about whether their organization has the mechanisms and people skills to translate potentially profitable but unfamiliar ideas into practice.

In chapter 7, Lynda Gratton discusses how internal exchange of information supports innovation. Her research shows a high correlation between cooperation within a group and knowledge transfer across group boundaries. According to her data, the smartest contributors to team efforts have strong contacts outside the team. Gratton suggests that leaders consider when organizational boundaries protect valuable knowledge and when they stymie it. Her even stronger advice is that leaders create projects that ignite the latent energy for cooperation found in every organization.

Eric von Hippel looks at how individuals innovate in a wide variety of situations in chapter 8. A diverse group of people responding to their own and others' needs is the source of smart ideas in his view. Many develop relatively minor innovations, but "lead users" tend to be more visionary and help organizational leaders understand trends in the market. This group is ahead of, but similar to, customers in the broader market. Examples in the chapter come from many organizations, from librarians to sports enthusiasts, that are interesting reminders that innovations occur in many different settings.

A closely related topic is covered in chapter 9, written by Frank Piller and Christoph Ihl. Piller's team does research on the tools available to companies that want to involve customers in decisions about product design, production, and marketing. The chapter shows how smart customers can be involved in co-creating new products and services. Leaders must decide, however, on suitable targets for co-creation. They must consider how to integrate co-creation with organizational processes. And they must be aware of and overcome the power of NIH "not invented here" reactions to these ideas.

Karim Lakhani moves to the contributors' point of view. In chapter 10 he describes modular collective problem-solving activity that is often motivated by intrinsic rewards. These development projects tend to have peer leaders who promote a common view of the work being done. They flourish in open organizational structures. The smart people in these projects are willing to work on problems outside of their specialty and build on solutions proposed by others. Leaders of organizations who want to tap this source have to learn to post problems to these diverse communities, rather than take on the problem-solving role themselves.

Chapter 11, on motivating firm-sponsored e-collective work, looks at an even broader range of contributors. Andrei Villarroel describes "crowdsourcing" projects carried out by large numbers of geographically distributed individuals acting independently but contributing to a collective whole. He then develops a model showing how OI squeezes firms to pay more attention to complex tasks that are less easily addressed by innovative individuals and groups.

Trends in Open Innovation

OI decentralizes innovation and potentially accelerates learning as it does so. That means formal training may be less important because many individuals find it easier to learn from seeing and responding to what others do than engage in theoretic discussion or adaptation of established vocabulary and techniques. The third section of this volume looks at this and other trends.

Chapter 12 by Anne-Katrin Neyer and Nizar Abdelkafi begins with the possibilities of open innovation for education. Their case study shows how large groups of students can learn by interacting among themselves and with outsiders to create solutions to real problems. As an extension, the authors also argue for a broader concept, open schools, in which students are considered active staff and integrated into the life of an educational institution. This is an example of how leaders (including instructors and policy makers) can discover new sources of creativity within their organization.

Catharina van Delden and Nancy Wünderlich report on the use of social media for open innovation in chapter 13. Few companies have an effective presence in social networks that might facilitate word of mouth or viral marketing. This chapter summarizes the authors' research on the effectiveness of four appeals aimed at students that was followed by a project involving Facebook fans in the development of a new mustard. The smart people sought in this kind of effort are potential customers with an affinity for a firm's product characteristics and links to like-minded individuals. Leaders are urged to find language and campaigns that attract their attention.

In chapter 14, Johann Füller, Katja Hutter, and Julia Hautz describe the rationale behind their software platform, *MASSive Ideation.* In contrast to currently popular idea contests, *MASSive Ideation* not only allows for generating and evaluating numerous ideas, it supports their further elaboration into promising concepts with the collaboration of a large and geographically scattered crowd. This resource aims to capture the advantages of both real-life innovation workshops and virtual online interaction. Leaders who organize such projects must be aware of participant characteristics and also deal with integration issues within their own organization.

In chapter 15, Mitchell Tseng describes an open manufacturing paradigm that builds on many principles of open innovation. Smart companies in his description temporarily unite to quickly respond to specific customer needs. Product specifications often build on ideas found in the mass market, including patented material. While problematic from an intellectual property point of view, Tseng nevertheless suggests that it is worth learning from the speed and adaptability of these "bandits." Those interested in using open manufacturing principles are advised to collectively (1) develop the means of tracing system components to assure accountability, (2) create standards to facilitate communication among different organizations, and (3) use established platforms to simplify and speed collaboration.

Most of the chapters in this volume were first presented at meetings of the Peter Pribilla Network. An epilogue to the volume summarizes conversation between three participants—Anne Huff, Yves Doz, and Karim Lakani. They discuss barriers to and facilitators of open innovation and describe successful leaders as finding a balance between competition and cooperation in OI projects. The future they envision, however, is one in which open innovation is fully integrated into a broader innovation strategy.

Potential Problems of Open Innovation

The tone and vision of this volume are basically positive, but all new efforts face difficulties; invention and innovation in particular are risky by definition. Well-publicized OI failures include BP's inability to process ideas suggested during the Gulf oil spill by scientists associated with InnoCentive[6] and Lego's decision to drop their Lego Universe game after an investment of 50 million USD.[7]

Many other disappointments are less well publicized. One generic problem associated with OI is the massive amount of material it generates. Too many organizations enthused about OI have been faced by a suggestion box crammed with unrelated, hard-to-process, and often irrelevant ideas, and abandoned their OI efforts. Those who continue can find that congestion means attention is given to only a subset of ideas, reducing arguments for the expanded solution space OI can provide while potentially demotivating and even angering those who took the time to make suggestions left unaddressed.

Then there is the problem that the definition of smart problems and smart answers depends on perspective. A fascinating aspect of Wikipedia's development, for example, has to do with the difficulties of handing different interpretations of "facts." OI projects typically use outsiders (including solution providers) to evaluate proffered inputs, even though these outsiders have less information about organizational resources and strategic commitments. This decision is very consistent with the basic assertion of OI that the crowd has wisdom (Howe 2009), but it is not problem-free. For example, ideas and rankings tend to become more homogeneous and less innovative as a community interacts over time. Wikipedia attracts such a large and diverse base of contributors it might be expected to avoid this problem, but its history exemplifies another problem: value differences make evaluation and integration of some inputs impossible.

Furthermore not all innovation issues are easily outsourced to open innovation. Problem modularity is often a pre-requisite for success, as is the broad distribution of relevant knowledge, but these are not the characteristics of all difficult problems. Furthermore, in chapter 2 Thomas Lackner indicates that companies like Siemens typically spend months generating the apparently simple questions asked of outsiders. The difficulties involved are one of the major reasons why brokers such as InnoCentive, yet2.com, and NineSigma are used. While these intermediaries are helpful, they increase the costs associated with a strategy often adopted because of limited funds for innovation.

Similar problems are likely throughout the innovation process. Once a promising idea is enthusiastically accepted, for example, a new idea can distract the organization from core activities. This is one way to lose competitive advantage, but there are others. Some organizations, including a significant number of startups, have become so deeply involved in outside alliances that they have given away intellectual property without sufficient return. Of equal concern, competitors can look for clues about market opportunities and the knowledge needed to address them from problems posted on public sites, potentially shifting competitive balance in their favor.

In short, invention and innovation are inherently risky endeavors. Opening the processes involved also opens new areas of risk. Of course, failure is part of learning and even expensive dead ends can be useful. Basically, successful OI requires maturity in processes and well as thought (Habicht, Möslein, and Reichwald 2012) and that is the product of failure as well as success.

The Promise of Open Innovation

Some OI failures may be the result of inexperience that lessens over time. In chapter 9, Karim Lakhani's study of 166 problems posted relatively early in InnoCentive's history showed a 29 percent success rate. An April 8, 2009, article in *Business Week* raised the success rate to 50 percent, a plausible indication that participants have learned to use the platform more effectively (Hagel and Brown 2009).

Enthusiasm and potential growth associated with innovation also help balance the problems of limited control over innovation processes and outcomes. Organizations need energy (Bruch and Ghoshal 2003). OI can be especially positive in this regard, in part due to technology that facilitates immediate and graphic communication. OI is also associated with other valued traits. Cooperation, for example, is essential to innovation, as many chapters in this volume explain. Lynda Gratton in particular focuses on cooperation in chapter 7, showing that valuable contributions to innovation often depend on broadly connected individuals.

The outputs of OI projects thus yield results that individuals are unlikely to achieve alone. In one study InnoCentive found that their most successful solver was in fact a group that discussed and developed solutions before the most promising were submitted (Hagel and Brown 2009). An obvious conclusion from these and other experiences is that interaction among promising problem solvers tends to improve ideas for innovation. Luckily new technologies facilitate the involvement of larger groups in this process.

Eric von Hippel has been among those who argue that innovation will accelerate even faster if governments change intellectual property rights laws based on processes and environments that are rapidly eroding. Significant changes are occurring. In the United States, the America Invents Act, the first significant change in US Patent law in 60 years, was signed into law in September 2011. One stated purpose was to streamline patent applications and increase certainty. While the results are currently debated, efforts to create common international procedures are also underway.

Nevertheless, learning and evolution continues. Supporters suggest that the many forces leading to innovation are growing stronger. Old ways of working therefore cannot be expected to be successful. OI is a necessary change in mindset. Leaders must clarify the kind of knowledge that might be gained from open innovation and where useful inputs are most likely to be obtained. They must also assess whether the organization has the capability to recognize and incorporate external ideas. John Bessant and Bettina von Stamm have evidence from workshops described in chapter 6 that many organizations are dissatisfied with their ability in these important areas affecting long-term viability.

Conclusion—Leading Open Innovation

A common definition of leaders, as opposed to managers, is that they are able to articulate an inspirational vision for action (Nanus 1992). In the case of open innovation we believe leaders must help others understand how this new way of working departs from well-established ideas about closed innovation. More specific tactics for leading open innovation presented in this volume are summarized in Table 1.1.

While these ideas seem promising, a major challenge for leaders involves resistance to new ideas, especially those that come from outsiders, a problem that is colloquially known as NIH (not invented here). This resistance can occur across the spectrum of

Table 1.1
Advice to leaders of open innovation

1	Define the knowledge needed through open innovation (chapter 2)
2	Bring knowledge-holders together within the organization and beyond (chapter 2)
3	Deliberately seek and manage tensions between established practices and ideas from outsiders (chapter 3)
4	Maintain energy for innovation via emotional commitment (chapter 3)
5	Make relevant operating information available to all innovators (chapter 4)
6	Accept the challenge of simultaneously addressing multiple tasks (chapter 4)
7	Search for and use tools for identifying new ideas and blending them with the ideas of insiders (chapter 5)
8	Consider successful OI practices developed in other organizations (chapter 6)
9	Assure that the organization has the mechanisms and people skills to put unfamiliar ideas into practice (chapter 6)
10	Create projects that ignite energy for cooperation (chapter 7)
11	Consider whether internal boundaries stymie rather than protect valuable knowledge (chapter 7)
12	Look to those who are highly motivated to develop solutions to problems they experience as users (chapter 8)
13	Work with customers to co-create new products and services (chapter 9)
14	Post problems to relevant but diverse groups of outsiders rather than assume to role of solution generator yourself (chapter 10)
15	Focus on tasks less easily addressed by innovating individuals and groups (chapter 11)
16	Treat employees and users as important sources for developing new solutions (chapter 12)
17	Seek ideas from potential customers with an affinity for your product or service, using familiar language and tone in your communications with them (chapter 13)
18	Facilitate collaboration from large groups via online tools that allow interaction among small groups (chapter 14)
19	Trace innovation components to assure accountability (chapter 15)
20	Create standards to facilitate communication among different OI participants (chapter 15)
21	Use established platforms to simplify and speed collaboration (chapter 15)

innovation activities, from initial ideation through development and evaluation. They can be as difficult for entrepreneurs as for established organizations because open innovation practices depart from assumed innovation procedures.

In other words, OI success seems to require "skunk works" procedures writ large. Skunk works typically succeed because they are championed by those with deep knowledge of potential support and resistance. The chapters in this volume suggest that successful leaders of open innovation projects must not only champion OI as a general approach but also help develop new processes and structures to help it succeed.

In short, leaders of open innovation are called upon to become involved in implementing new ideas. As Neyer and Abdelkafi say in chapter 12, they must teach the teachers. While this is again a familiar concept about leadership, open innovation pushes boundaries. Few are eager to learn from unfamiliar, often younger innovators or adapt practices developed in resource-strapped developing countries; yet open innovation has shown how rich these resources are.

As we consider the daunting tasks summarized in table 1.1, we are nonetheless encouraged by a cluster of arguments. Open innovation potentially is a cost-effective approach to finding and developing new solutions. It often is emotionally energizing for those involved. Furthermore, successful experiences are accumulating to give confidence and some direction to those who wish to experiment with OI. We hope this volume inspires its readers to take up the challenges and promises of this innovation in innovation.

Notes

1. http://en.wikipedia.org/wiki/Reliability_of_Wikipedia.

2. See http://news.pg.com/pg_views, http://www.annualreport.pg.com/annualreport2009/letter/lead.shtml, ahttps://secure3.verticali.net/pg-connection-portal/ctx/noauth/PortalHome, all accessed April 25, 2010.

3. http://www.generalmills.com/en/Company/Innovation/G-Win.aspx.

4. For a description of the America Invents Act, the first significant change in US Patent law in 60 years see http://www.uspto.gov/news/speeches/2011/kappos_georgetown.jsp.

5. Henry W. Chesbrough, The era of open innovation, *MIT Sloan Management Review*, Spring 2003, p. 38.

6. Alissa Walker, BP to InnoCentive: Sorry, we don't want your 908 ideas for saving the Gulf. *Fast Company*, June 23 2010. Accessed at http://www.fastcompany.com/1663156/bp-innocentive-sorry-we-dont-want-your-908-ideas-saving-gulf.

7. http://www.innovationexcellence.com/blog/2011/11/18/legos-50-million-open-innovation-failure/.

References and Further Reading

Bruch, H., and S. Ghoshal. 2003. Unleashing organisational energy. *MIT Sloan Management Review* 45 (1): 45–51.

Chesbrough, H. 2006. *Open Innovation: The New Imperative for Creating and Profiting from Technology*. Cambridge, MA: Harvard Business School Publishing.

Habicht, H., K. M. Möslein, and R. Reichwald. 2012. Open innovation maturity. *International Journal of Knowledge-Based Organizations* 2 (1): 92–111.

Gilles, J. 2005. Special report: Internet encyclopedias go head to head. *Nature* 438 (December 15): 900–901.

Hagel, J., and J. D. Brown. 2009. The next wave of innovation. *Business Week* April 8. Accessed at: http://www.businessweek.com/innovate/content/apr2009/id2009048_360417.htm.

Howe, J. 2009. *Crowdsourcing: Why the Power of the Crowd Is Driving Business*. New York: Crown Business.

Huston, L., and N. Sakkab. 2006. Connect and develop: Inside Procter & Gamble's new model for innovation. *Harvard Business Review* 84 (3): 58–66.

Johnson, B. 2010. Shanzhai! *Wired UK,* December 7. Accessed at http://www.wired.co.uk/magazine/archive/2011/01/features/shanzai?page=3.

Lakhani, K. R., and Z. Kanji. 2008. Threadless: A Business Community. Multimedia Case 608707, Harvard Business School. Accessed at http://cb.hbsp.harvard.edu/cb/web/product_detail.seam?R=608707-MMC-ENG,

Lakhani, K. R., and A. McAfee. 2007. Case study on deleting "Enterprise 2.0" article. Courseware 9–607–712. Harvard Business School. Accessed at http://courseware.hbs.edu/public/cases/wikipedia/.

Lindegaard, S. 2010. *The Open Innovation Revolution*. Hoboken, NJ: Wiley.

Nanus, B. 1992. *Visionary Leadership*. San Francisco: Jossey-Bass.

Seybold, P. B. 2006. *Outside Innovation: How Your Customers Will Co-design Your Company's Future*. Hammersmith, UK: Collins.

von Hippel, E. 2006. *Democratizing Innovation*. Cambridge: MIT Press.

von Hippel, E., J. P. J. de Jong, and S. Flowers. 2010. Comparing business and household sector innovation in consumer products: Findings from a representative study in the UK. Available at SSRN: http://ssrn.com/abstract=1683503.

2 Open Innovation at Siemens AG

Thomas Lackner

Introduction

In 2009 Siemens had around 56,000 active patents and spent €3.9 billion on R&D, or 5.1 percent of its revenue. This was accomplished in large part by 30,800 R&D employees based in 176 locations worldwide, a huge community in itself, with its own size-centric challenges. In this chapter, I focus on the vast open innovation program in Siemens that augments the internal research community in churning out successful product and service innovations.

Siemens has always had a strong, historical emphasis on innovation. The company was started 150 years ago with a telegraph line from India to England, which it prefinanced, so the idea of a business model was understood even in the company's very early days. From that point forward, people at Siemens have known that it is not always easy to innovate, but innovation must be central to the way the company does business. Accordingly, when I talk about either R&D or innovation in the context of Siemens, I am talking about transforming knowledge into money. At Siemens we further distinguish between research and innovation. This difference and its consequences are illustrated in figure 2.1.

The Innovation–Market Connection

As is often seen, it is not always the best technology that leads to business success. One of the most quoted examples of a better technology losing to inferior is the famous Betamax–VHS battle, where the inferior VHS technology, thanks to better marketing, decimated the Betamax offering. Hence, what is crucial for a market success is to make the most effective connection between innovation and market. Generically speaking, there are four options (quadrants I to IV) to make an innovation-market connection as shown in figure 2.2.

Consequences

- Research is a neccessary but not a sufficient condition for innovation
- Economic value is only created by successful innovations
- Business strategy drives R&D strategy

Figure 2.1
Research and innovation are complementary
All figures © Siemens AG

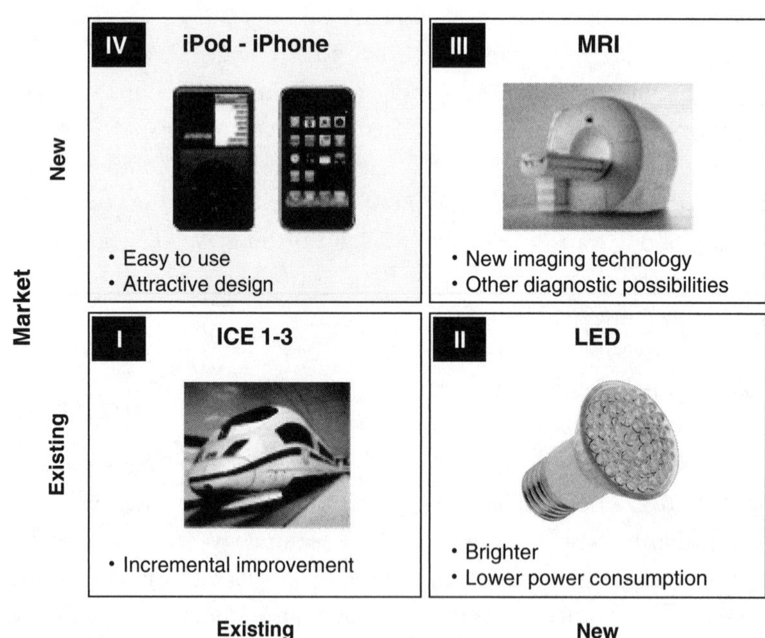

Figure 2.2
Different paths from innovation to the market

Penetrating existing markets with existing technology (quadrant I) has played a big part in Siemens' current success. For example, the high-speed intercity-express (ICE) trains now running in Germany, Switzerland, Austria, Belgium, and the Netherlands can travel at the top speed of 300 km/h due to enhanced aerodynamics and braking technology developed at Siemens. The trains also are exceptionally efficient. They consume, on average, a mere 0.33 liters of gasoline per passenger for every 100 kilometers. We have developed special trains to endure extremely cold temperatures in Russia and just announced another Chinese contract worth €750 million for 100 high-speed trains to run from Beijing to Shanghai, the most vital high-speed train connection in mainland China. Clearly, this is an important way of using our innovative capacity to continuously improve and adapt existing offerings to better meet the demands of our diverse customers..

Siemens also is strong at taking a new technology to an existing market (quadrant II). LED lights, for example, are based on a new physical principle that led to the development of a new technology. This has brought us new advantages such as developing innovative lighting that evokes emotions with a continuous spectrum of color lights. Siemens also is adept at entering new markets with new technologies (quadrant III). For example, our state-of-the-art magnetic resonance imaging (MRI) technology is novel and unique when compared to x-ray and other similar devices. With MRIs, we have created and entered a new market, as our technology displays tissue with greater accuracy and finer resolution than any other available alternative.

Siemens is often not so strong in bringing existing technologies into new markets (quadrant IV). While many other companies have a similar weakness, we need to learn from innovators like Apple. An iPod, for example, used existing technologies but was a new product that became a huge market success. Why does Siemens have problems doing the same thing? In part, it is because we have very good R&D people who are, not surprisingly, most focused on developing their products and technologies. This is sometimes an obstacle.

Leveraging Existing Technology into New Markets

As figure 2.3 shows, there are several possibilities for moving into new markets. There is the strategy of being the first mover, that is, not only fast (and often first) at developing new technologies but also fast at seeing discontinuities and changing the rules of the game. For example, ten years ago Cisco bought all of IBM's networking patents, products, and customers. They began to dominate networked communications before other firms realized how big the market would grow.

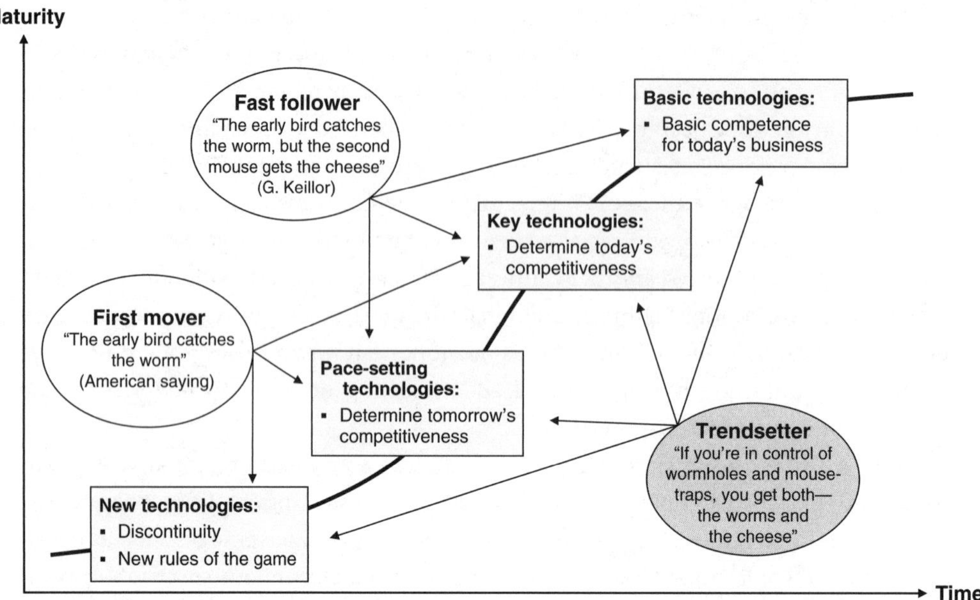

Figure 2.3
Most important innovation strategies and their positioning along the technology life cycle

There is a saying that the early bird catches the worm. That is true. Cisco was fast and they got the worm. But there also are fast followers. The companies following this strategy rely on basic technologies but make improvements on them. Garrison Keillor, a famous columnist, recently said, "The early bird catches the worm, but the second mouse gets the cheese." That means that the first mover is often in the trap, while the second captures the market.

A third trendsetting strategy, shown on the right in this figure, seems to be the most versatile. This strategy controls both the wormholes and the mousetraps. If one can do that, one gets both the worms and the cheese. That is what Siemens systematically strives for. In the following, I will describe how Siemens is using open innovation approaches to be a formidable trendsetter.

Innovation at Siemens

Different people mean different things when they say "open innovation." Currently there is no common understanding, even in the academic world, on how porous an innovation process should be in order to be defined as an open innovation process. At Siemens we follow a generic map (see figure 2.4) to structure our endeavors to innovate. The *x*-axis follows the innovation process from generation of ideas, to selection of concepts, to technical development, to market launch—typical phases in any innovation process. The *y*-axis shows the level of openness during these steps from a seemingly closed business unit level to completely open sourcing of knowledge from any available external person or firm. At Siemens, for example, one can run innovation development within a business unit, which is typically a closed process. Or one can operate within a sector, say energy or health. One could also go cross-sector, which is often termed a companywide activity. An even broader option is to develop an innovation within one or more value chains, including customers. Finally, at Siemens, one can source knowledge from external communities to complement or substitute internal research.

As seen in figure 2.4, the R&D and Sales and Marketing departments at Siemens are typically run within the boundaries of a business unit and are considered examples of closed innovation. Interestingly, some activities such as licensing and transaction activities conducted at this level are considered examples of open innovation at many

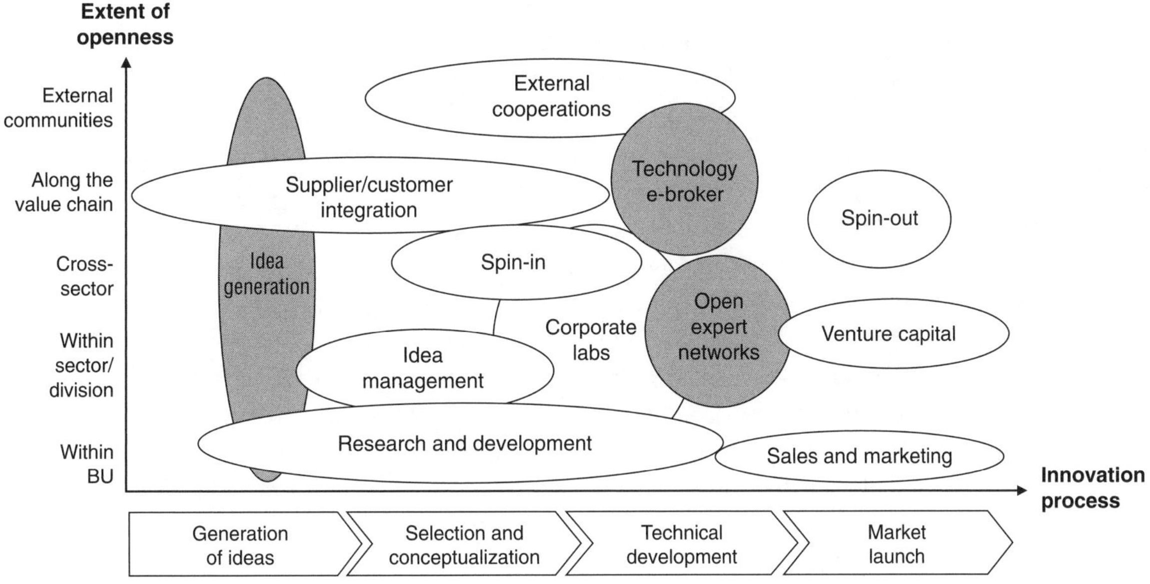

Figure 2.4
Generic map with different paths to innovation at Siemens

other companies. In total, Siemens has been successful with traditional innovation activities.

In addition Siemens is regularly engaged in venture capital activities, to not only identify but also invest in the next big idea on the market. Simultaneously the company runs corporate labs that provide a platform for the transfer of knowledge and ideas between the various sectors and divisions of Siemens.

Siemens also has spin-offs. The spin-off enterprises come under the purview of the Siemens Technology Accelerator (STA), a unit that was established in 2001. These enterprises have technologies that could not be commercialized internally by Siemens, for reasons that are not connected to the innovation or technology. During the early phase of a spin-off, STA plays the role of a mentor and provides legal, financial, and organizational support in every possible way to help the spin-offs become successful.

For example, EnOcean, a battery-free sensor company was the first company that was spun off with the help of STA in 2001. This new firm, started by three former Siemens employees, quickly developed a viable business model targeting the building installation sector. But, with its scalable products, the company had the vision to enter other markets such as the automotive sector, in this case promoting a battery-less tire pressure senor. The start-up company soon acquired venture capital, now employs over forty people, and has expanded its markets to the United States and elsewhere. EnOcean has a great new technology, and continues to be important as part of the sustainability movement. Today it has more than 300 interoperable products offered by 70 OEM customers.

Siemens also regularly cooperates with universities, with around 8,000 projects run by 800 university partners. To complement this, Siemens also has structured spin-in activities based in Berkeley and Shanghai. The company is in direct three-way relationships with universities and entrepreneurs. These Technology-to-Business programs source the brightest ideas and help found companies at an early stage. The companies are brought to a point where they add value to Siemens. This companywide idea management effort, called the 3i-program, has a long history and generates over 100,000 ideas every year. The ideas developed have ranged from improvement suggestions up to new business proposals. They are usually thought up by one person, sent to a department, and then evaluated. There are also many other programs within Siemens that attempt to improve interactions with suppliers and customers. What Siemens does not have—and what I am talking about in this chapter—is a good collaboration process for generating new ideas. The chapter shows the extent of our current efforts to generate good technological ideas and improvements by connecting external and internal sources.

Open Innovation

This point is illustrated by the dark gray bubbles in figure 2.4—the use of idea generation processes, open expert networks, and technology e-brokers. Siemens started open innovation activities in these areas in 2008. There was some benchmarking. Lots of other companies were asked what they were doing to stimulate innovation. It became clear that every company had to develop an open innovation strategy that would fit their requirements best. Open innovation was not a standard approach that could be successfully replicated in different companies. First, one needed to analyze the external environment a company finds itself in, and the internal processes and procedures that it uses to conduct business. Second, depending on these external and internal conditions, companies would need to identify and customize specific open innovation methods to meet their specific goals.

Procter & Gamble was the first, I would say, to emphasize an open innovation strategy. Hewlett-Packard partners with universities in a unique way. BMW focuses on idea generation with external partners. Every organization has to find a way to develop its own means of innovation.

At Siemens we are just beginning to develop open innovation activities based on web 2.0 technologies. We simply post a question, a challenge, or a business question to a huge community. That is the gist of open innovation. It is not a "simple" cooperation with a university, or with a partner, where we formalize the cooperation. It is an open cooperation. We are working to complement our existing, relatively open processes to address unsolved business challenges.

You might ask why we are developing these new activities. The answer is that there is a lot of knowledge, good people, and untapped brainpower outside of Siemens that we would be foolhardy not to access. By reaching out, we can access not just 30,000 plus Siemens R&D workers, but 1.3 million experts in the United States and many more around the world, as shown in right-hand side of figure 2.5. In the bar chart on the left, one can see a global trend toward a proportionate shift in R&D spending from large enterprises (≥ 25,000 employees) to smaller companies.

At the same time we keep in mind that innovations are no longer the product of small solitary workshops. Rather, innovators are working with networks to access knowledge that is distributed among people spread across national boundaries. There are new ways to access global talent, both through the Internet and with the help of search technologies but using these resources requires a strategy.

If you raise the issue of open innovation in a big company, you usually get the response that "We are doing everything already." But if you ask management, "Do

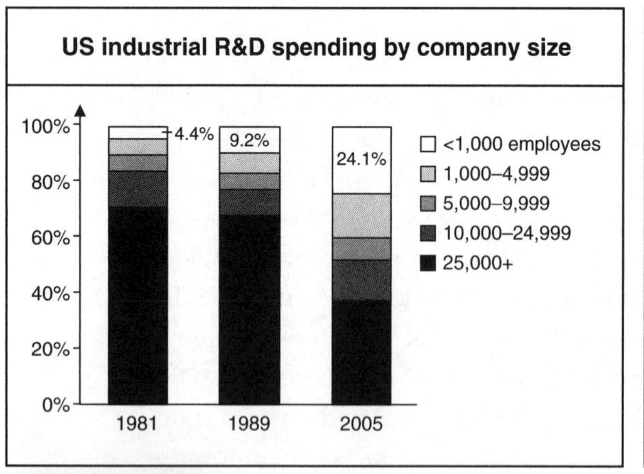

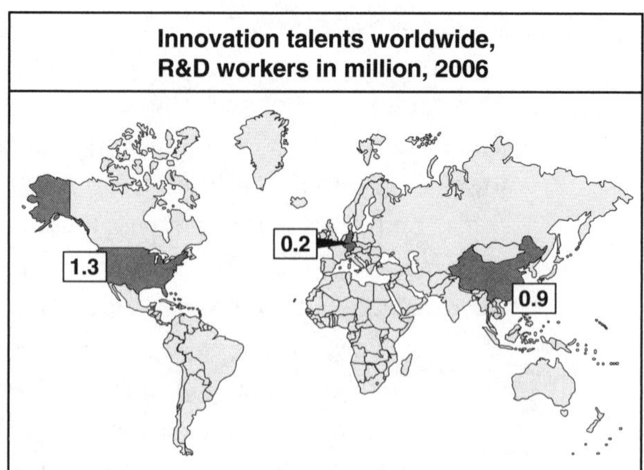

Drivers

- Internet and search technology
- VC and government spending enables small company innovation
- Asia, India, and ex-USSR technology becoming available
- Emergence of private research institutes
- Talent mobility

Figure 2.5
Increasing innovation generated outside of large enterprises

you really exploit the creative potential of your employees? Really exploit?" they get a little unsure. Because, of course, we have good top management and we communicate everything, but do we really tap the potential of our 30,800 R&D employees (let alone the 400,000 employees), asking them to be more innovative? And, do we always develop technology in the most effective way? I don't think so.

These are some of the key questions where open innovation approaches could be beneficial:

- Do we always develop technologies in the most effective way?
- Does our corporate culture promote a spirit of openness and create a desire for proactivity?
- Do we have a corporate innovation identity?
- Can we separate our core business and the information we can share?

As I said, a strategy is needed. For example, if Procter & Gamble wants to develop something new, they first look internally and ask is it available? If not, the second aspect of the P&G strategy is to look externally to see if what they want is available. Why look externally? There are millions of bright people out there: what is wanted could be readily available. If P&G cannot find what they want internally or externally; only then do they commit resources to develop the required product internally. It is a very simple strategy. I can imagine that if departments within Siemens would pursue a similar strategy, they could be more focused. But at Siemens, we have a special challenge: "Wenn Siemens wüsste, was Siemens weiß." Very simply it means, "If Siemens only knew what Siemens knows." It is a true challenge within our company.

Potential Problems of Open Innovation

No strategy is without risks. Open innovation is a strategic opening of the company. It moves from the idea "the lab is our world" to the idea "the world is our lab." This is an important figure of speech we are using to communicate the change that is required in Siemens. It sounds very reasonable, but it means, in depth, a culture change in our company. In "the lab is our world" view you have people who are renowned and rewarded for doing R&D on their own. A change to "the world is our lab" means you need people who find a solution as fast as possible, wherever available. It is a different mindset.

You have to have both in a company. You need to have people who are really doing in-depth work and people who have real fun in finding something very fast. But it is not so easy to find a balance between these two groups of people.

Procter & Gamble had the goal of sourcing, within five years, 50 percent of its new technologies from external sources. They achieved it and brought down their R&D costs substantially. And at the same time they improved their innovation success rate by 100 percent. Of course, if you are telling these stories to an R&D department, they are not very happy, but nevertheless, if management is talking about these examples, R&D departments do pay attention.

The details help people who are oriented toward internal processes start thinking. For example, Procter & Gamble was looking for a technology that would allow them to print on Pringles, a potato chip, because they thought it would allow them to expand their market. First they looked internally for a process, but it was complicated to print on dough, and they did not find a good solution. Then they partnered with a printer company. That did not succeed either. Finally, they used an open innovation approach. They asked worldwide: Who has a technology that can print on food? They found a professor in Bologna, Italy, who had developed an ink-jet technology, for a small bakery, that could print on cookies and cakes. P&G sourced this technology, made modest changes in it, and succeeded.

The critical mindset is always: What is my core business? What is my core R&D and what is not? These are the questions you have to ask yourself. To ask this question in

Siemens at the company level is stupid. We have to go down and ask at the business unit level: What is core and what is not core?

That is the process we are pursuing in Siemens, as we look for new technologies and ideas both externally and internally. My job is to go to business units and tell them the stories that I have just told you. A little bit more in-depth, of course, with some best-practice examples. We have a tool box to help them start their own open innovation processes. We point to pilot projects in the areas you see in dark gray on figure 2.4. We ask, "Do you have a topic for one of these open innovation approaches?"

Examples of Open Innovation Projects Underway at Siemens

We are running quite a few external idea contests. For example, some years ago, Fujitsu-Siemens had a question: What services could be offered by next generation IT centers? If you are posting such a question you have to ask yourself: what is the right way to express this question? Whom do I address it to? Do I want to post a question with the branding of Fujitsu-Siemens? Would I be selling a secret if I sent it to an open community? What would I do with the ideas that come in? Is my organization prepared to digest novel ideas? What does an innovation idea contest cost? How do I approach an open community? And so on and so forth.

The challenging problem is "how should I ask this question?" If our business development people want to find interesting services for an IT center, they have to decide what they are really looking for. If you try to nail them down to formulate a precise question, they are likely to run into difficulties. But that is precisely what they have to do. First, keeping the goals in mind, they have to formulate a question appropriately. Second, only then should the question be broadcasted to a wide community.

Here is another example of an idea contest in Siemens. OSRAM was seeking input from a large external community to help them emotionalize light, what might be called "mood lighting." The company wanted to know how people would use light to make them feel better and energize themselves. They did not want to develop these ideas just within the OSRAM community; they wanted to get a lot of people from different walks of life to get involved in their project. The contest was opened to general public (http://www.led-emotionalize.com/). In the first phase, ideas from all participants are collected and discussed. In the second phase, the best ideas were jointly developed by the community. It was a very simple and open process. The winners received attractive monetary and nonmonetary prizes amounting to just €7000. Traditionally, to achieve similar results, OSRAM would have conducted such a brainstorming process internally or outsourced it to a design firm. This would have

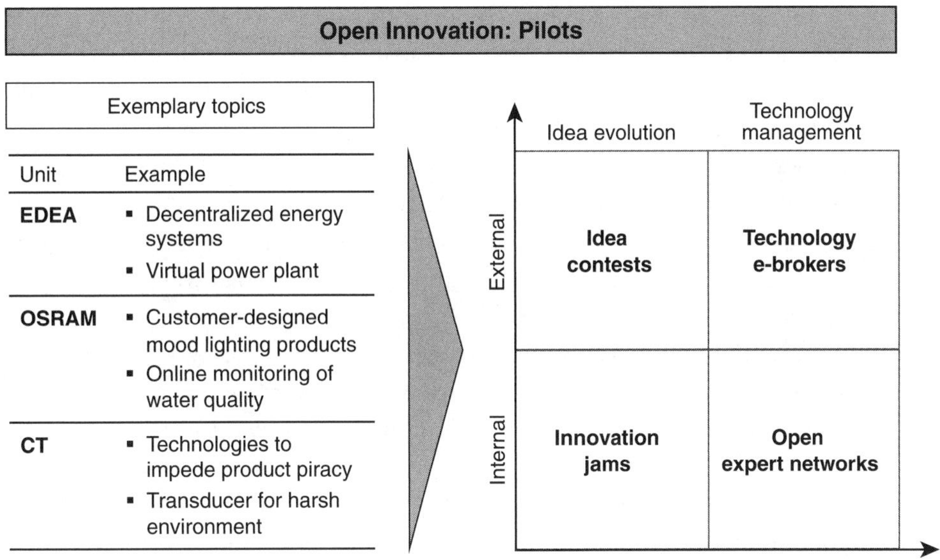

Figure 2.6
Sector-sponsored pilot tests for open innovation approaches

been a lot more expensive. These are known as external idea competitions/contests. They require a concrete business idea, where you can specify what you want.

This is not the only way to develop ideas. Another option is shown in figure 2.6. During an innovation jam, a form of internal idea generation, we do not specify criteria; rather, we conduct an open online discussion. A jam is not something that you spread on bread; the word is a musical term. Sometimes an ad hoc group of people come together to play jazz. That is exactly what we intend to do across different business units: specify a topic that is interesting enough to draw a wide variety of people to talk together. Jams have been run by other companies with perhaps 500 to 150,000 people. Our strategy so far has been to involve around 1,000 people from Siemens worldwide.

We put a lot of work into communication when setting up a jam—making people aware of the topic, inviting them to participate. We ask some clear questions on a specific topic, and invite responses that are typically 50 to 500 word posts. As one comment leads to others, categorization may come from pre-defined forums, but user-generated tags are also helpful. Typically, an innovation jam is limited to duration of three to five days.

For example, we conducted an innovation jam on anti-piracy. Piracy has been huge issue for Siemens, especially as many intermediaries that market Siemens' high-tech products—in secondary markets—have been replacing some genuine components with counterfeits. This consistently hurts the Siemens image as a producer of high-quality goods. In a worst-case scenario, people using Siemens products have been physically hurt. This online jam brought together people from all sectors of the company worldwide faced with this specific challenge. It provided a discussion board where piracy problems encountered were listed and ideas to counter piracy were developed. Collectively, we have a lot of expertise in IP law protection and IP rights enforcement. This innovation jam helped channel the scattered knowledge and expertise to solve current piracy problems and prevent future piracy.

As our experience with this innovation jam was very positive, we intend to run more on other topics. A number of very interesting ideas are currently floating within the company, including a discussion on new business ideas for services in the health care industry and on cooperating beyond the boundaries of our firewall. We can also use open innovation tools to develop precompetitive ideas, for example, in the area of robotics. We can imagine developing a lot of ideas, but it is not so easy to get them implemented.

Now let me address the tools of figure 2.6, where we are using open innovation to develop and manage technologies. For example, a unit with special applications is looking for a decentralized energy storage system, another for a special sensor system. We assumed that there was a huge group of people outside Siemens working on relevant ideas who might offer a solution, a product, maybe even a prototype. We are using expert networks to find these innovations rather than spend more money on new internal solutions.

Finally, we are partnering with technology e-brokers such as InnoCentive, NineSigma, and Yet2.com. The benefit of using these kind of companies is first the large communities they help us access. Second, they have the experience to customize our questions to reach a certain group. If you address an abstract question to a crowd, usually you get answers that are not useful. So the trick is to specify your question and, more important, address the right people. For example, NineSigma has a target group of two to three million people. We might post a question through them that they channel to approximately 100,000 relevant solvers. By doing so, we collect feedback from perhaps fifty or hundred people. Then we can select the best three or four solutions, and sometimes combine the input to come up with one best solution.

We have some performance indicators that show collaborating with these technology e-brokers can increase our speed of innovation. For example, a company in the automobile sector was looking for oil sensor technology; through an e-broker, they found the technology they needed in the Ukraine from a supplier who catered to the food industry. This type of cross-sector contribution is typical with technology e-brokers.

The intermediaries we work with operate in somewhat different ways. NineSigma, for example, is running a typical M&A business with a focus on technologies. They help us primarily connect with small and medium enterprises, universities, and independent R&D organizations. They have an open process: they help us to write professional requests for proposals and they provide excellent and confidential feedback from the solution providers. But they stay away from the actual contract between the seeker and the selected solution provider. InnoCentive, in contrast, runs a confidential process. They act as an Escrow agent, which is legally speaking a little bit more complicated. I will not go into any details about this process as it is described in chapter 10.

An Ideal Picture of Siemens as an Open Innovator

My overall message to Siemens, and people with an interest in open innovation more broadly, is that the world is changing. Siemens wants to be, and I hope can be, a networked company. There is hard work to be done in opening doors while maintaining some control. Even more difficult, we have to change our culture to succeed in a networked world. We believe that culture change is necessary at Siemens and we hope that in five years we will see some success. One picture I show at Siemens is figure 2.7. I hope that our people look at it and wake up a little. I hope they say: "We can do a better job of bringing our brains together. Let's do something different."

Better yet, we could end up with another picture. Figure 2.8 was a present to a manager within SIS, our Global IT Solutions and Services unit. He was leaving, and about 3,000 people were asked: "Just send an e-mail and write down who has helped you considerably within the last twelve months. We would like to give this picture as a present to our boss." I would say that this is a real picture of Siemens' brainpower. Information is being exchanged that we have not directly measured, but it has value. Although I cannot claim that we would find a similar picture in all sectors of Siemens, clearly we are already networked in some important ways.

Idea for Innovative Leaders: Bring Knowledge-Holders Together

Midway through this chapter I bluntly said: "If Siemens only knew what Siemens knows." "What we know" is a huge problem for us and, I believe, for almost all companies of any size. There is relevant knowledge in different suborganizations within Siemens. Figure 2.9 illustrates the complexities involved. Knowledge can be found in different business processes and different projects. It is in different geographical locations and a function of different languages and cultures. As a result "what we know" is fragmented. Our challenge is how to bring this knowledge together.

- Think creatively or "outside of the box"
- Think in networks, not in organizations
- Create open doors with well-defined access controls
- Foster open market innovations
- Connect the best with the best

Create competitive advantage by managing complexity of internal and external know-how and flow of information

Figure 2.7
At Siemens—networked, different, and open approaches to innovation

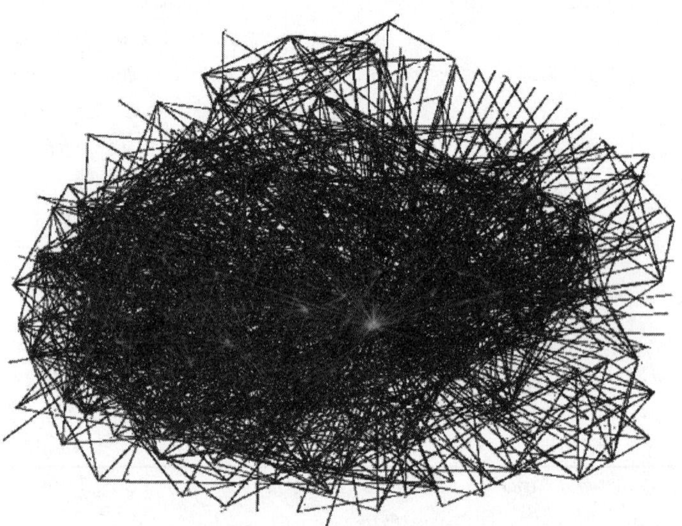

"Who has helped you in your professional work during the last 12 months"

Figure 2.8
Knowledge networking across Siemens that already works

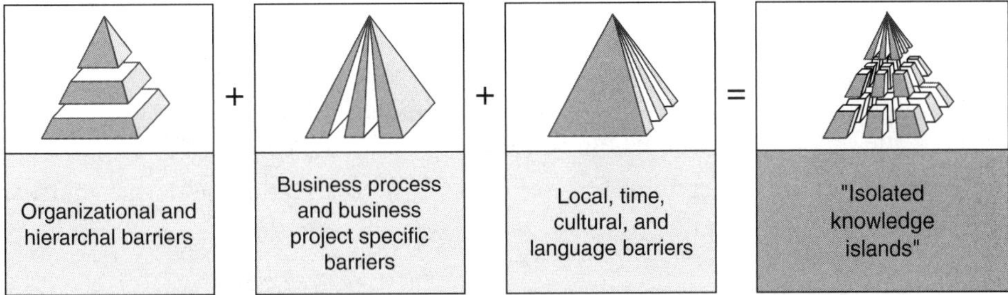

- Open expert networks **connect existing knowledge** within the company
- Employees with different expertise contribute their knowledge **voluntarily**
- Focus is on technologies with clear **business impact**
- Cross-sector networks **leverage competitive** edge of an integrated **technology** company

Figure 2.9
Open expert networks for enterprises—Why do we need communities?

Social networking may be part of the solution. We did a study and found out that presently more than 10,000 people in Siemens are exchanging information on social sites, but we don't know what they are exchanging. We believe that a social network site within Siemens would facilitate exchange of knowledge with respect to technologies.

We developed such a platform ten years ago in a web 1.0 technology for the information systems sector, so we know what we are talking about. We want to develop something like it for the company as a whole, with web 2.0 features like tagging. It is no longer necessary to start with a big pre-defined structure of interesting technologies. Today there are rating mechanisms that allow the most important technologies to emerge. We also hope that people will be able to establish their own profile. IBM has done that, and we hope to get the momentum within Siemens to do something similar.

I believe that companies can learn from each other as they improve their knowledge management capacity in this and other ways. I hope that academics with an interest in this area will also be involved and share the outcome of their studies. As I said, this is a serious problem for almost all companies.

Further Investigation

A list of organizations involved in open innovation can be found at http://www.15inno.com/2010/03/02/open-innovation-examples-and-resources/. You can use this and other resources to compare open innovation programs by three or four multinational firms.

• How would you suggest Thomas Lackner expand Siemens' open innovation efforts over the life cycle of developing and delivering products and services?

• What more might be done at the sector level, across sectors, and with outside participants?

References and Further Reading

Achatz, R. 2009. Open Innovation bei Siemens. In A. Picot and S. Doeblin, eds., *Innovationsführerschaft durch Open Innovation: Chancen für die Telekommunikations-, IT- und Medienindustrie*. Berlin: Springer, 43–68.

Chesbrough, H. 2006. *Open Innovation: The New Imperative for Creating and Profiting from Technology*. Cambridge: Harvard Business School Publishing.

Chesbrough, H. W. 2007. The market for innovation: Implications for corporate strategy. *California Management Review* 49 (3): 45–66.

Christensen, J. F., M. H. Olesen, and J. S. Kjær. 2005. The industrial dynamics of open innovation—Evidence from the transformation of consumer electronics. *Research Policy* 34 (10): 1533–49.

Eberl, U., and A. F. Pease, eds. 2011. *Pictures of the Future—The Magazine for Research and Innovation*. Munich: Siemens AG.

Enkel, E., O. Gassmann, and H. Chesbrough. 2009. Open R&D and open innovation: exploring the phenomenon. *R&D Management* 39 (4): 311–16.

Lakhani, K. R., L. B. Jeppesen, P. A. Lohse, and J. A. Panetta. 2006. The value of openness in scientific problem solving. Working paper 07–050. Harvard Business School.

Lichtenthaler, U., and H. Ernst. 2007. External technology commercialization in large firms: Results of a quantitative benchmarking study. *R&D Management* 37 (5): 383–97.

Lindegaard, S. 2010. *The Open Innovation Revolution*. Hoboken, NJ: Wiley.

Perkmann, M., and K. Walsh. 2007. University–industry relationships and open innovation: Towards a research agenda. *International Journal of Management Reviews* 9 (4): 259–80.

Prahalad, C. K., and V. Ramaswamy. 2004. *The Future of Competition: Co-creating Value with Customers*. Boston: Harvard Business School Press.

Vanhaverbecke, W., V. Van de Vrade, and H. W. Chesbrough. 2008. Understanding the advantages of open innovation practices in corporate venturing in terms of real options. *Creativity and Innovation Management* 17 (4): 251–58.

3 The Need for Speed: Fostering Strategic Agility for Renewed Growth

Yves Doz

Introduction

Mikko Kosonen and I looked at how successful, innovative companies become victims of their success and then attempt to regain strategic agility. Our book *Fast Strategy*[1] reports on the causes of such failures, provides a model of strategically agile companies, and explains how some maturing firms recapture the strategic agility that once allowed them to innovate while others do not. We believe strategic agility requires a form of strategy making that has similarities with open innovation. We were particularly concerned that there was an increase in corporate rigidity across organizations at the very time more agility was crucial. This concern emerged from my research, teaching, and consulting on strategic commitments and from Mikko Kosonen's insights as the man at the center of the strategy process of Nokia for over a decade—from the mid-1990s.

Research Approach

We first developed a very rich history of the 1990 to 2005 period at Nokia as a research case from which to articulate interpretations, tentative conceptualizations, and theoretical propositions. Once we had a summary and tentative conceptual understanding from Nokia's experience, we gathered more data. Was Nokia a unique case, or a representative example of a wider phenomenon? We also asked ourselves about boundary conditions and limits.

The answers required theoretical, purposive sampling. That means that we chose additional companies to study as a function of the theory we were trying to build: Was their experience going to challenge and inform our emerging conceptualizations, or support, enrich, and nuance them? We went to leading exemplars such as Cisco, Intel, and SAP—companies we believed had faced similar challenges and experiences to Nokia. We also looked at companies with a broader range of activities, such as HP and IBM, to see the extent to which strategic agility—or rigidity—was a corporate or business unit level issue. With the additional data gathered in this research, we were testing and refining our initial theories. We were asking, what conceptualizations fit many situations? What are the critical contingencies? As we developed more robust theoretical statements, we tried to make predictions and build deductive propositions that could then be tested on a larger sample. The process is captured by the arrow on the left side of figure 3.1.

Before explaining our work in more detail, it may be useful to reveal our results, and how they fit with the open innovation agenda of this book. Figure 3.1 shows our general approach toward observing what we call "strategic sensitivity." All companies need this. Most have it in the early days but tend to lose it. A major message of our book is that success tends to erode strategic sensitivity over time.

In this chapter I argue that openness is critical to achieve and maintain agility, or strategic sensitivity. This comes from open processes with multiple stakeholders. The richness and diversity they bring to company dialogue is critical.

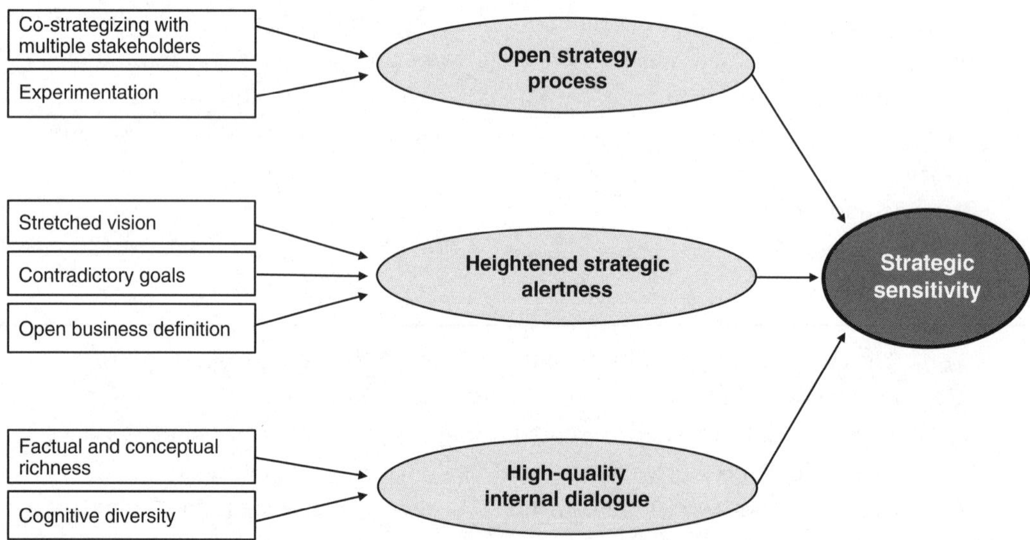

Figure 3.1
Open processes that drive strategic sensitivity
All figures © Yves Doz and Mikko Kosonen, *Fast Strategy*, Wharton School Publishing, 2008

Focus on Successful Competitors in the IT Industry

The data I examine comes primarily from the IT industry, which is wonderful territory because things change relatively quickly there. With the rise of the Internet, the industry has had to adapt quickly and often to the convergence between communication, computing, and entertainment; there is also the ebb and flow between network and devices as repositories of applications and intelligence. The IT industry has experienced revolutions, like the shift from centralized mainframes to client-server networked computing.

Somewhat jokingly, Mikko and I wrote in *Fast Strategy* that we went to the IT industry just as scientists trying to unravel genetic codes go to fruit flies. In both cases the objects of study reproduce very quickly. To discover the challenge of strategic agility as an organizational capability, we wanted to look at companies that pursued an integrated strategy. Although dynamic portfolio management does provide strategic agility for a diversified company, portfolio companies investing in and divesting from different businesses were not terribly interesting to us. They achieve a form of strategic agility not by transforming the businesses they are in, but by changing the composition of their portfolios, an exercise that can be carried out from corporate headquarters without engaging the organization and its members.

Mikko and I wanted to investigate companies that had been challenged by discontinuity and disruption to see how they responded when their strategic agility was tested by outside forces. We also wanted companies that were leading incumbents in their industry, or at least in a particular segment, because we were particularly interested in the risk and toxic side effects of becoming overly self-confident, of possibly becoming rigid without knowing it.

Although we did exploratory interviews at over a dozen companies, we focused our in-depth analyses on five companies that best fit the criteria discussed above: Cisco, IBM, Intel, HP, and SAP. And of course Nokia, which was the starting point of this research project. This selection was partly choice on our part, partly result of various constraints, but we are very happy with the set and what they represent.

A Successful and Widely Accepted Recipe for Success

We asked many executives at our case study sites why and how their companies had been successful. There was significant overlap in the answers we received, in the main along a few key themes. In summary, corporate leaders said, "We succeeded because we had a clear vision about the future of our core business." They stressed they made sustained efforts toward product innovation and had a tight focus on continuous improvements. They were ambitious and aspired to become leaders in everything they did. Or as the Americans would say, they had "the guts to do it." But these are not the only sources of success. Company leaders said, "We were organized in a way that allowed growth. We had strategic partners. We made great efforts to understand and collaborate with our customers. We created business units, we gave them autonomy, and we gave them the ability to be entrepreneurial. At the same time, we built on our experience. We developed efficient business systems and processes." Equally important, the leaders we interviewed made comments that had to do with being able to move fast. They said, "We succeeded because we had clear definitions of overall responsibilities for individual units. We had strong leaders. We had systems that allowed us to promote the best people."

Who would disagree with these statements? I am sure that most corporate and company leaders would support these claims, along with almost all strategic management or organization theory researchers. In fact these summary statements go beyond what the executives we interviewed told us. Table 3.1 describes good management practices collected during this research project. You will find one variant or another of all these directives in a number of strategy textbooks and in executive development courses for managers. This has become the conventional wisdom for excellence.

Table 3.1
Corporate beliefs about sustained growth and high performance

Clear direction and focus
- We should have a clear vision for the future of our core business
- We should have a sustained effort at maximally leveraging our core business
- We should have a tight focus on continuous improvement
- We should have leadership in everything we do
- We should have self-confidence and an action orientation

High efficiency
- We should have strong business units with sufficient autonomy as they grow
- We should have highly efficient business systems and processes
- We should have deep collaborative relationships with our key customers and partners
- We should learn by doing and build on our experience

Quick commitment
- We should have clear charters for all organizational units
- We should have strong and experienced leaders with proven track records
- We should make decisions fast
- We should promote successful leaders

The Relationship between Past Success and Current Difficulties

Unfortunately, there is a problem hidden at the heart of corporate success in the companies we studied. A primary conclusion from the study is that the practices of our leading incumbent companies, and the beliefs of both company leaders and management researchers about what will make a company succeed, are both right and wrong. The statements found in table 3.1 are right because they have to be followed to succeed. And yet we found that they also set the stage for later failure.

Look at the first statements about the importance of providing clear direction and focus in table 3.1. These ideas are both right and wrong because a sense of direction, though it seems hard to fault, narrows the field of vision, especially if a company becomes successful and begins to move more quickly. It is not very different from what most of us have experienced driving a car. When you drive a car at a high speed you discover there are so many stimulants coming your way so fast that you can only look at what is directly in front of you.

In a company that grows big fast, this and other sources of success, like a focus on continuous operational improvement or concern about maximizing the success of the core business, turn into implied dominance. They transform a well-earned success into hubristic arrogance, which tends to have disastrous side effects over time, as shown in table 3.2.

The table also describes the tyranny of the core businesses. It is hard to quarrel with sustained effort at developing a core business, but we found it also can limit vision.

Table 3.2
Toxic effects of single-minded attention to clear direction and focus

Driver	Consequence	Toxic side effect
Clear vision for the future of our core business	Clear vision for the future	Tunnel vision
Sustained effort at maximally leveraging our core business	Framing everything in the light of the core business	Tyranny of the core business
Tight focus on continuous improvement	Short-term internal orientation	Strategic myopia
Leadership position in everything we do	Reluctance to open collaboration and experimentation	Dominance mindset
High action orientation and self-confidence	Action hero syndrome; no time and interest for alternatives	Snap judgment and intellectual laziness

The more successful a company is in its core business, the more dependent it becomes on the perspectives and the framing provided by the people who run the business. In a sense the perceptions, the framing, the way managers perceive reality, are increasingly shaped by their success.

In addition a tight focus on continuous improvement leads to what might be called "strategic myopia." Companies are well-advised to keep improving on an ongoing basis, of course, but to some extent they tend to lose direction in the process. Furthermore, achieving a leadership position tends to be followed by what you could call a "dominance mindset"-- excessive self-confidence, or hubris. People who have been building a business successfully for a long time tend to be very action oriented. They make very quick decisions. These snap judgments help them succeed in areas they know well, but are dangerous in areas they do not know.

There is an interesting set of issues around each aspect of a company's success. We found a pattern around efficiency, for example, that is very similar in its toxic side effects to what we observed around focus. As summarized in table 3.3, strong and autonomous business units often imprison resources. Each business unit is pursuing its own objectives, has its own resources. Almost inevitably, there is a bit of resource holding and defensiveness on the part of senior executives. As a result the more efficient the business system, the more rigid it may become.

Collaborative relationships similarly create ties that bind, sometimes in a very down to earth, operational way. For example, when Motorola introduced folding phones a few years ago, Nokia was rather slow in responding to the challenge. One shouldn't be surprised to learn that the head of design at Nokia did not have a positive feeling

Table 3.3

Toxic effects of single-minded attention to high efficiency

Driver	Consequence	Toxic side effect
Strong business units with sufficient autonomy as they grow	Core business managers "sitting on their resources"	Resource imprisonment
Highly efficient business system processes	Increasingly differentiated and specialized ("fit for purpose") activity systems	Activity system rigidification
Deep collaborative relationships with key customers and partners	Customer and partner "lock in;" decreasing strategic freedom	Ties that bind
Learning by doing and building on experience	Forgiven and hidden misbehavior and shortcomings	Management mediocrity and competence gaps

about the new folding design and was reluctant to imitate it. But there was an even deeper and more serious roadblock. Nokia's mobile phones were designed around a particular type of circuitry, which happened to be a little over a centimeter thick. It could not be redesigned. It could neither be split in two to fold, nor easily be made thinner. Hence the company could not quickly escape its dependency on the particular supplier that provided this rather thick circuit. It took Nokia a couple of years to develop new products around a redesigned circuitry. Similarly, when the bottom fell out of the market for Internet telephony, Cisco, used to years of high growth and the need for a secure supply of components for its routers, could not cut back production without incurring huge penalties to its suppliers, with whom it had engaged in long-term contracts.

Such patterns were identified again and again. For example, learning by experience often is not a good predictor of long-term management success. First of all, corporate success heightens reputations independent of causality. What could have been serendipitous luck is interpreted as judicious management choice. Hubris and misplaced self-confidence prevails. Similarly, recruiting a large number of people and promoting them very fast does not give them enough time to learn. We found managers who were pretty good at running after their old success. But after a while they discovered that they were not as good as they wanted to be, or were expected to be, when facing new strategic challenges or implementing new business models. Success and familiarity with the territory had hidden management weaknesses and capability gaps.

Further observations are summarized in table 3.4 on the capability for top management to make bold strategic decisions, a capability that naturally erodes over time. Once top management teams no longer need to make shared strategic decisions, merely growing an existing business along a well-charted course, their thinking tended to go

Table 3.4
Toxic effects of single-minded attention to quick commitment

Driver	Consequence	Toxic side effect
Clear charters for all organizational units	Declining intensity of dialogue and decreasing need for collective commitments	Management divergence
Strong leaders with proven track record	Inflated egos; overly bold commitments; implicit pecking order	Heady charm of fame and power
Preference for fast decision-making	Decisions elevating to the top team; decisions made by the same leaders	Expert management
Successful leaders	Tired hero syndrome; future opportunities looking less thrilling than past experiences	Emotional apathy

in divergent directions. Each person had their own priorities, and ran their business, or played their specialized expert role, in their own way. In the process they lost sight of the integration of the whole company. The richness of dialogue that characterized the company when it was young and entrepreneurial was often lost.

Strong leaders can become overconfident. They sometimes have inflated egos, and often do not tolerate dissenting voices. Over time they are more likely to make commitments and throw challenges to their managers that do not make sense. That's what we call "the heady charm of fame and power." Leaders become unrealistic in their expectations, and sometimes irrational in their behaviors.

Rapid decision-making is often required in today's world. It is obviously a good thing, as we all know, but it also leads to what is known as "expert management," in which people no longer really challenge each other: the CFO does finance, the operations type takes care of operations, the head of X business does X business, and so on. Members of the leadership team avoid venturing on each other's turf and challenging one another. Companies can succeed for a while with this kind of arrangement, but that too has a downside. Mutual deference and specialization of roles and skills deprive the organization of much needed checks and balances in decision-making. Decisions are made fast, but badly, and that process fails when complex collective choices have to be made. These require careful dialogue and thoughtful consideration, not merely the juxtaposition of expert opinions.

Last, executives may lose some of their enthusiasm over time. If you had led Nokia's growth, you would have had a tough but exhilarating life for 15 years. At 50, success secured, you would look for self-renewal in a different challenge. We saw emotional apathy at Nokia and other leading companies.

The Cumulative Effect of Growing Rapidly

Many very successful companies come to the problematic point shown in figure 3.2, which is the sum of what I have been describing. First, what we call "strategic sensitivity," meaning leaders' ability to be in touch with strategic developments around them, tends to decline. Second, resource fluidity, the ability to re-allocate resources in a fast but committed fashion, also tends to slow down. Finally, leadership unity is undermined, without anyone noticing until difficult and complex strategic decisions have to be made.

This figure provides an organizational, evolutionary explanation for the fact that many companies succeed, but in general not for long. That means there is some kind of life cycle to management: quantitative researchers who look at statistical data on

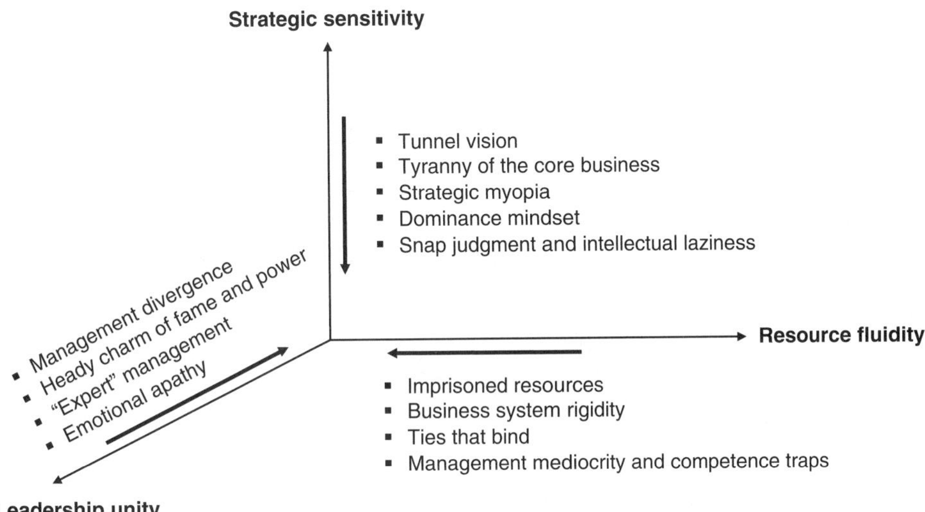

Figure 3.2
Curse of success

the performance of businesses will observe a "regression to the mean." In other words, excellent companies seldom stay excellent for long. Mikko and I provide a tentative systemic explanation in *Fast Strategy*. As change calls for strategic agility, these companies no longer have it, and their performance deteriorates. Dealing with this life cycle is the real challenge for leaders.

Where any one company is on the life cycle is uncertain, as shown in figure 3.3. This is another important observation from our study. In a way, the strategic rigidity or strategic paralysis described previously is like slowly losing physical fitness in midlife. If we discover as individuals that we have lost agility and engage in strenuous exercise, we may hopefully regain health but not by doing exactly what we did when we were young.

Many successful companies are facing something similar. In order to renew themselves, they have to become fit in middle age for a world that is more complex in markets and technologies, more demanding of leadership in stock performance terms, and more rapidly changing than the world they were used to in the past.

Taking the example of Nokia, a company that makes something like 1.5 million phones a day, one can imagine that they have a well-honed business system. Yet that system became inadequate for the challenges they faced. They had to go into Internet services, work with complex advertising-based revenue models, and figure out more

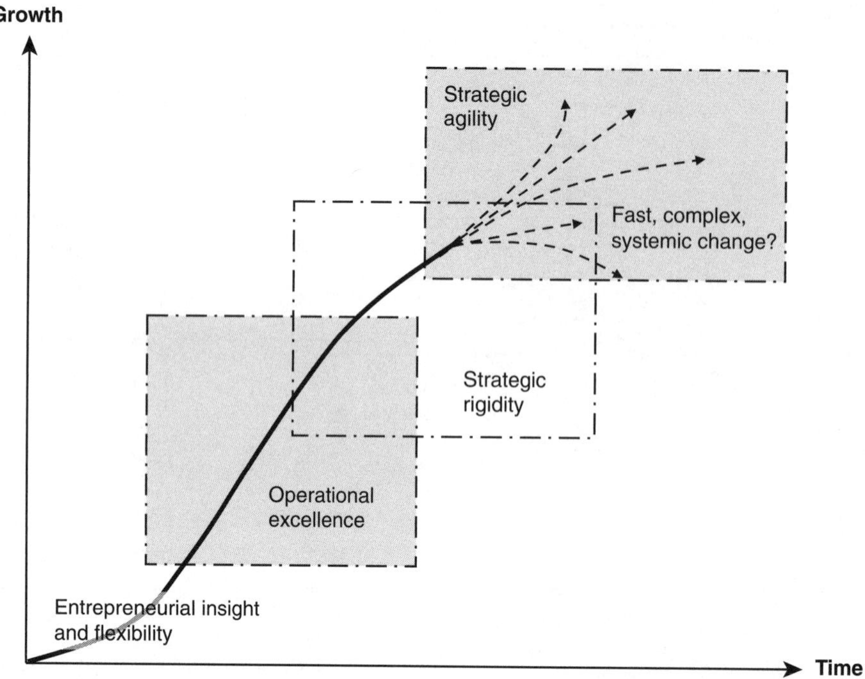

Figure 3.3
Where is strategic agility most needed?

than Google has already figured out. Google is a "pure play" Internet services company with a very simple business model—reap the increasing returns of search engines (the bigger and more widely used, the better they get, attracting further use, and growth) and monetize unused screen space with paid advertising in a personalized way. Nokia attempted to combine its strengths in devices, software platforms, and mobility applications to create innovative services in collaboration with telecom network operators. This is a considerably more complex business model proposition than Google's or Facebook's. It put Nokia in a very complex, very fast, very systemic environment with complex transaction models, ecosystems, and open innovations. It is several orders of magnitude more complex than the world of making phones and selling them in bulk to telecom network operators just a few years ago. We know they could not address the new challenge successfully.

Just as Nokia's strategists have a harder job than when they were faced with simple challenges like the trend toward folding phones, we observe that many well-known and successful companies confront a similar situation today. They have reached a

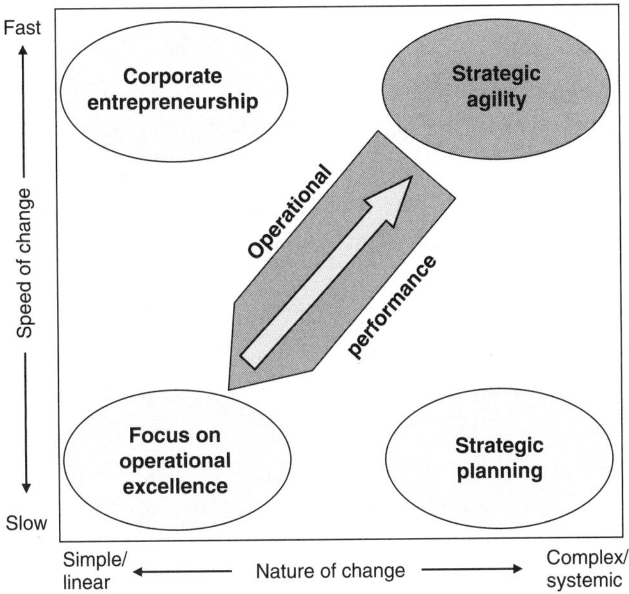

Figure 3.4
Why strategic agility now? Why so hard?

point of relative rigidity that is a direct outcome of their past success just when they have to deal with a faster, more complex world. It is not easy, as suggested by figure 3.4. The planning and entrepreneurial solutions developed in companies, and by researchers who study companies, are no longer sufficient.

Strategic agility is especially important when companies must simultaneously make rapid and complex changes in their core business model. In some industries it may be enough to focus on operational excellence alone and not be really concerned with strategic agility. The 100th anniversary of the first mass-produced car, the Ford Model T, was in 2008. Your neighbors who have a BMW or a Mercedes are likely to say cars today are fundamentally different from a century ago. Think twice. They would be right about some details we all value about modern cars such as air conditioning or electronic driving assistance, but today's cars are not so fundamentally different from the Model T. The basic architecture of a car and the basic way cars are made has not changed in the last century. Cars and the assembly lines required to produce them have merely become much more complex, and companies have to focus on operational excellence.

Other companies face terribly complex and uncertain situations, with huge stakes and risks, but these situations unfold slowly. Take the oil industry, which has very long cycles. Development of an oil field takes years and costs billions, production runs for decades, oil prices fluctuate wildly, and new energies appear, some to stay, others (like bio-fuels) with a more uncertain potential. Traditional strategic planning works well in this kind of industry, as suggested in figure 3.4 at the bottom right. It is possible to thoughtfully develop strategies, test them against multiple scenarios (it is no coincidence that Shell is famed for the development of scenario planning methods), and turn them into long-term strategic plans that one updates every year, or every other year.

Conversely, at the top left in this figure, entrepreneurial companies and the things they offer often are not very complex at the beginning. However, speed is paramount. Leaders in this situation are obsessed with finding new opportunities, creating more ventures, or developing new units in an established company. New startups that grow big fast, like Google, are demonstrating the importance of discovering and quickly elaborating offerings that capture customers, yet this is far from obvious. Beyond its core business, despite its famed innovative culture and intensive efforts, Google's success so far has not exactly been stellar. Creating new ventures and maintaining an entrepreneurial culture are the key levers of success. From the corporate standpoint, the company is run like a very dynamic portfolio company.

Strategic agility becomes really important when companies have to quickly respond to very complex systemic changes. However, there always remains a huge tension between the pressure of operational performance and the ability to build and maintain strategic agility. Take Nokia in the mid-1990s. It suffered a logistics crisis, namely an operational breakdown of its supply chain and manufacturing network. The sudden takeoff of mobile phones as a mass market caught the company by surprise, and it cobbled a response to increase production fast, but in a poorly coordinated manner. It sorted out the crisis quickly, but one lesson learned was that operations needed to be better planned and managed with greater discipline.

Another lesson was to launch new ventures as renewal options, in the hope of building a third leg to Nokia. This set up a high level of tension between operational excellence and strategic renewal. What you typically find in these circumstances is that strategic agility is constantly being eroded. Inflexibility—rigor mortis at the extreme-- is produced by the very real need for operational excellence. It is an ongoing tension within most organizations.

Escaping the Rigidities Caused by Success

A key thing Mikko and I point to in *Fast Strategy* is the need to increase strategic sensitivity, or if you wish "strategic alertness." This requires something very similar to descriptions of open innovation found in this volume. To have an advantage, companies must maintain a strategic process that is open to the outside but is also enriched by being highly participative internally. This is not what happens in companies where strategy remains the purview of a very small group at the top.

Because the more interesting innovations and disruptions tend to happen at the periphery of an organization, in new markets and emerging technologies rather than in the center, companies must be open to a great variety of information sources. To take a classic example, Xerox was for decades mesmerized by IBM and Kodak—new competitors in photocopiers that also were its neighbors in upstate New York. Only because of its joint venture with Fuji in Japan did it finally become aware, reluctantly, that a new breed of competitors, led by Canon, was emerging in Japan and mounting a very fundamental challenge to Xerox's very existence. This is an example of why strategic agility requires strategic processes to be decentralized, distributed, internally participative, and (selectively) open externally.

IBM provides a tangible example. They have replaced the traditional executive committee at the top of the organization with three different teams. The first is operational, basically led by operational managers, closest in composition to an operating committee. Then there is a technology and innovation team, and a strategy team. Each of the three teams includes key people from the top of the organization but also a selection of the best and brightest younger executives in the organization. There is a rotating membership, so that every year half of the members on a given team are replaced. But it is not a "let's meet to take on this or that assignment" situation. It is a fulltime or nearly full-time appointment—the individuals involved are detached from their usual responsibilities for two years.

Another important thing to mention is that alertness is partly the result of entertaining contradictory goals and tensions. SAP, for example, has been managing a major transition. They decided to move from serving Fortune 1000 companies to also serving one or two hundred thousand smaller or mid-size enterprises. For the traditional software development engineers at company headquarters in Walldorf, Germany, that meant providing Internet-based service that would be even better than the in-person service they were providing onsite to a small group of large corporate clients.

Establishing Internet-based services for a large number of smaller corporate customers was a complementary goal for SAP, one that created tons of tension in the organization. Making it happen was complex because some of the new Internet models were coming from the periphery of the organization, mostly from acquisitions and R&D work in California. They challenged the beliefs, practices, and status of the traditional research and development establishment in Walldorf. What had created a high level of internal tension, also created a high level of strategic alertness over the past few years.[2] SAP formed a corporate consulting team, a group of around 30 people recruited at a relatively young age from consulting and investment banking. This is somewhat similar to what IBM has been experimenting with, assigning younger "best and brightest" executives to its three corporate teams, with similar effects.

When SAP's CEO Henning Kagermann was asked about the main contribution of young people in key assignments, he had an interesting answer. "They are very bright," he said, "they bring in lots of new ideas." But then another SAP executive added something more intriguing: "They keep us honest." By this he meant that not only did they feed insightful information and analyses to the top team, they also checked on the quality and openness of the strategic dialogue at the top.

Our conclusion from this and other companies' experience is that the quality of dialogue created is quite critical. It is almost as if the leaders at the top have to operate in a kind of fishbowl. Ideally, increased visibility and increased tension lead to increased strategic alertness. There are many ways to achieve strategic sensitivity. I have just mentioned a few. In our *Fast Strategy* we break every driver of strategic agility into component parts, but then it quickly becomes relatively complex, as shown in figure 3.5 and explained in much more detail. We have very specific findings behind each of these points that I do not have room in our book to discuss in this chapter.

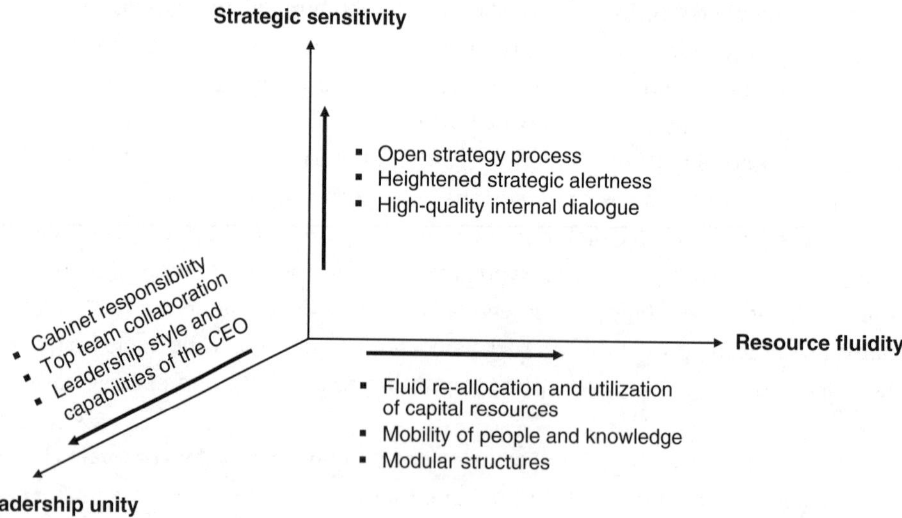

Figure 3.5
Key capabilities enabling strategic agility

Table 3.5
A peek into the microscope

	SAP	NOKIA
Heightened strategic alertness	• Stretched goals/CEO promises • Multidimensional organization • Assigned designated corporate and business level strategists to drive and facilitate corporate wide strategic collaboration with key partners	• Stretched goals/CEO promises • Open "business" definition—life goes Mobile • Systematic recruitment from other businesses
Quality of dialogue	• Corporate strategy group (30-person strong internal consultancy team) recruited from consulting and investment banking to improve the quality of strategic dialogue common frameworks and concepts that allow rich interpretations of strategic issues in a common language • Create an environment where everybody has the freedom to speak up, criticize, be out of the box • Discuss first as a team at the top; "openness to disagree forces a true team"	• Strategic agenda: 10 major strategic issues that are continuously followed on emerging technologies, business models, and other important trends relevant for more than one business group. "Handpick" 10 of the most capable individuals from any part of the organization to work on selected vision themes. • Strategy process: Involve thousands of people, supported by web-based dialoguing tools

Table 3.5 provides just a brief look at two issues under strategic sensitivity, in two companies: heightened strategic alertness and quality of dialogue. For example, Dr. Kagermann at SAP increased the freedom to speak, the ability to disagree, and so on. These are critical to internal dialogue. We provide many more details in *Fast Strategy* so that it is possible to get a sense of similarities (and differences) across companies. As academic researchers we then want to articulate this in a more rigorous fashion, as a model or as a framework. Hopefully others will also be interested in following up on this line of inquiry.

Achieving Greater Resource Fluidity and Increasing Teamwork at the Top

There are all kinds of organizational mechanisms that need attention if an organization is to create the building blocks required for strategic agility. You can think in terms of a LEGO® block metaphor. An organization has to be able to be assembled, disassembled, and reconfigured in various outcomes, around key processes and information systems, producing various products, responses to using various structures. All this allows the company to make rapid entry and rapid exit in specific businesses or specific types of activities. The process also needs greater mobility of people and greater mobility of knowledge.

This is important, as the process of becoming fast is a slow process. It takes a lot of cognitive work to rebuild strategic sensitivity. It takes a lot of organizational work to rebuild resource fluidity, create common business infrastructures, create modular organizations, and modular elements of business systems. Leadership unity would seem to be a necessary force pulling disparate resources together. That is true, and creating leadership unity that is interpersonal and relational is also a slow process. It usually requires a mix of the intellectual and emotional, almost a psychodynamic intervention. One finds that it is essential to have coaching, monitoring, and advising on different ways of working together at the top of the organization.

The critical point is that the top team must be able to function as a true team. That may sound like a tautology, but it is not. In most organizations the closer you get to the top, the less teamwork there is. The more you find a tight one-on-one relationship between the CEO and trusted barons, who essentially each run their own fiefdoms (perhaps regional, functional, product lines, or business), the less likely that the organization will enjoy the leadership unity needed to create agility.

Typically corporate reward systems operate to the detriment of collective decisions because they emphasize individual performance, discipline, and control. That encourages standoffish behavior. In all the agile companies that we studied, we found a shift in incentives at the top from strategic performance to overall corporate performance. It varied from company to company, it was perhaps fifty-fifty at HP and perhaps 100 percent at SAP, but clearly there is a realignment of incentive systems to create more cohesive leadership.

There is also an interesting shift in the kind of leaders companies are choosing. Think of Samuel Palmisano, CEO at IBM, as compared to his predecessor Louis Gerstner. Think of Henning Kagermann, CEO at SAP, compared to Hasso Plattner. On television, Gerstner and Plattner were much more exciting types than their successors. However, when it actually comes to creating the collective, participative processes needed to make an organization work, our conclusion was that the duller, quieter successors were actually a lot more effective than more flamboyant leaders. A very peculiar form of leadership is developing. It is not quite servant leadership. It is a more complex form. We call it "adaptive leadership." It is essentially the capacity to help teams work as a collective.

Conclusion

In summary, we found that strategic agility results from strategic sensitivity; it needs to be combined with resource fluidity as well as leadership unity. Figure 3.6 has two

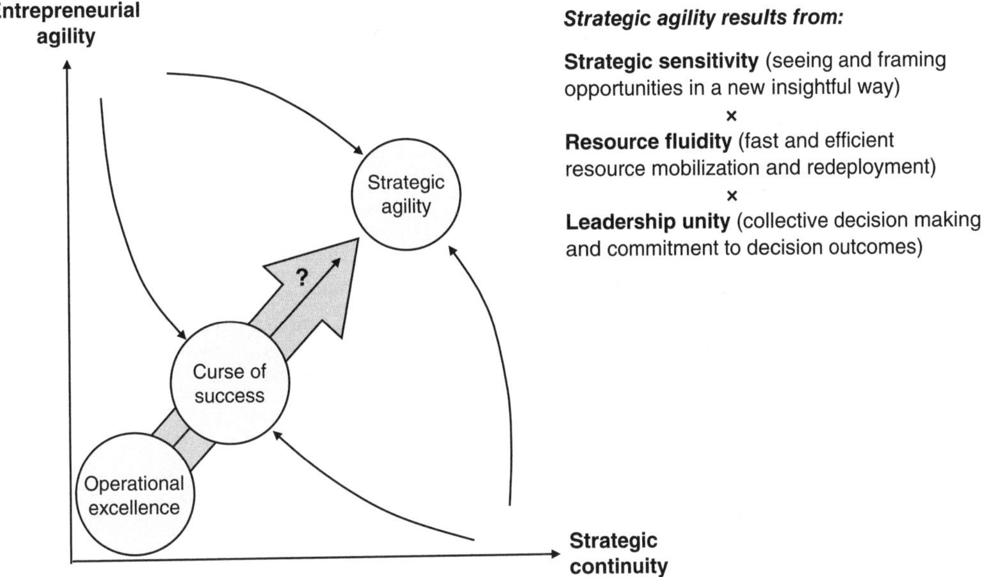

Figure 3.6
Summary

small x's that are multiplicative signs, meaning that any one positive factor without the other two, or even two without the third, does not get you there. If one of them is zero, the sum is zero. Or, if one of them is very low, the whole thing becomes very low. That is essentially the strongest set of findings of this research project.

From a broader perspective, we believe that agility is required to achieve two things that are increasingly important in a globalizing economy but are very difficult to address simultaneously. On the one hand, companies have to become more entrepreneurial. They must recognize new opportunities and respond to them before others do. On the other hand, strategic continuity is required to help the organization's many stakeholders understand their relationship to the organization, and to improve operational performance.

Idea for Innovative Leaders: Pay Attention to Emotion

How does an organization become healthy again? What is the equivalent for companies to your doctor telling you as an individual that you should stop smoking and drinking, start exercising, avoid stress? Of course, some of us will die of a heart attack,

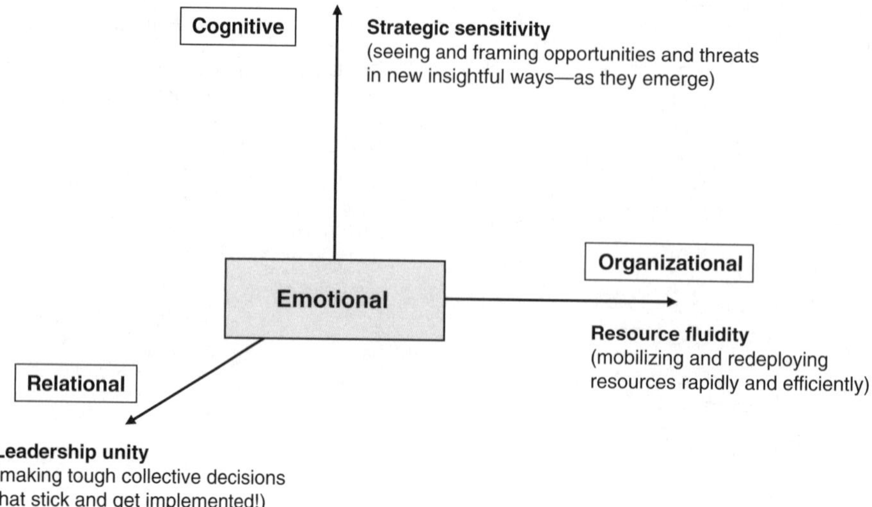

Figure 3.7
Key levers of strategic leadership

like some companies fail to renew themselves and disappear, despite extensive efforts. It's worth working hard to keep that from happening.

We found that rebuilding strategic sensitivity calls for a lot of intellectual and cognitive work. It calls for really slowly, painfully reshaping the way a fairly large group of senior executives and managers in an organization relate to create their own future. It is particularly interesting that emotional issues are at the heart of this transition, as shown in figure 3.7.

Mikko and I feel strongly that the real energy for strategic agility comes from emotional commitment. Yet emotion tends to be neglected in organizations. Many executives feel that playing on emotions is too dangerous, while others have a sense that it is not proper to talk about emotions. For these and other reasons emotions are ignored.

There is equal neglect from academics. Not enough research has been done on emotional commitment in organizations. And therefore we have tended to focus too much on extrinsic rather than intrinsic rewards. But extrinsic rewards in most organizations are relatively primitive for two reasons. First, measurement is difficult. Second, and more important, thinking about extrinsic rewards leads to a very cynical view of the human being, a very mechanistic view of the human being. So one last comment for both executives and researchers: Do not ignore the emotional dimension!

Notes

1. Download an MP4 video or and an MP3 audio discussion by the authors at http://knowledge.insead.edu/faststrategy080101.cfm?vid=16

2. For decades Intel has similarly maintained a tension between the chip-making side of its organization, essentially very competitive, and the chipset development and platform organization, which is much more open to collaboration.

References and Further Reading

Bower, J. L., and C. G. Gilbert, eds. 2006. *From Resource Allocation to Strategy*. New York: Oxford University Press.

Doz, Y. L., and M. Kosonen. 2008. *Fast Strategy: How Strategic Agility Will Help You Stay Ahead of the Game*. Upper Saddle River, NJ: Wharton School Publishing.

Doz, Y. L., and M. Kosonen. 2008. The dynamics of strategic agility: Nokia's rollercoaster experience. *California Management Review* 50 (3): 95–118.

Doz, Y. L., and M. Kosonen. 2010. Embedding strategic agility: A leadership agenda for accelerating business model renewal. *Long Range Planning* 43 (2–3): 370–82.

Noda, T., and J. L. Bower. 1996. Strategy making as iterated processes of resource allocation. *Strategic Management Journal* 17 (7): 159–92.

Staw, M. B., and J. Ross. 1987. Knowing when to plug the plug. *Harvard Business Review* 65 (2): 68–74.

Van de Ven, A. H. 2007. *Engaged Scholarship*. Oxford: Oxford University Press.

4 Leading Innovation

Rudolf Gröger

Introduction

As a company CEO I can get all of the technological expertise I want. If I need fifty A-rated electronic engineers, it is easy to hire them. If I need 500, I just hire 500. And if I want more, I go to China. Obviously, if these resources are available to everybody, the difference between an average company and a very successful company is not technology, but due to the "soft factors" that leadership must provide. By extension, innovation is much less about technology than about the capacity to lead innovation.

The iPhone is not a product of the twenty-first century in terms of technology, there is something else going on. The phone started out with poor quality and poor service. The battery life was not good. You could not fold it. You could not change the loudness of the ringtone, and so forth. But everyone says, "I have to have one." Just like everyone says, "I drive a BMW" or "I drive an Audi." No one is saying, "I drive an Opel."

I suggest that if you want to be a leader, the only thing you have to do, logically, is bring your company into a position where it has the competitive advantage of people wanting to buy what you have to offer. This must be the reason why you get out of bed in the morning.

Background to Becoming CEO of O_2

I worked almost twenty years at Siemens. At the end of that time I was the German boss of the information and communication business and my biggest customer was Deutsche Telekom. Of course, I paid a visit to my biggest customers twice a year just to make sure that everything was going well. After my second visit, the head of Deutsche Telekom called my boss and said, "I want to hire that guy, and we'll pay him this much. Don't make him a counteroffer. Then you will have somebody with a Siemens heritage in Deutsche Telekom, which is as good for you as for us."

So the two made a deal and I was sold like a football player to Bonn. If you are based in Munich you are not too excited to go to Bonn. But I did it and I was relatively at ease because I thought that after eighteen years in Siemens, I understood the culture of big organizations. I thought that if I went from Siemens to Deutsche Telekom, there would not be a big cultural change. In fact the differences could not have been bigger.

After six months in Deutsche Telekom, I founded the company that today is called T-Systems—a worldwide ICT company. To make that happen, I tried to acquire a big IT systems house. In the end I decided to buy DaimlerChrysler's IT arm, a company that had 25,000 people working in 22 countries. Once again, I was sitting in Bonn and I thought to myself, if I bring a company from Mercedes into Deutsche Telekom, the culture must be similar, but again the differences were very big.

In all of these businesses, and again when I went to Viag Interkom, which soon became O_2, I thought that the network was the asset and would make the difference. None of that turned out to be true. In all of these businesses, the only differences were the people. My lesson is: if you run an infrastructure business, the infrastructure itself is not a competitive differentiation. People make the difference—the engineers planning the network, the people in the shops, your employees are your ambassadors —or not.

Therefore I say—a bit provocatively—forget about innovation. There is no customer who wants to buy your innovation, as your innovation. If you go to a coffee machine, you will likely push the cappuccino button. The more creative among you may choose to drink the latte. The innovation in that machine is not the technology that brings milk and coffee together. The innovation is demand for cappuccino, which was not there five years ago. That alone is the innovation.

The Most Important Characteristics of Leadership

If people make the difference in every business, the core competence of leaders must be managing people. I feel the biggest problem in our education system at the moment is that we are teaching a lot of theory, but we are not training people to deal with situations, change companies, and find innovation. I have been saying to professors for some time, "All the people you sent me were worth very little. I had to train them a second time. I had to drill the importance of working with people into them."

The most important thing students of business must learn is how to be authentic as a leader. I mean by that authentic not only as a person, but also as a person who

Figure 4.1
Basic beliefs about leadership

is part of an authentic company culture. One of my first lessons about leadership was that people were watching me. Even if they are at the lowest education level, they felt whether I was authentic in what I was doing. They knew whether there was a difference between brain and heart. All successful companies have leaders. Especially the deutsche Mittelstand, the middle-sized companies that dominate our economy. These companies tend to have leaders you have never heard of, but they are leaders by birth. They have authenticity in their genetic code.

In bigger organizations, I think there are three things that must be given attention, as shown in figure 4.1. The first has to do with vision, the second with culture, and the third, leadership. These are the things that shape a leader's behavior, general direction, and motivation.

Vision Is Central

When I started working for Siemens, the American business school message that "you must have a vision" was beginning to influence the average working person. As a result company managers started asking, "Could someone in this office please write a vision?" The result was very nice sentences. They were printed and then hung in meeting rooms so that everyone knew the company's vision.

This is not my understanding of a vision, or how it is achieved. If vision is authentic and seriously meant, you must describe every single word and what you mean by it. You have to break down what vision means in terms of behavior. The process gives people an example of whether top management's actions are consistent with the professed vision.

After vision, you have to think about culture. How are people dealing with each other? How open are people when they deal with each other? This tells employees what is okay and what is not. I learned from being in Siemens, Deutsche Telecom, and then O_2 that different companies have very different cultures. Linking vision and culture therefore is not simple. It has to be tailored to the situation, but it must be done. The goal is leadership that allows you to bring motivation into the organization.

Vision must be able to transmit thoughts about the normal world into something better.

Market Position Is Important

One of my rules is that there is no Olympic ideal—I do not agree with the belief that being part of the Olympics is more important than winning. Everybody wants to be the winner. What if I had said, taking over the company that became O_2, "We are the smallest in Germany and the latest in the market, number four out of four"? That is not an inspiring message. People want to have targets. If you cannot change your number four position to number three position, change the focus. Then say you want to be number one in the American segment, if you can't improve your overall place.

Towers Perrin, a global consultant company specializing in salary schemes, did a survey in 2004 in which they asked "What is important for you in your company?" Salary was number ten. The most important for employees was something like: "Senior management is interested in what I am doing. They ask me how I feel. They motivate me." If a leader is able to do these things, the people who work for them will go to every fight. If you have a vision, if you know what your targets are, there is no need to say, "I will give you a hundred bucks more if you do what I ask." They would, of course, take the money, but that is not the real motivation.

Becoming CEO of VIAG Interkom

To understand even the very short version of my experience at O_2, you must know that in Germany there were four mobile licenses awarded in 1998. In those days we were all sitting on piles of money, having no idea what to do with it going forward. Everyone thought that if they entered the mobile industry they would have a license to print money. The two clear market leaders were T-Mobile and D2 Vodafone, each with about 40 percent of the market share. There was no need for a fourth network, since we already had a third as well. This was the starting position for me in 2001 when I became the head of VIAG Interkom. As fourth contender the company had a market share of 6 percent. We had 3,400 people, revenue of 1.1 billion euros, and earnings before interest, taxes, depreciation, and amortization [EBITDA] of minus 270 million euros.

Even worse, a couple of days after I joined the company, on the first of October 2001, our shareholders said they wanted to close and sell. My boss, the CEO of British Telecom, gave this news to the press, not to me. When I found out, I called and said,

"Was this really necessary? You bring me out of my comfort zone in Deutsche Telekom and then you say close the company. That's not fair." And he said, "Rudi, business is not always fair. You have two weeks. Calculate what it costs to shut down the whole company."

The number came to 500 million euros: letting 3,400 people go, getting out of contracts, and so on. But then my boss said, "No, sorry, I cannot give you 500 million." That was the opportunity for me to propose a deal: I would try to improve the business, quarter by quarter. If that happened and if at least one of the first four quarters EBITDA was positive, we would be allowed to survive.

It was not an easy game. In the first stage of this kind of business, companies put as much money as they can into infrastructure. Then the second step is to get customers. Otherwise, the infrastructure doesn't make money. But when the first early adopters, the people for whom price is not so relevant (let's say in this situation the business people), have already been absorbed, this first stage is over. In the next stage market share goes to brands. The brand becomes extremely important because customers really cannot decide whether the Vodafone network is better than T-Mobile or something else. So you buy a brand. And with the brand, you buy trust, a perception of quality, and good feeling.

VIAG Interkom entered the market at exactly that point. Branding had started. But we had financial difficulties. Extremely high investments had been made. We had spent 1.8 billion euros year after year on the network because in an infrastructure business you cannot wait. You have to have a network or you are out of business.

There were some bright spots. We were a startup company. We had startup processes, structures, and mentality. If something was not working, we were likely to say, "We are a very young company. You competitors cannot do what we do. You are a hundred years old; we are two years old."

There was, however, a lot of uncertainty around new technology. 3G services were really taking off, but it was not clear if it was worthwhile to go there, market-wise, especially for us because we had poor market position. And this was late 2001; do not forget the financial crisis. The Internet bubble had burst six or nine months earlier. A lot of people had lost a lot of money

Vision as the Basis of Turnaround

To improve VIAG Interkom, we started with the question of why we were in the market. Finally, we arrived at the sentence: Be an innovative company. That sentence cost me 48 hours of continuous meeting, boxes of Weißbier, and six dictionaries. I was reading the dictionaries to find out what "innovative" means and more important what it might mean for us.

I also had to think about how we might measure whether we were innovative. You have to remember that we were buying network equipment from today's Nokia-Siemens Networks, phones from Motorola, Sony Ericsson, and Nokia—so what could innovation mean for us? And if it was to make sense, every word we used in our statement had to be a performance indicator that we could measure. What would it mean if we had said, as we did, "We want to enrich our customer's lives, whatever they do, wherever they are"? Vision has to be measurable. We had to set targets, and we did. We concluded, for example, that we wanted to have 100 percent network coverage because, if we want to enrich your life wherever you are, we have to be there with our network.

Ultimately the basis for the O_2 turnaround was the structured set of statements shown in figure 4.2. If we had not been able to translate our vision in this way, we might just as well have said that our vision was that we all want to be forever young, rich, and healthy.

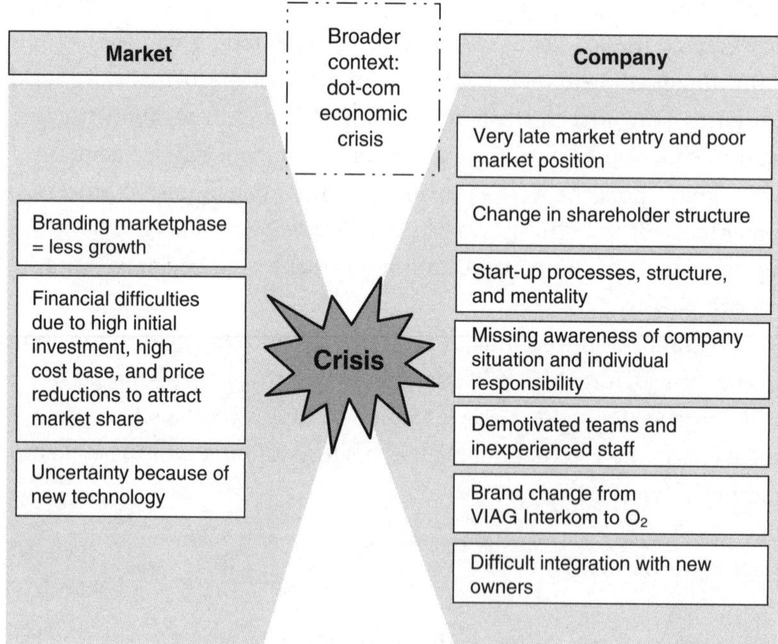

Figure 4.2
VIAG Interkom challenges

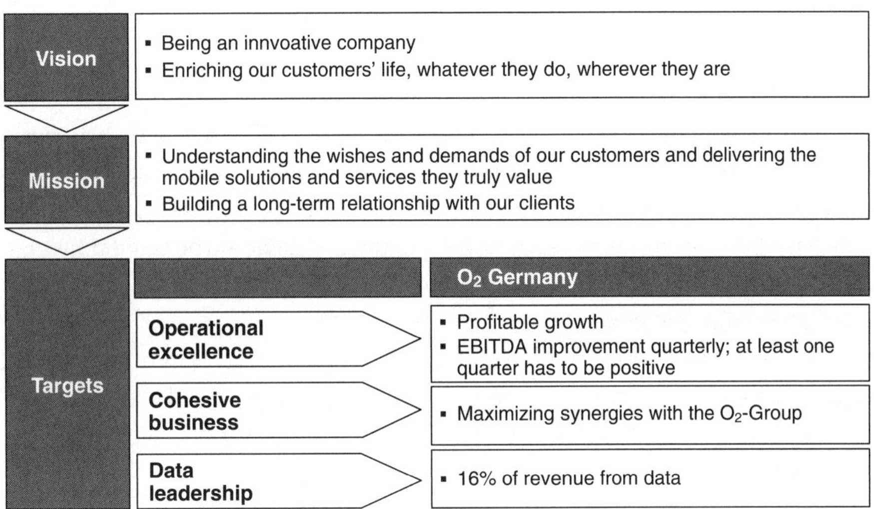

Figure 4.3
O_2 vision, mission, and targets that led to the turnaround

Actions after Targets Were Established

I had agreed on some targets with British Telecom, including growth in EBITDA (at least one of the first four quarters had to be positive). Figure 4.3 shows the vision, mission, and the goals of the rebranded company O_2. These were the things we looked at first. But I discovered you never have one problem alone.

I went, first, to the sales department and said, "Guys, why are you not selling enough?" They said, "Rudi, we are great salespeople. But, to be honest, our network is not the best. We know that already. No wonder people do not buy from us."

Then I moved to the network department and said, "Hey, network department, the guys in sales say you are responsible for our underperforming in sales because the network is not good." But the network people said, "We have built a wonderful network."

"Who is it then?" I asked them. Perhaps you will not be surprised to find what they suggested, "The real problem is IT. Our planning tools are poor. We sometimes build a network where no customer is sitting, and on the other hand, where customers sit, we do not have something to offer. You know, it's IT." But then IT said, "We are running the best systems ever!"

So I said, "Who the hell is it, then?" and all three groups agreed: it is the new shareholder. They said, "We have a British shareholder, you know. They drive on the wrong side of the street. They have their own currency. They are hard to understand. The Brits are guilty."

What I concluded is that you can't save a company by finding a critical problem. You can't save a company by saying to people "You are no longer allowed to fly business class." These are not your real problems as a leader. Your problems are that your production is too slow and too expensive. Your people are demotivated. Your sales force is targeting the wrong customer. You have many problems at the same time that you must focus on. And therefore you have to deal with everything at the same time. This is the leadership challenge.

In our turnaround and I think in many other cases of turnaround as well—leadership requires that everything has to be repaired at the same time: product roadmaps, quality, technology streamlining—everything. You cannot say this or that is a priority because everything has to be addressed tomorrow.

Communicating a Complex Agenda

Some people say there is complexity reduction for decision-making at the top, but this is wrong. Every reduction in complexity leads you in the wrong direction. You have to learn to deal with more complexity. Also, going forward, what you deal with today does not become easier, it becomes more complex. You have to think about processes and methodologies to deal with more complexity, not reduce it. This is fundamental.

The biggest problem I faced as a leader is shown in figure 4.4, a slide I used at O_2. As boss, I had to come out of a secure office, stand in front of three or four thousand people, and say, "I have a plan. I'll tell you what you and I will do." You have to do that, because otherwise why should people have faith in what you want them to do?

The thing that makes life uncomfortable is when you have to say, as I did, "Look, on this first arrow from 15th of December 2001 to the end of May 2002, we will do cost-cutting, and this will mean some jobs will be lost." But I also said, "I swear to you that nobody will be fired on the 1st of June. That is my commitment. Commitment number two: the money we are saving in cost-cutting will not just be added to the bottom line. So you have to save money, but you can reinvest some in the future survival of the company." That is what we did at O_2. We took one-third of the money we saved and spent it in the market, on our future.

The big problem was that the slide shown in figure 4.4 was shown to everyone. From a leadership perspective, this is quite a difficult situation because everyone in

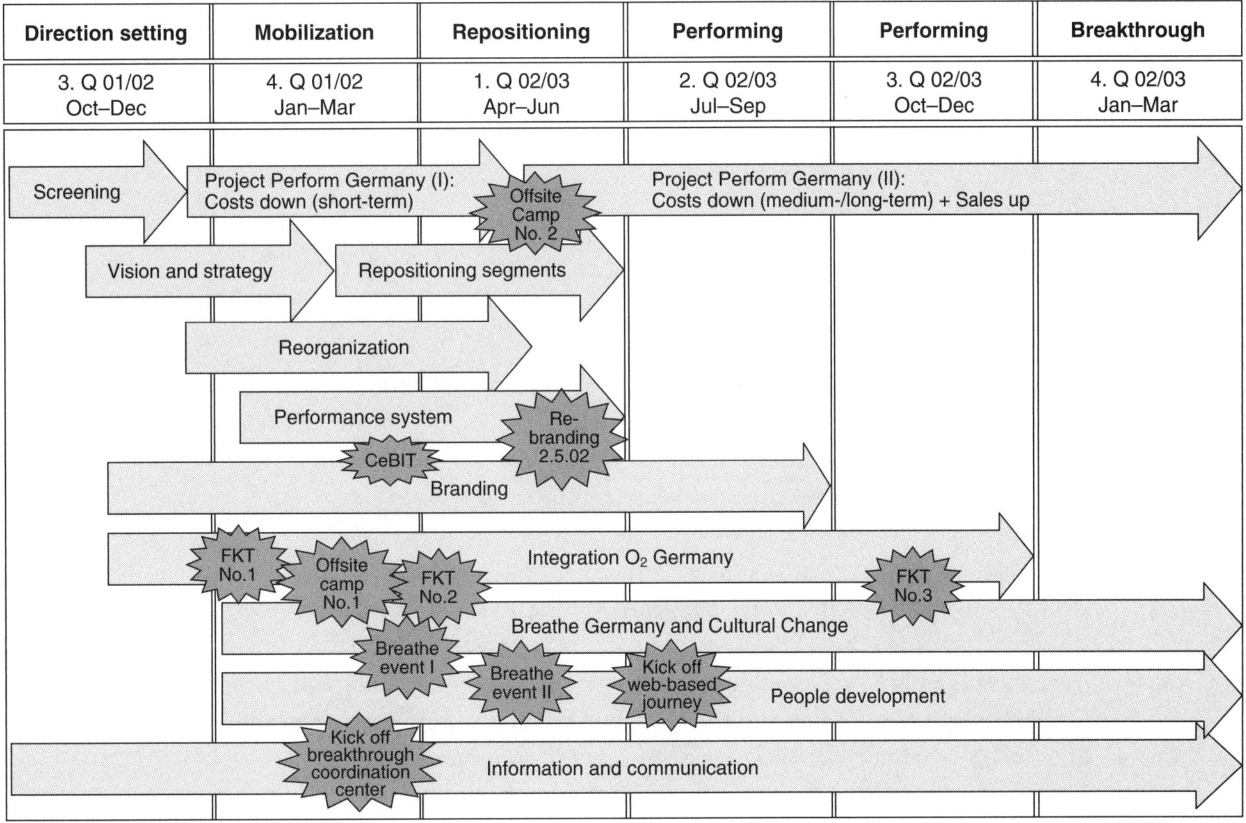

Figure 4.4
Detailed roadmap for change process

the company knows your deadlines. And everyone in the company therefore knows whether or not the boss is working according to what has been promised.

Leaders are too often represented as miracle workers, as wizards. Some may think they can just say, "I am the boss. I'll tell you tomorrow what I think." But why should people trust that kind of a leader? Isn't it better to say, "This is my plan; I don't have a better one. Stand up if you think you have a better one, I'm happy to talk to you. But if not, please, let us execute my plan."

It is not comfortable, but openness is the key tool to being authentic when having to ask people to follow your plan. It is the only way. And if you can't deliver on a promise, you have to go back to people and say, "I tell you what. I failed. And the reason is this and this. Tomorrow, I'll do it better."

This is of great importance because, especially in developed countries, the workforce is quite well educated. They are not silly. And the younger workers, who have grown up using the Internet, expect all information to be available at any time, at any place. Why do we think that when these people walk into a company, they will switch off and say, "Now I'm spending 40 hours a week in my company. I am no longer competent. I am not informed. I do not have access to relevant data, but I should be motivated 40 hours a week. That's impossible.

The Centrality of Open Leadership

I gave people all of the tools they were used to using outside the company and then said, "There is no information in this company that you do not have. Nobody has more information than anyone else." Then I said, "Using this information, I'll tell you exactly where we are. Whether you like it or not, this is the next step."

However, if you do this kind of thing as a leader, one interesting consequence is that it tends to trigger what I call the "Perestroika" phenomenon. Mikhail Gorbachev used this word to describe what happened during the mid-1980s when the Soviet Union was restructuring. The Perestroika phenomenon goes like this: In big organizations there is a tendency for middle management to have more information than the people beneath them. Therefore they are more powerful. Not top management, but some levels of middle management have the most information.

If you say you want to have the kind of democracy in a company where everyone has every number, then middle management worries that you want to get rid of them. You take them out of the system because everyone knows what's going on. And then, the Perestroika effect kicks in: people go out on the streets and say, "This is crazy." Just as they did in Moscow.

Many people who resist change were part of the company elite. A leader destroys that elite if they inform everyone in the organization. But, again, you need open leadership if you want everyone's motivation, everyone's commitment. People grow up having information available outside of their office. This means that the most important thing for leaders is communication, communication, communication.

I believe this is a fundamental change for leaders going forward. We have put a great deal of educational effort into our workforce and now we must deal with them accordingly. We must respect them. We must inform them. We have to present deeper approaches where we say, "I am one of you. I am the boss, yes. I get more money than you do. But only if we work together will we be able to change the thing that blocks us." The old attitude that I have more information and so you will always do what

I say is absolute nonsense. Maybe this attitude worked in the 1960s or 1970s, but not in the type of business I am talking about today.

Dealing with Resistance to Change

The toughest job is cultural change. There is no Excel sheet helping you, there are no rules. It's only you and the people. And you have to go through a rollercoaster, as shown in figure 4.5, which will happen; like it or not. The open leader tells people, "I have a new vision to move us to a better place than we are today." First, they love it; they follow you. Then, to a certain extent they become inactive, less enthusiastic, disgruntled, and noncooperative. They ask, "Is this really true? Do we have to do this hard work?" The open leader has to work through that ordeal. To just decide that we need a culture change next month simply will not work.

The truth is that, even if your company is in trouble, only 5 percent of your people are putting in the effort to help you. The vast majority is skeptical, resistant, or at least putting on the brakes. As a leader, you have to find the 5 percent. The only people who can make culture change is that 5 percent.

Forget about the rest. You must find that 5 percent. And you must be aware of the many, many reasons why others will resist. I had a poster like the one shown in figure 4.6 in all O_2 offices. We also put it on trays in the canteen where people put their dishes every day. It shows 44 very familiar arguments. If someone suggests a change, you will hear things like: "We need to have a working group study it. We are too small

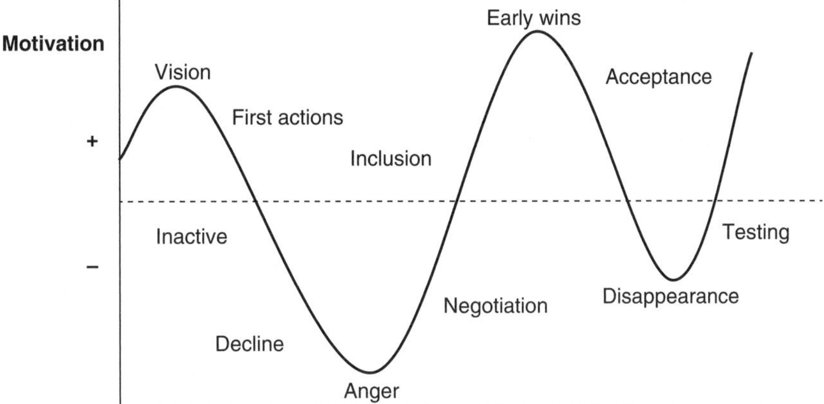

Figure 4.5
Emotional rollercoaster of the turnaround

We tried that before
This place is different
It costs too much
That's beyond our responsibility
We're all too busy to do that
That's not my job
It's too radical a change
We don't have the time
There's not enough help
Our place is too small for it
It isn't practical for operating people
The folks will never buy it
The union will scream
We've never done it before
It's against regulations
It runs up overhead
We don't have the authority
That's too ivory-tower-like
Let's get back to reality
That's not our problem
Why change it?
It's still working okay
It's hopelessly complex
You are right, but ...
You're two years ahead of your time
We don't have the personnel
It isn't in the budget
It's a good thought, but impractical
Let's give it more thought
Top management would never go for it
Let's put it in writing
We'd lose money in the long run
It's never been tried before
Let's shelve it for the time being
Let's form a commitee
Has anyone else ever tried this?
What you are really saying is ...
Maybe that will work in your department, but it won't in mine
The executive committee will never ...
Don't you think we should look into that further before we act?
Let's all sleep on it
It won't pay for itself
I know a fellow who tried this way
What would the president say?

Figure 4.6
Short list of the usual arguments used to slow the change process

for that. We tried that last year. This is out of our territory. This is too complex. I don't think our shareholders will like it." And on and on. As a leader you have to help the 5 percent understand these ready excuses and help develop processes to overcome them.

You take the first five people, train them, and make sure that they think and behave in a way that supports the turnaround. Then you send them out in the organization. As you do that you say, "I need five more people who are very much like you. Enlist the guys you know or find someone else who thinks like you." In that way five people become twenty-five and then a hundred and twenty five.

Conclusion

Many more things happened in turning O_2 around that I do not have space in this chapter to tell about. We broke all the rules on branding. We changed our name overnight. We switched Viag Interkom off on the 30th of April; we switched to O_2 on the 1st of May. In the beginning most Germans said, "Oh Zwei" or "Ooh Zwei." No one said O_2. But from the beginning we intended our name to be pronounced in English. This is against the "rules" of branding, which say you should choose a name that is easy to say. We broke another rule when we chose a name that might seem more like mineral water than a mobile operator. We also used celebrities; it was the first time in the industry to do branding this way. And we did it all with the smallest marketing budget ever.

I became manager of the year three times after rebranding, the first time that had happened since the Second World War—so it went relatively well. Soon we were the fastest growing mobile operator ever for sixteen consecutive quarters. We were growing, quarter on quarter, by at least 25 percent and at the same time improving our financial performance from –270 to +800 million, which had never happened before.

We were awarded any prize that was available, and the best prize was that Telefónica, the biggest telecom outside China, said, "You are so great, we want to buy you." We sold the company for 26 billion euros, in cash, within one week. It was the biggest cash transaction ever done, at least in Europe, or even on a global scale.

Idea for Innovative Leaders: Share the Need to Do Everything All at Once

A major challenge for leaders is to deal with everything at the same time. The requirements of open innovation add significantly to this challenge, but they also offer something important. Once information is shared, the search for solutions is shared.

5 Open Innovation: Actors, Tools, and Tensions

Kathrin M. Möslein

Introduction

How can patients with an orphan disease stimulate research activity to help solve their daily, but often almost unknown health problems? How can a city or region create a mindset of energy-efficient behavior among its citizens? How can a firm find solutions to R&D problems that could not have been solved within its own R&D department? How do individuals with unsolved needs find solutions developed by others, or failing that, design and potentially market their own unique ideas?

Fifty years ago, the answer to all these questions would have been that solutions for such difficult problems were almost never available. Even ten years ago, it would have been quite a task to find solution examples. Despite the World Wide Web offering information on every imaginable topic, stimulating activity, creating awareness, or raising attention beyond the obvious boundaries of a given budget, these questions are still far from trivial. But along with the rise of web 2.0 applications, individuals, firms, and the online population in general increasingly use social networking sites to find solutions to such problems.

Today more and more individuals and firms are participating in open innovation offerings. As a result the patient with an orphan disease in Germany can engage in the open innovation platform for rare diseases www.gemeinsamselten.de and create his or her own innovation challenge. City governments can run an innovation contest following Munich's example found at www.save-our-energy.de. A firm's R&D department can liaise with an innovation marketplace like www.innocentive.com, or even set up its own innovation challenge. Finally, we all can join innovation communities such as those described in this volume, namely www.quirky.com (chapter 9) or https://unseraller.de (chapter 13) to create exactly the kind of products and services that we would like to see in the market.

Three Types of Innovators in Open Innovation

Open innovation is not new. Innovation has always been a multiplayer game that has been professionalized and institutionalized over the last century by corporate players into R&D departments, streamlined R&D processes, defined stage-gates, and specific job descriptions. This streamlining process in my opinion has reached its limit and no longer allows for effective or efficient coping with innovation challenges. More specifically, people outside R&D departments have been step by step excluded from innovation processes.

Organizations that open up their innovation processes beyond the inside-out processes of corporate R&D departments typically involve external experts like customers, suppliers, value partners, and members of universities or research institutions. These external actors, also called *outside innovators*, are a promising pool for generating design ideas, innovation concepts, or even well-rounded solutions. The goal is to complement the innovative power of a firm's researchers and developers, who are called *core inside innovators*. These are the people who innovate by "job specification" or "per definitionem."

There is also an interesting third and often neglected group of innovators who can be essential for innovation success: *peripheral inside innovators*. These are employees within the organization who are not directly involved in the innovation process of their organizations by job description or formal role, but who nevertheless have enough information about needs and solutions to act as innovators. They innovate mainly due to confidence, curiosity, and pro-active interest in the well-being of the organization. The following story (see table 5.1) illustrates their potential role and importance.

The bubblegum story shows that important innovators in a firm are not just those with a title in the R&D department. Employees from all functions, levels, and units of an organization often show extraordinary engagement, motivation, creativity, and talent for innovating. I know from various research activities I have directed that if organizations open up their innovation processes and extend their focus from core inside innovators toward outside innovators and also peripheral inside innovators, they are likely to find new successful innovations. Furthermore employees within the organization are particularly important in open innovation projects as a bridge between innovations inside and outside the organization. Table 5.2 summarizes the characteristics of these players.

All three types of innovators play a crucial role in innovation processes:

• *Core inside innovators* are, by definition, entrusted with developing new products, processes, services, and strategies. While organizational R&D departments were widely organized as closed departments at the heart of organizational innovation, responsibil-

Table 5.1
Bubblegum story reported in http://www.ideafinder.com

In 1928, bubblegum was invented by a man named Walter E. Diemer. Here's what Walter Diemer, the inventor himself, said about it just a year or two before he died: "It was an accident." "I was doing something else," Mr. Diemer explained, "and ended up with something with bubbles." And history took one giant pop forward. What Mr. Diemer was supposed to be doing, back in 1928, was working as an accountant for the Fleer Chewing Gum Company in Philadelphia; what he wound up doing in his spare time was playing around with new gum recipes. But this latest brew of Walter Diemer's was—unexpectedly, crucially—different. It was less sticky than regular chewing gum. It also stretched more easily. Walter Diemer, 23 years old, saw the bubbles. He saw the possibilities. One day he carried a five-pound glop of the stuff to a grocery store; it sold out in a single afternoon.

Before long, the folks at Fleer were marketing Diemer's creation and Diemer himself was teaching cheeky salesmen to blow bubbles, to demonstrate exactly what made this gum different from all other gums. The only food coloring in the factory was pink. Walter used it. That is why most bubblegum today is pink.

Gilbert Mustin, president of Fleer, named the gum Dubble Bubble, and it controlled the bubblegum market unchallenged for years, at least until Bazooka came along to share the wealth. Walter Diemer stayed with Fleer for decades, eventually becoming a senior vice president.

He never received royalties for his invention, his wife told the newspapers, but he did not seem to mind; knowing what he had created was reward enough. Sometimes he would invite a bunch of kids to the house and tell them the story of his wonderful, accidental invention. Then he would hold bubble-blowing contests for them.

Table 5.2
Three types of innovators in open innovation

Type of innovator	Where to find them
Core inside innovators	Employees of the R&D department or the strategic innovation unit for whom "innovation" is part of the job description
Peripheral inside innovators	Insightful employees across all functions, levels, and units of an organization for whom "innovation" is NOT part of the job description
Outside innovators	Creative customers, suppliers, value creation partners, universities, institutional research departments, and other units that reside outside the boundaries of the focal organization

ity for innovation is broadening to include designers, researchers, developers, and innovators in other departments as well, including marketing, business operations, and corporate strategy.

• *Outside innovators* are largely comprised of customers, suppliers, and other value creation partners, as well as university members, researchers from research institutes, and even competitors. Within the strategy of open innovation, organizations implement methods and tools to integrate these outside innovators into the innovation process. Often the greater public is explicitly invited to participate.

• *Peripheral inside innovators* generate new ideas based on self-motivation, engagement, intrinsic interest, and confidence, but they are rarely supported by tools or other resources. The suggestion box and more recent idea management systems still prevail in companies as the main mechanism to integrate peripheral inside innovators. Although modern updates include elements of social software and web 2.0, they are usually not well integrated in organizational innovation strategies.

Unfortunately, it is rare that all three types of innovators are incorporated into an integrated innovation strategy and they are rarely supported by integrated tools and platforms. This situation poses essential constraints for the innovation capacity of organizations. As early as 1984, Robert Rosenfeld, founder of the office of innovation at Kodak, is credited with the following prophetic words: "The failure of large organizations in America to innovate is primarily the result of a communication gap, not a decline in ingenuity" (Rosenfeld and Servo 1984). Furthermore a growing variety of communication technologies and innovation tools have tended to intensify rather than reduce specialization.

Approaches that include a richer and more inclusive pool of innovators are still at the experimental stage. Combining these tools into well-integrated, effective, as well as efficient business models is currently a matter of experimentation and exploration. This chapter introduces five basic categories of tools to strategically implement open innovation and to help integrate all three types of innovators in open innovation initiatives.

Tools for Open Innovation

As shown in figure 5.1, the tools of open innovation can be connected. Their development, diffusion, and implementation are mainly driven by the attractiveness, usability, and inclusiveness of web 2.0 and social software, which is evident when looking at the features of each tool in open innovation processes.

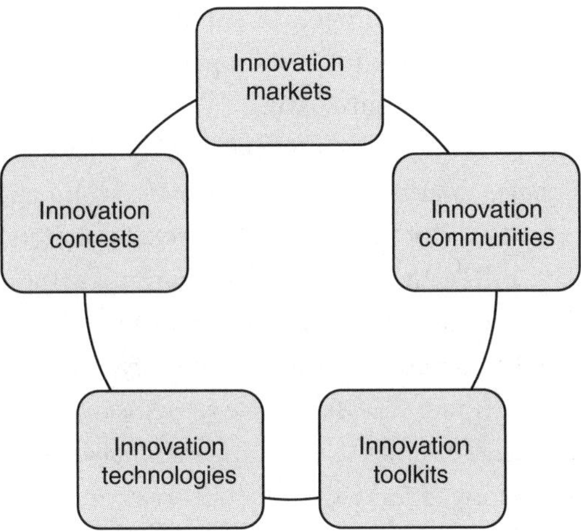

Figure 5.1
Tools for open innovation

Innovation Contests

Innovation contests in their basic structure have a long-standing tradition and have influenced industries or even societies for a long time. For example, in 1869, Emperor Louis Napoleon III of France offered a prize to anyone who could make a "satisfactory substitute for butter, suitable for use by the armed forces and the lower classes." Still, neither Michel-Eugene Chevreul nor Hippolyte Mege-Mouris (historians are uneven about the inventor) were paid when they came up with margarine, since Napoleon died before the prize was awarded.

In the nineteenth century, innovation contests leave the realm of political organizers as they are increasingly adopted by industrialists as a powerful means of problem solving. Famous examples of this period (Haller et al. 2011) include the "Rainhill trials" (1829), which were used by the directors of the Liverpool and Manchester Railway Company to decide whether hauling trains should be powered by stationary engines or locomotives. During the next century, realization of innovation contests slowly entered average business: An early example can be identified in 1997, when the "Fredkin Prize for Computer Chess" granted 100,000 USD for building the first computer to beat world chess champion Garry Kasparov.

So, what is actually new and what makes innovation contests an important tool for open innovation? Social software features and web 2.0 enable a multitude of actors to announce contests for exciting innovation challenges, with global reach at minimal costs. We define an innovation contest[1] as a web-based competition of innovators who use their skills, experiences and creativity to provide a solution for a particular contest challenge defined by an organizer (Bullinger and Möslein 2010).

Innovation contests can stimulate research in new, especially challenging or under-represented fields. Great examples are the Google Lunar X PRIZE—"a $30 million competition for the first privately funded team to send a robot to the moon, travel 500 meters, and transmit video, images, and data back to the Earth" (www.googlelunarxprize.org.). Two sites mentioned in the introduction of this chapter provide further examples: the Rare Disease Challenge—a community-based innovation contest to identify, address, and potentially solve challenges associated with rare diseases (www.gemeinsamselten.de), and the Save-Our-Energy Contest to engage Munich citizens in the challenge of becoming a role model for energy efficiency among cities (www.save-our-energy.de).

Innovation contests also are implemented in various ways. Many go far beyond targeting product or process innovations, but address innovative services, broader solutions, or whole business model innovations. Formulating the innovation challenge for the contest is crucial. As experience is the best guide to help designing innovation contests, my research team and I have collected and analyzed more than 400 innovation contests. They have been systematized according to key design elements and success factors and are made available to the public via the Innovation Contest Inventory (ICI): at www.innovationresearch.de.

Innovation Markets

Innovation markets are virtual places where innovation supply and demand meet. In general, they are realized as web 2.0 supported online platforms, on which innovation seekers (typically organizations) announce innovation challenges and innovation providers (typically individual innovators or teams of innovators) propose concrete solutions or concepts. Innovation markets act as intermediaries, connecting innovation seekers and innovation providers (often called "solvers"). A growing number of innovation markets are available online.

Figure 5.2 depicts the basic pattern of innovation markets as intermediaries for open innovation and shows selected examples of such intermediaries. InnoCentive, founded in 2001 (the same year as Wikipedia) by Eli Lilly might be the most well-known and frequented innovation market. It declares itself as "the world's first open innovation marketplace." And while it originally focused on innovations in the chemical industry; today it serves not only companies in all kinds of industries, but also nonprofit organizations and governments. Among their partners they list Eli Lilly, Life Technologies, NASA, nature.com, Popular Science, Procter & Gamble, Roche, Rockefeller Foundation,

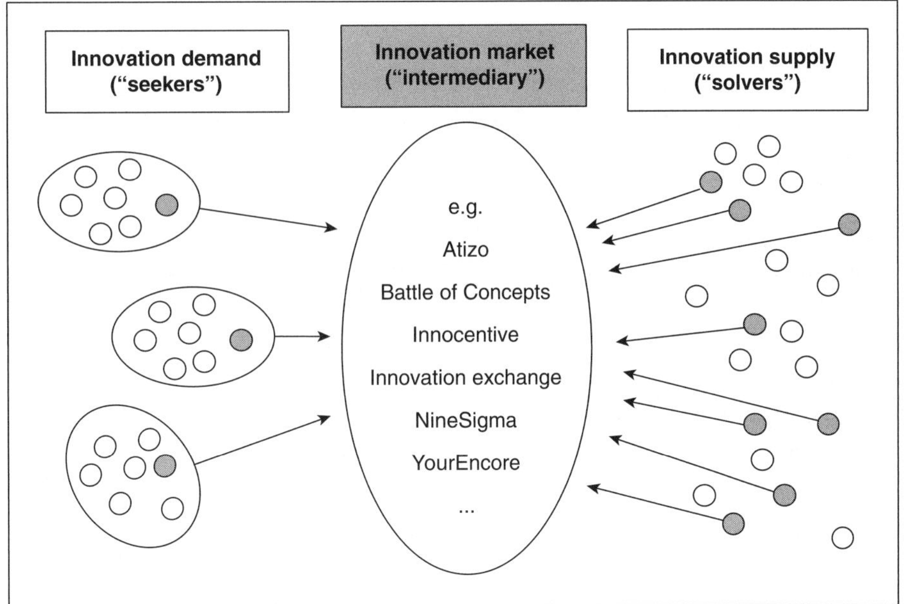

Figure 5.2
Innovation markets as intermediaries for open innovation

and The Economist. As of mid-2011, InnoCentive reported approximately 250,000 registered "solvers" from nearly 200 countries, a total of more than 1,300 challenges posted with an average success rate of 50 percent, more than 339,000 project rooms opened for collaborative innovation, more than 24,000 solutions submitted, 866 awards with a range of awards from about 5,000 to $1 million based on the complexity of the problem and a total of more than 28 million USD award money posted. More details can be found in chapters 10 and 11 of this volume.

Other examples of innovation markets include NineSigma (www.ninesigma.com), Innovation Exchange (www.innovationexchange.com), Atizo (www.atizo.com), YourEncore (www.yourencore.com), and Battle of Concepts (www.battleofconcepts.nl). While these markets focus on organizations publishing innovation problems, www.innovationsupplychain.com establishes a solver-driven innovation market. Here, solution providers get the possibility to look for both a suitable problem and a possible purchaser for their innovative solution. Organizations directly search for promising innovative concepts, an approach especially attracting small and medium-size organizations. Other innovation markets allow user definition of the purpose and range of outreach, including iBridge (www.ibridgenetworks.org) and Brainfloor (www.brainfloor.com).

Innovation Communities

Innovation communities enable innovators to collectively share and develop ideas, discuss concepts, and promote innovations. Web 2.0 and social software based innovation communities normally bundle interested and specialized innovators for particular issues and thus support collective development and enhancement of innovation concepts. These communities group together voluntarily and independently to create innovative solutions in a joint effort, embracing a family-like spirit. Open source development communities are well-known examples, as explained by Karim Lakhani in chapter 10. The great success of these communities has led to issue-related communities in specific industry sectors.

One interesting example is the Internet-based innovation project, *OScar* (www.theoscarproject.org). The project was launched in 1999 on the basis of a published manifesto: "To build a car . . . without any factory, any CEO, any funds, any boundaries . . . but instead with the support of lots of creative people in the web . . . with a global spirit of optimism . . . representing absolute empowerment." This meant the community faced huge challenges, but as described in their website: "The idea behind the *OScar* project is simple: A community of people virtually plans and develops a new car. The idea is about the goal to develop a simple and innovative car, but also about the way this goal is achieved. We would like to convey the idea of open source to 'hardware' and we want *OScar* to be the precursor for many different projects in this field."

OScar is one example, extreme in its ambition, but not yet in its success. Meanwhile LocalMotors (www.localmotors.com) under the leadership of John B. Rogers Jr. has already proved that even a product as complex as a car can be created by a community. Many other successful examples deal with less complex innovations, among them UnserAller a Facebook-based online innovation community founded in 2010 that so far aims for simple products—mustard, salad dressing, snacks, shower gel, and the like—and does it with impressive success, as described in more detail by cofounder Catharina van Delden in chapter 13, and illustrated in figure 5.3. The site was recognized as the best ICT related start-up in Germany by the German Federal Ministry of Economics and Technology in 2011.

More and more companies are using innovation communities as a tool for strategically creating innovations. While in the early days emergent and self-organized innovation communities were the typical pattern, today we see a trend toward strategic, firm-sponsored innovation communities. One example of such an innovation community is the *Apple Developer Connection* (developer.apple.com). It invites innovators to offer solutions around Apple products. What makes this community special is that external enthusiasts do not contribute free of cost. In fact there are different types of

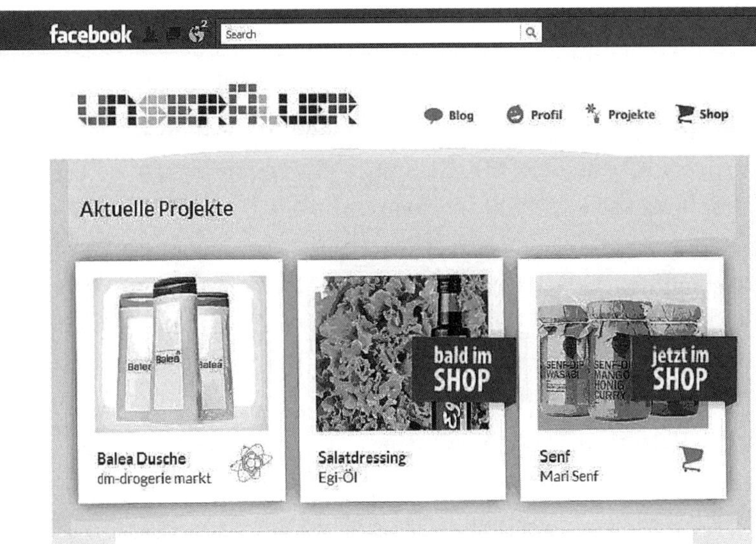

Figure 5.3
unserAller—A Facebook-based open innovation community

community memberships, which imply subscription fees. Apple in turn offers its members access to a range of technical resources, support tools, or pre-releases. Thus the community is not only a tool for creating innovations but also a business model for increasing revenues as well as focusing inputs.

Innovation Toolkits

Innovation toolkits provide an environment in which users develop solutions in prescribed steps. For example, toolkits are available to customize your new car or its equipment (e.g., www.mini.ie), or to design a product to your own specifications (e.g., the LEGO Cuusoo approach, accessible at www.lego.cuusoo.com). The idea is that basic knowledge about desired innovations is available in literally every household. However, while the application of toolkits is quite widespread for the configuration of predefined solutions, the mass-customization of predesigned products, and the selection of variants from a broad range of offerings, the application of toolkits for more innovative solutions is still in its infancy.

In order to implement toolkits for open innovation on the seeker's as well as on the solver's side efficiently, toolkits have to fulfill five basic requirements (see Reichwald and Piller 2006):

• *Full line of trial and error:* toolkit users tend to be more satisfied with their developed solution when they can go through the entire cycle of problem solving. This requires that users receive simulated feedback at each step of the development process. Simulations enable users to evaluate the current solution and improve on it in an iterative process. This way cognitive and affective learning processes are activated (learning by doing), which improves the quality of the solution.

• *Defined solution space:* A toolkit's solution space defines all variations and combinations of feasible solutions. Basically the solution space only permits innovation solutions that take specific technical restrictions into account and are "feasible" from a technical point of view. Depending on the type of toolkit, these constraints are more or less strict (as I will discuss below).

• *User friendliness:* User friendliness describes how users perceive the quality of interaction with the toolkit. The challenge is to find the right degree of complexity (between over complexity and over simplicity), openness, and interactivity as to perfectly stimulate the innovators creativity and motivation. If expectations or capabilities are heterogeneously distributed among the potential innovators, the seeker may want to make different types of toolkits available to the potential target groups of innovators.

• *Modules and components:* Modules and components are the basic building blocks of a toolkit (programming languages, visualization, help menus, drawing software, text boxes, libraries, etc.); these make up its operational functions and are available to potential innovators for supporting innovation activities. Modules and components comprise the toolkit's solution space and determine its user friendliness.

• *Solution transfer:* After innovators have developed a toolkit-based innovation, their concept or solution is transferred to a seeker or manufacturer. This toolkit-based transfer has to allow for a perfect translation of the solver's or user's solution in the "language" of the seeker or manufacturer.

Toolkits differ in their strategic goals, design principles, and users to be targeted. Those currently available in the market also can be broadly classified into the three categories, as shown in table 5.3.

Through feedback and simulation, toolkits enable users to create possible solutions with relevant attributes (e.g., design, performance, and price) themselves. This way users venture on a learning process similar to the learning process offered to kids through chemistry experiment kits, Lego kits, simple blackboards, or Plasticine. Users experiment with the toolkit's solution space until they reach an ideal solution for a given problem. The solution, which contains needs and solution information, is trans-

Table 5.3
Current categories of toolkits

	Tool kits for user innovation	Tool kits for user co-design	Tool kits for idea transfer
Goal	*Creation* of ideas and concepts as well as new features or designs	*Customization* through product configuration (sales tool)	*Transfer* of existing innovation ideas and concepts from solvers/ users to seekers/ manufacturers
Design principles	• Compares to a "chemistry kit" • Broad solution space • High cost of usage • Complete trial-and-error	• Compares to a Lego kit • Restricted solution space • Low cost of usage (due to standard modules • Only partial trial-and-error	• Compares to a blackboard • Unlimited solution space • Low cost of usage • No trial-and-error (only feedback from other users)
Users	Solvers or innovators with lead-user characteristics	All kinds of solvers/ innovators	Solvers or innovators with lead-user characteristics

Source: Reichwald and Piller (2006).

ferred (mostly automated) to the seeker or manufacturer. Among the three described categories of toolkits only the *toolkits for user innovation* allow for a certain degree of innovation. In the future a more intense use of innovation-oriented toolkits for broader application areas of open innovation can be expected.

If we look, for instance, at Gene Designer www.dna20.com/genedesigner2, a bioinformatics software package that is mainly used by molecular biologists from different industries to design, clone, and validate genetic sequences, we can easily imagine the future of innovation toolkits for open innovation. On YouTube a range of video tutorials is available that guides potential gene designers worldwide through the process of cloning so-called BioBricks with this free-of-charge software package (see also http://en.wikipedia.org/wiki/Gene_Designer). It is not hard to imagine how this kind of software could be further developed in an even more user-friendly, web-based interactive open innovation toolkit.

Innovation Technologies

Innovation technologies enable progress from the conceptualization of an innovation to prototyping or even producing a product or service. Innovation technologies like 3D-scanners, laser cutters, or 3D-printers allow even individual users to fully develop new products and services. All these technologies are associated with the prospect of an ongoing democratization of innovation activities and with the often proclaimed trend toward "personal fabrication."

In developing open source software, programmers globally cooperate on their software code. Now innovation technologies enable us to collectively and globally develop intangible specifications for real products, services, and solutions. Two-dimensional software controlled cutting with CNC-cutters allows the creation of furniture, fitments, and accessories (e.g., www.ronen-kadushin.com and www.movisi.com). 3D-printers (i.e., printers that create three-dimensional objects out of plastic powder under CNC-control) allow a fast and immediate "printing" of prototypes during development processes, thus enabling "rapid prototyping" directly from ordinary household computers.

Visionaries like Neil Gershenfeld, director of the MIT's Center for Bits and Atoms, anticipated this trend of a future of "personal manufacturing" or "personal fabrication" quite a while ago. His 2005 book, *FAB: The Coming Revolution on Your Desktop—From Personal Computers to Personal Fabrication*, vividly describes a future where anyone can become a producer or manufacturer, even at home. Just as many did not believe in the proclaimed revolution of "personal computing" when computers were mainframes and only available for companies or governments, today we struggle to imagine a future of "personal manufacturing" or "personal fabrication" where every household can become a production unit in a future world of value creation.

From a technical perspective this future is less hard to imagine. Additive manufacturing (as opposed to our traditional subtractive manufacturing) is mainly digital manufacturing as 3D-computer models are translated in 3D-printouts. These 3D-printers are already available, prices are falling, and application areas growing. While current home 3D-printers like the RepRap (www.reprap.org) are only able to print plastic objects, an engineering student project at the University of Exeter is experimenting with printing chocolate (*ChocALM—Chocolate Additive Layer Manufacturing*) and an MIT student project is exploring food printing more generally in the *Cornucopia: Digital Gastronomy* project (http://web.media.mit.edu/~marcelo/cornucopia/index.html).

It is obvious that CAD software or 3D-scanners in combination with laser cutters or 3D-printing open up new possibilities of potential personal production. The analogy between personal computing and personal fabrication is a helpful one to understand anticipated future developments. Similar to current printing with simple printers at home, with better copies widely available in offices or copy shops, we can expect cheap and easy-to-use 3D-printing (and other manufacturing) facilities if not at home then at least in "fabbing" shops around the corner. Fab labs are already present worldwide.

While they mainly target a young generation of hobbyists, production-oriented "service bureaus" target a more professional audience.

In addition Internet companies are starting to offer manufacturing services for the products and innovations created by simply anyone. A telling example is the Internet company Ponoko (www.ponoko.com), which makes it possible to create, manufacture, and distribute design concepts. With the help of Ponoko, basically everybody can become a competitor of the very largest companies, like IKEA. The innovation technologies that will make this possible are still in their infancy, but they can be expected to become powerful tools for open innovation that reaches far beyond the fuzzy front end of idea creation to innovation implementation and commercialization.

Conclusion: Inherent Tensions of Open Innovation

All tools and platforms for open innovation presented in this chapter include four common and novel effects. As summarized in figure 5.4, they (1) allow for large numbers of innovators to contribute, (2) empower these innovators to collaborate in widely distributed settings, (3) foster high-speed interaction that radically accelerates innovation processes, and (4) provide a global memory for innovators to build on. These four characteristics clearly facilitate collaboration across organizational boundaries and create new opportunities to create innovations. Additionally the five categories of innovation tools reviewed in this chapter open up space for novel strategies

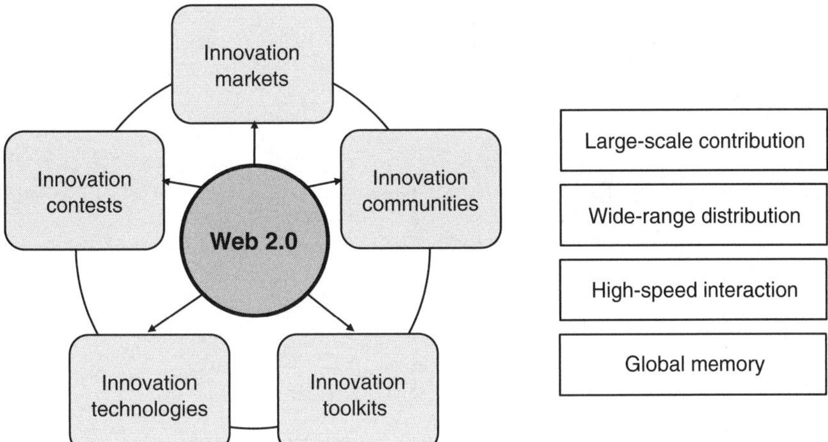

Figure 5.4
Tools for open innovation and their effects

that make it possible to integrate the different types of innovators necessary to meet today's innovation challenges.

The challenge of how to apply these tools in concert to effectively and efficiently cope with open innovation is far from being solved. Today we see open innovation tools mainly used separately. Often they target only one specific innovator group. For the future, however, we should look at these tools as the basic building blocks of integrated open innovation platforms. To combine these building blocks wisely requires a better understanding of their modus operandi, but also of the tensions that open innovation creates in all kinds of value creation settings.

The key characteristics of open innovation are shown in three boxes on the right of figure 5.5, which also outlines tensions that have to be managed for leading innovation. Only aspects of these tensions can be sketched out here. However, these and related issues are addressed explicitly, as well as implicitly, in the remaining chapters of this volume.

- *Single innovator versus teams of collaborators:* Is the individual genius more innovative than innovation teams? This traditional conflict between individual innovation capacity and team innovation is paradoxically intensified in open innovation. Additional and globally dispersed innovators (individuals as well as teams) are integrated in organizational innovation activities. Furthermore the community of innovators, an increasingly Internet-based innovative community, is achieving more status. Overall,

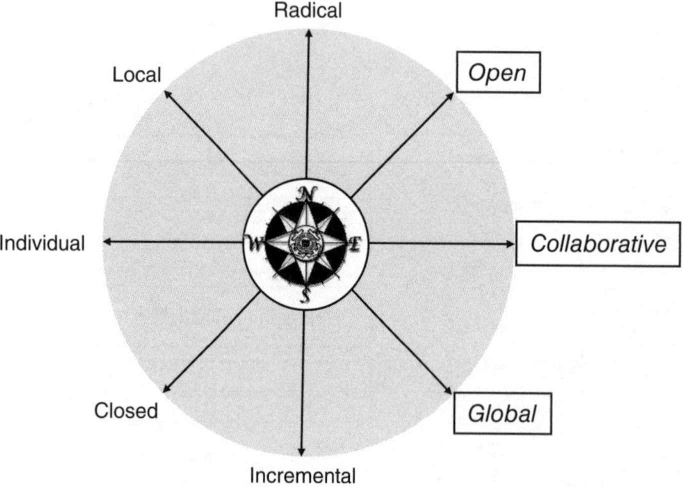

Figure 5.5
360 Degrees of tension for innovation

a need for more collaborative innovation efforts is generally recognized as innovation complexity increases and the global knowledge base grows.

• *Local innovation clusters versus global innovation communities:* It is not clear that globally distributed, collaborating individuals can generate the same innovative power as regional clusters. The question between local pooling versus global dispersion of innovation activities has long been regarded as an "either–or" question. However, successful cases of globally supported innovation in this book offer clear evidence of the innovation potential of dispersed participants. This step in innovation is enabled by the tools presented in this chapter. Nevertheless, handling these tools successfully and to gain competitive advantage remains a core challenge for strategy and leadership.

• *Evolution versus revolution:* While the opinion prevailed for a long time that outside innovators or employees who are not trained as researchers could only contribute to continuous (evolutionary) innovations, many examples show that they support both continuous and discontinuous (revolutionary) innovations. Organizations have to deal with the predominant challenge of how to design, implement, and strategically incorporate open innovation, so as to involve innovators according to their strengths and not according to common prejudice.

• *Closed innovation versus open innovation:* Besides opportunities to reshape innovation activities, organizations have to face challenges of strategically handling conflicts between closed and open innovation. One main challenge lies in the decision about the degree of open innovation activities to support. Total openness cannot automatically be assumed to be the right strategy.

In short, balanced strategies are needed that combine the advantages of opening innovation activities with the strengths of cohesive R&D departments. Moreover the decision to use open innovation has to be integrated with the organization's strategy, as further described in the epilogue of this book.

Idea for Innovative Leaders: Learn from Those Who Successfully Balance Open and Closed Innovation

The development story of Apple's iPod in combination with iTunes is an impressive example of discontinuous innovation that involves individuals, affects boundaries of business sectors, and even changes the economic rules of whole industries (see table 5.4).

This story is an excellent example of discontinuous innovation that involves individual innovators, companies, business sectors, and even the economic rules of whole

Table 5.4
Apple iPod story from Kahney (2004)

. . . The iPod originated around a business idea dreamed up by Tony Fadell, an independent contractor and hardware expert who helped develop handheld devices at General Magic and Philips. "Tony's idea was to take an MP3 player, build a Napster music sale service to complement it, and build a company around it" Knauss [a close companion of Fadell's] said: ". . . Fadell left Philips and set himself up as an independent contractor to shop the idea around."

Apple hired Fadell in early 2001 and assigned him a team of about 30 people. . . . Fadell said, "This is the project that's going to remold Apple and 10 years from now, it's going to be a music business, not a computer business." Tony had an idea for a business process and Apple is transforming itself on his whim and an idea he had a few years ago.

Fadell was familiar with PortalPlayer's [at the time a cooperation partner of Apple] . . . designs for a couple of MP3 players, including one about the size of a cigarette packet. And though the design was unfinished, several prototypes had been built. "It was fairly ugly," he said. "It looked like an FM radio with a bunch of buttons." The interface, Knauss said, "was typical of an interface done by hardware guys."

"(PortalPlayer) was attractive to Apple because we had an operating system," said Knauss. "That was a real selling point for Apple. We had the software and the hardware already done, and Apple was on a tight schedule."

Knauss said the reference design was about 80 percent complete when Apple came calling. For example, the prototype would not support playlists longer than 10 songs. "Most of the time building the iPod was spent finishing our product" Knauss said. At the time, PortalPlayer had 12 customers designing MP3 players based on the company's reference design. Most were Asian hardware manufacturers, Knauss said, but also included Teac and IBM.

Big Blue planned a small, black MP3 player, based on the company's own mini hard drives, which featured a unique circular screen and wireless Bluetooth headphones. "The design for IBM was a lot sexier," Knauss said.

industries. It is also a perfect example is of successfully and strategically combing open and closed innovation in an overall innovation strategy. It is the kind of story that must be closely examined to learn how innovation can succeed.

Note

1. The term "innovation contest" is used instead of "idea contest" to illustrate that a contest is suited to cover the entire innovation process from idea creation and concept generation to selection and implementation (Tidd and Bessant 2009).

References and Further Reading

Berger, C., K. Möslein, F. Piller, and R. Reichwald. 2005. Co-designing modes of cooperation at the customer interface: learning from exploratory research. *European Management Review* 5 (2): 70–87.

Bessant, J., and K. M. Möslein. 2011. *Open Collective Innovation: The Power of the Many over the Few.* AIM Research Report, Executive Briefing, 2011. London: Advanced Institute of Management Research.

Bullinger, A. C., and K. M. Möslein. 2010. Innovation contests—Where are we? AMCIS 2010 Proceedings. Paper 28. http://aisel.aisnet.org/amcis2010/28.

Chesbrough, H. 2003. *Open Innovation: The New Imperative for Creating and Profiting from Technology*. Boston: Harvard Business School Press.

Gershenfeld, N. 2005. *FAB: The Coming Revolution on Your Desktop—From Personal Computers to Personal Fabrication*. New York: Basic Books.

Haller, J. B. A., A. C. Bullinger, and K. M. Möslein. 2011. Innovation Contests—An IT-Based Tool for Innovation Management. *Business and Information Systems Engineering* 3 (2): 103–106.

Huff, A., T. Fredberg, K. Möslein, and F. Piller. 2006. Leading open innovation: Creating centripetal innovation capacity. AOM Presenter Symposium Paper, Atlanta.

Kahney, L. 2004. Inside look at birth of the IPod. *Wired,* April 21.

Möslein, K., and B. Bansemir. 2011. Strategic open innovation: Basics, actors, tools and tensions. In M. Hülsmann and N. Pfeffermann, eds., *Strategies and Communications for Innovations: An Integrative Management View for Companies and Networks*. Berlin: Springer, 11–24.

Neyer, A.-K., A. Bullinger, and K. Möslein. 2009. Integrating inside and outside innovators: A sociotechnical perspective. *R&D Management* 39 (4): 410–19.

Piller, F. 2005. *Innovation and Value Co-Creation: Integrating Customers in the Innovation Process.* München.

Reichwald, R., and F. Piller. 2006. *Interaktive Wertschöpfung—Open Innovation, Individualisierung und neue Formen der Arbeitsteilung*. Wiesbaden: Gabler.

Robinson, A., and S. Stern. 1998. *Corporate Creativity*. San Francisco: Berrett-Koehler.

Rosenfeld, R., and J. Servo. 1984. Business and Creativity. *Futurist* (August): 21–26.

Schumpeter, J. 1934. *The Theory of Economic Development*. Cambridge: Harvard University Press.

Tidd, J., and J. Bessant 2009. *Managing Innovation: Integrating Technological and Organizational Change,* 4th ed. Chichester, UK: Wiley.

von Hippel, E. 2005. *Democratizing Innovation*. Cambridge: MIT Press.

Zerfaß, A., and K. Möslein. 2009. *Kommunikation als Erfolgsfaktor im Innovationsmanagement.* Wiesbaden: Gabler.

II WHO CONTRIBUTES TO OPEN INNOVATION?

6 Opening Organizations for Innovation

John Bessant and Bettina von Stamm

Introduction

It is not easy to recognize a currently successful innovator, in part because a good reputation can hide problems. We know a well-known Danish medical devices producer, for example, that enjoys a dominant market position and has received multiple awards for innovation. It has deep competencies around skin/wound care, in part because of its active user paradigm, which regularly draws on panels of nurses for input.

Yet when we visited the company, managers were not as happy as we expected them to be. One manager said, "People get all these good ideas, but there's nowhere to take them." There also seemed to be general agreement with the observation that, "The improvements have just been minor things in the past few years—not big innovations. It's been a long time since we've had a really new concept."

What is the problem? An employee said, "We are too busy." Another thought "It's so structured here. There's no real room for radical ideas." That fits with the observation that "The words 'out of the box' are here, but there is no commitment." This company is facing the challenge that many successful companies face. They do what they do very well, but have a problem with discontinuous innovation; they cannot re-create the fluid innovative state that created their current success. The situation is so pervasive that we have each spent years investigating it.

Exploration versus Exploitation

We have all seen good companies stumble and fall as their environment changes. We have been working with companies that want to discover what they can do to anticipate and avoid that disaster. But if a company is seeking a discontinuous innovation that will have spectacular effects, should it not also keep using established innovation procedures that have already been proved successful?

Most companies should try for a balance in our opinion, but it is not easy. A core theme in discussions of innovation relates to the tensions between "exploitation" and "exploration" activities. *Exploitation* essentially involves leveraging what the firm already knows. Firms need to produce a steady stream of incremental product and process innovations that effectively "do what they do better." This is often a good thing, but the innovation that results is not that far from what is already being done.

In increasingly competitive and fast changing environments firms also need to "do something different." They have to find radical product or process innovations rather than imitations and variants of what they and other competitors are already offering. *Exploration* is necessary to find less familiar knowledge that will support big departures from the status quo. The innovation space that firms must thus try to encompass is large. It is not just about products and processes, but about the paradigm the firm uses to conduct its business, and the positions it takes with respect to buyers, competitors, suppliers, and other players in the marketplace.

While firms ideally cover the large space shown in figure 6.1, the organizational routines needed to support the two kinds of innovation are quite different. On the one hand, incremental exploitation is facilitated by structured processes, which typically results in many small-scale changes carried out within operating units. This is what established and well-regarded companies know how to do very well. Radical innovation, on the other hand, is occasional and high risk. It typically requires a cross-functional combination of resources and a looser approach to organization and management, as shown in table 6.1.

There is no easy prescription for carrying out these two types of innovation simultaneously, given the tensions between them. Many organizations aim for a degree of ambidexterity, a word popularized by Professors Tushman and O'Reilly in 1996 and used more recently by Professors Julian Birkinshaw and Christina Gibson. For example, a firm may invest in a few "blue sky" or high-risk outside bets but concentrate on a larger number of projects around their core technology. Market research might similarly search for a few new markets but also focus on developing deeper understanding of established key market segments. The difficulty is often doing both exploitation and exploration at the same time. Too often the more radical projects never see the light of day in organizations that try to be ambidextrous.

Based on years of observation, we think most companies begin to have problems with exploration right at the beginning of the innovation process, as they search for the ideas that will feed radical type 2 innovations. We know firms increasingly face

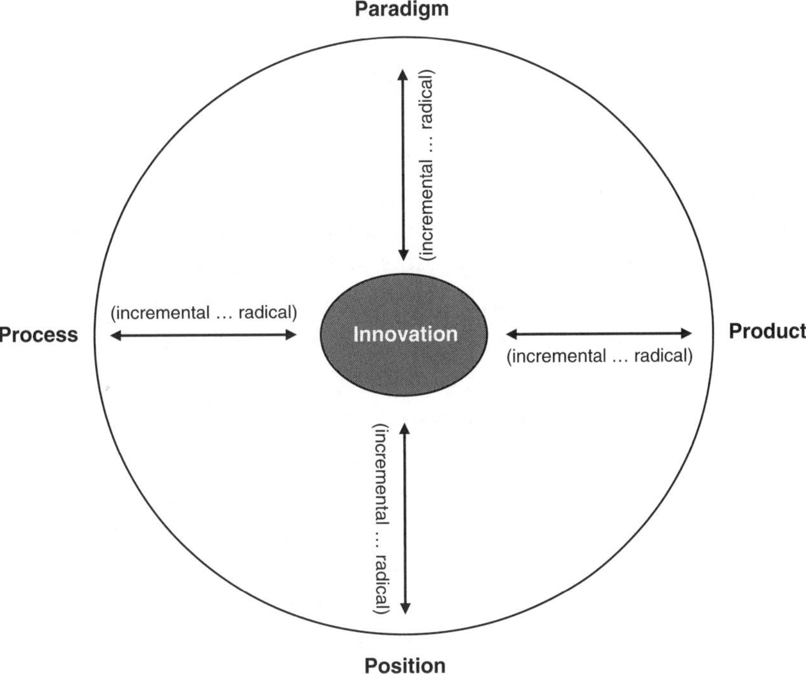

Figure 6.1
Space within which firms can innovate

Table 6.1
Differences between exploitation (type 1) and exploration (type 2)

Type 1—Exploitation	Type 2—Exploration
Clear and accepted rules of the game	No clear rules—these emerge over time. High tolerance for ambiguity
Path-dependent strategies	Path-independent, emergent, probe-and-learn strategies
Clear selection environment	Fuzzy, emergent selection environment
Selection and resource allocation linked to clear trajectories and criteria for fit	Risk taking, multiple parallel bets, tolerance of (fast) failure
Operating routines refined and stable	Operating patterns emergent and "fuzzy"
Strong ties and knowledge flows along clear channels	Weak ties and peripheral vision important

discontinuities in their environment, including major changes in technology, significant political shifts, and redefinitions of the regulatory environment. Under such conditions it is clear that local search for new ideas will not be helpful.

However, observation and research reveals that most firms' attempts at *exploration* behavior continue to be bounded and path-dependent, even though conditions indicate a need for radical change. Because of their success with *exploitative* innovation, firms continue to focus on regions believed to hold promise and search along trajectories which are relatively stable. Open-ended research may be carried out, but in zones that are perceived as having connections to the current knowledge base.

We argue that these firms are rather like the drunk who has lost his keys on the way home and is desperately searching for them under the nearest lamppost "because there is more light here." Despite increasing change and uncertainty, firms have a similar, natural tendency to search in spaces they already know and understand. Unfortunately, the weak early warning signals that reveal the emergence of totally new possibilities—radically different technologies, changing public opinion, new political contexts, regulatory threats or opportunities, and (most important) possible new product or service offerings—are unlikely to be discovered under the firm's particular lamppost. Instead, firms must move out to the darkness. They need to develop ways of searching that cover 360 degrees of the innovation space!

Figure 6.2 highlights the search challenge. The routines required to develop innovations in the bottom left quadrant are (relatively) straightforward—they involve sys-

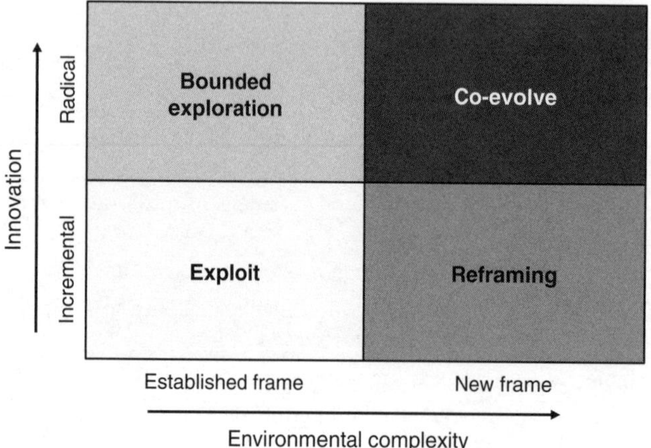

Figure 6.2
Conditions under which different kinds of search behaviors are important

tematic consideration of new developments in a space the firm already understands. Key lines of enquiry have been established. Members of the firm understand basic technology, are familiar with current markets and their competitive dynamics, know a lot about regulatory conditions, the political framework and its constraints, and so on. With skill they are able to exploit what they are already doing and find better solutions over time.

When uncertainty increases, the firm has a more difficult innovation problem—but if it remains in the same environment, searchers have a good idea of the directions in which to place their bets. In the upper left quadrant of figure 6.2 search goes beyond current technological or regulatory pathways into new but promising market opportunities. Search for new ideas is certainly required, but it is bounded by rules of a business game with which the firm (and its competitors) are relatively familiar.

Innovation tends to be more difficult as the environment becomes more complex. As new markets and technologies, competitors, regulators and other players emerge, innovation is likely to require reframing and unlearning old "rules" of the game as shown at the bottom right of figure 6.2. For example, the revolution created by low-cost airlines some years ago introduced a new business model. It was not simply a matter of low prices—but a complete reframing of the way different elements of the air travel business might interact. Successful low-cost airlines had to develop rapid turnaround capabilities, sophisticated pricing models, flexible and multi-skilled working arrangements, and so on. They moved beyond the routines of established airlines. Still, they were working with many understood dimensions of competition.

That kind of challenge, though significant, is now being eclipsed as companies find themselves in the upper right quadrant of figure 6.2. Here the environment is complex, but knowledge is low. For example, the rapidly growing field of VoIP (voice over Internet protocol) communications is not developing along established trajectories toward a well-defined endpoint. It is merging. The broad parameters are visible—including the rising demand for global communication, increasing availability of broadband, multiple peer-to-peer networking models, and growing technological literacy among users. Yet the dominant design for VoIP is not yet visible. Instead, there is a rich fermenting soup of technological possibilities, business models, and potential players from which a new competitive arena is gradually emerging.

Search for information in this kind of situation must explore new territory. There is unpredictability and no clear place to start—companies are in an unexplored space where completely new games can emerge. The challenge for Skype and other contenders is to do something different—something that no firm has yet done. Searchers seeking a position in this and other emerging situations must ask whether any of their prior assets are useful. They must search for answers in unexpected places, picking up and learning about radically different and unimaginable possibilities. Searchers are groping forward in a fog.

Our research suggests companies in this situation use a mixture of judicious experimentation and a lot of fast adaptive feedback to emerging situations. They essentially "probe and learn." Firms need to acquire two core skill sets underpinning these experiments: the ability to reframe existing elements in new combinations and the ability to co-evolve new knowledge elements. Success requires searching in unlikely places, building links to strange partners, allocating resources to high-risk ventures, exploring new ways of looking at the business—all of which challenge the "normal" way companies have approached the innovation problem.

Figure 6.3 revisits the idea of type 1 and type 2 innovations. While we know a lot about how to manage the steady state kind of innovation (doing what has been done, but better), we are much less clear about where and how to start building is continuous innovation capability for doing things in new and different ways. Smart firms are carrying out various experiments in this direction, but no one can claim to have found the answer for dealing with discontinuous environments. We're all still learning—and that's where the *Innovation Labs* come in—they focus on discontinuous innovation.

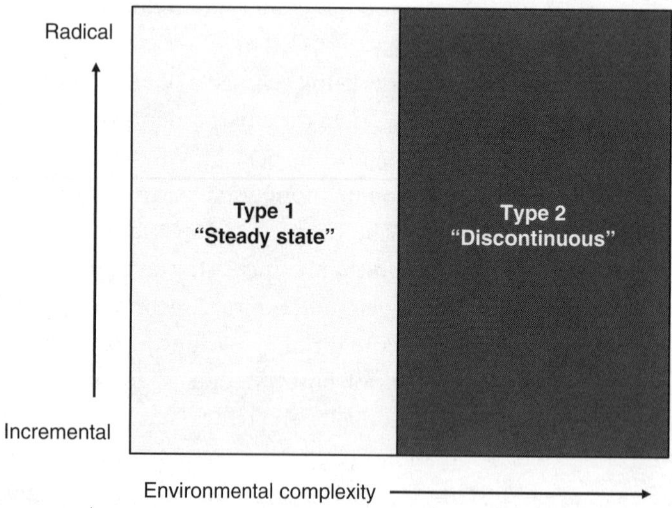

Figure 6.3
We need two types of innovation organizations

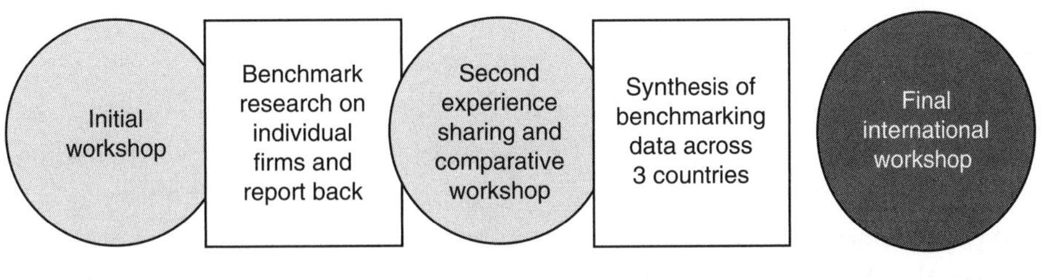

Figure 6.4
Outline of Innovation Lab network meetings

The Innovation Lab

Very simply, the *Innovation Lab* is an experiment in open innovation. It is an opportunity for firms to learn together about managing discontinuous innovation: sharing experiences, trying new things out, reflecting on what has and has not worked, and looking at new ideas and models. The workshops provide a chance to compare, contrast, share, and develop understanding of the major challenges of discontinuous environments by linking up with other noncompeting firms, working with (practically minded!) academic researchers and drawing on experience in different sectors and countries.

The Innovation Lab has a simple structure with four elements, as shown in figure 6.4, and further outlined at http://innovation-lab.org/.

- Recruiting companies in each country is followed by an initial workshop, surfacing discontinuous innovation challenges and capturing experiences, as well as issues and experiments in progress within participating firms.
- A data collection phase follows, using a short benchmarking framework. This results in a snapshot of each firm in terms of its approaches to dealing with key challenges of discontinuous innovation.
- Each firm's snapshot is the subject of a review meeting with the firm, followed by a second networking workshop that facilitates sharing experience and identifying cross-company learning opportunities.
- Finally, once a year the results of networking activity across countries (there are now labs in ten European countries, Australia, and Tunisia) provide the basis for a larger workshop to which participating firms and researchers from around the world are invited.

Firms get the chance to share ideas and network with other firms from very different sectors but facing common problems. They hear about new ideas and tools, new approaches, and have an opportunity to reflect and explore in a safe and confidential environment. By bringing together the experience of many organizations in different sectors and countries, we can build a simple benchmarking framework that will help firms identify what they could learn and from whom.

Participating organizations are investing time and commitment. We look for their active involvement in the workshops and for help with case study interviews—they identify who we should talk to and help us set up the research agenda. The Innovation Lab is meant to be an effective learning network rather than a public relations showcase, which is illustrated by the results of our first research project on innovation search, which yielded information about 12 search strategies for discontinuous conditions.

Search Routines to Support Discontinuous Innovation

Not surprisingly, different firms had different approaches to exploring new ground for discontinuous innovation and potentially benefit and had expanded their repertoire in different ways. Upon discussion, many realized they were doing more than they initially thought, especially when they counted less formal activities, as summarized in table 6.2.

Some of these search methods don't sound that fancy and there can be some overlap, but as I found more and more examples among large and small firms, including firms that are included on lists of the most innovative companies in the world, I became increasingly interested in the result of this first effort at open sharing. Because more information is available (as listed under resources below), I will give you only a brief account of the detail I have in my database.

Sending out Scouts

A number of firms have established specific projects to identify and process new ideas. For example, the O_2 in Germany has a trend-scouting group of about ten people that interprets externally identified trends in terms of the firm's specific business context. Once a year the group meets with the board to discuss and select ideas. Other Innovation Lab firms recognize that researchers and other employees attending professional conferences can be idea hunters and have put systems in place for collecting the insights they gain.

Exploring Multiple Futures

A second approach to finding innovation triggers is to consider alternative futures, especially those that do not follow current assumptions. One effective way of creating

Table 6.2
Searching for discontinuous innovation

Search strategy	Mode of operation
Sending out scouts	Dispatch idea hunters to track down new innovation triggers.
Exploring multiple futures	Use futures techniques to explore alternative possible futures, and develop innovation options.
Using the web	Harness the power of the web to detect new trends.
Working with active users	Team up with product and service users to see the ways in which they are changing.
Deep diving	Study what people actually do, rather than what they say they do.
Probing and learning	Use prototyping as a mechanism to explore emergent phenomena, and bring key stakeholders into the innovation process.
Mobilizing the mainstream	Bring mainstream actors into the product and service development process.
Corporate venturing	Create and deploy venture units.
Corporate entrepreneurship and intrapreneuring	Stimulate and nurture entrepreneurial talent inside the organization.
Using brokers and bridges	Widely cast the ideas net to connect with other industries.
Deliberate diversifying	Create a diverse workforce and diverse teams.
Using idea generators	Use creativity tools.

and exploring such futures is scenario planning, as pioneered by Shell. Innovation Lab firms emphasized that predicting possible futures is just the beginning of the search process. It is important to discuss actions that could be taken to make any particular future a reality. The Danish pharmaceuticals company, Novo Nordisk, provides a good example. It uses a companywide scenario-based program to explore radical futures around its core business. One interesting outcome of such a scenario plan led to the setting up the Oxford Health Alliance by the company. The Alliance is a nonprofit collaboration bringing together key stakeholders—medical scientists, doctors, patients, and government officials—who often have divergent views and perspectives. The goal is the prevention or cure of diabetes, which if achieved, would potentially kill off Novo Nordisk's main line of business. But, as CEO Lars Rebien Sørensen noted, that outcome might also create new opportunities.

Using the Web

The web is an additional space into which the firm can send its scouts. Increasingly firms use professional organizations that have search capabilities to help hunt for ideas in this complex environment. However, some participating companies are more active. For example, BMW makes use of the Web to support its Virtual Innovation Agency—a forum where suppliers from outside the normal range of BMW players can offer ideas. The inputs sought are both product and process-related: a recent suggestion was for carbon-neutral recycling of factory waste.

Working with Active Users

In a significant number of cases external innovators are becoming more active players in the innovation process. Companies using this strategy indicate that customers at the fringes of the mainstream tend to be more tolerant of early project limitations and more willing to work to discover something better. This makes them an ideal target group for beta testing. For example, after LEGO® launched Mindstorms Invention Systems—the programmable LEGO toys—in the late 1990s advanced users quickly cracked the code and developed updated versions that were superior to the original. While this was unexpected, in 2006 LEGO launched a radical new Mindstorms product—the NXT. This time the company invited some leading users to participate directly in product development. In recognition of the success of this program, LEGO stated that it was looking for 100 more "citizen developers" (http://mindstorms.lego.com/en-us/Default.aspx). It is interesting to note that while the issue of intellectual property came up regularly as Lab participants discussed similar outreach efforts, most companies did not view it as a major problem. Being able to visit the company's design studio (BMW) or having one's name associated with a product (LEGO) were viewed by active users as sufficient reward for their engagement.

Deep Diving

A fifth powerful source of demand-side innovation triggers is to take a much deeper look at how people actually behave—as opposed to how they say they behave, or company insiders believe they behave. For example, to ensure that its new terminal at London Heathrow would address user needs well into the future, BAA (the company that manages many major British airports) commissioned research into what users in 2020 might look like, and what their needs might be. The aging population came up as an issue. Focusing on the behavior of people at their current airports, BAA managers noticed that older people tend to go to the toilet more frequently than other customers. As a result they planned for more toilets at Heathrow's Terminal 5. However, further research showed that many people going to the restrooms did not actually use the toilet—they went there because it was quiet and they could hear announcements more easily. This observation led to other modifications of the new terminal and shows that it is not only important to observe, but even more to be able to understand and interpret observations appropriately.

Probing and Learning

It is often difficult to imagine a radically different future, and even harder to predict how things will actually develop. In order to get a better understanding of promising but radical innovations some participating companies have started to use an approach we call "probe and learn," which can be described as "trying something out and learning from the result, even if the result represents a failure." Novo Nordisk is making extensive use of probe and learn approaches as they try to understand the possible evolution of new diabetes-related services and care pathways, especially where very different conditions apply. In Africa, for example, there is a need for holistic solutions involving education, clinics, and prevention methods—all delivered from a very low-cost base. The company is involved in a process of prototyping and modification to develop responses that fit this environment.

Mobilizing the Mainstream

The seventh strategy confronts the tension between the need to search for ideas that might support discontinuous innovations and the fact that most organizations are already stretched, and lack resources for new and different search activities. I found that some participating companies had developed ways to amplify their search capacity by making better or different use of existing resources. For example, at Bang & Olufsen a number of "inspiration clubs" have been formed, each with a chair whose role is to facilitate and drive new innovations. The setup increases the likelihood that ideas from across the organization are identified, connected, and elaborated.

Corporate Venturing

In contrast to strategy seven, the next strategy involves setting up special units with the remit and budget to explore new diversification options. Typically these efforts are ring-fenced so that participants can consider opportunities that may not be acceptable in the parent organization (perhaps because they are too small, reflect badly on existing brands, or do not relate to existing businesses). Most setups mentioned by participating companies had provisions for acquisition as well as spin-outs. The degree of parent control varied from tight to a hands-off policy. Large corporations also have multiple ventures, with different control policies. Unilever, for example, has three schemes for corporate venturing: (1) a fund 40 percent owned by Unilever (with the rest owned by banks and investment funds) to buy companies from entrepreneurs and see whether they can be scaled up and turned into a larger success; (2) Unilever Technical Venture (UTV), which is wholly owned by Unilever and takes a minority stake in early-stage technology start-ups; and (3) Unilever Venture, which invests in technical spin-outs and other businesses that are close to the company's core activities.

Corporate Entrepreneuring/Intrapreneuring

The ninth strategy is a different take on corporate venturing often referred to as corporate entrepreneuring or intrapreneurship. This strategy attempts to build a culture where new ideas are generated within and across the organization. Many such schemes provide strong incentives for those willing to take the lead in moving ideas into marketable products from the company's core. Intrapreneuring aims to nurture entrepreneurial drive inside the organization. However, workshop participants pointed out that doing so often brought out fundamental tensions between creativity and control and between playing by the rules and creating new ones. Participants emphasized the importance of informal networking and other mechanisms to take ideas forward below the radar screen of formal corporate systems. For example, BMW has a strong commitment to bootlegging—encouraging people to try things out without necessarily asking for permission or establishing a formal project. In BMW these are called "U-boot" projects. A good example is the Series 3 Estate. The mainstream thought the model conflicted with the image of BMW as producing high-quality, high-performance, and sporty cars. However, a small group of staff worked on a U-Boot project to make a prototype, using parts cannibalized from other cars. The model was ultimately accepted and opened new market space for the company.

Using Brokers and Bridges

A tenth search strategy is based on the insight that interesting innovations often develop at the boundary between one knowledge set and another. People who can see how ideas in one area might connect with another are invaluable. Organizations interested in more radical innovations are using social networking tools and other techniques to map networks and connections outside their normal knowledge zones. For example, the UK engineering services company Arup has done extensive work on mapping networks inside and outside the business to better exploit potential connectivity. The result is a map of the Arup "brain," which indicates where connections might be made and who might engineer new links.

Deliberately Diversifying

Many Innovation Lab participants indicate that "fitting in with the culture" has been a recruitment criterion in the past, but some are placing greater emphasis on diversity (both in hiring and when setting up project teams) in the hope of supporting more discontinuous innovation. For example, the design and innovation consultancy IDEO hires people from backgrounds as diverse as medicine, engineering, anthropology, and physics to create teams with a strong track record in coming up with groundbreaking new ideas. The German auto supplier, Webasto, provided a complementary discussion on the topic of "querdenker" (people who think against the grain). Not long ago mangers in this company realized that they had stopped recruiting such people, one reason being that they can be quite demanding on resources. Today the company sometimes uses consultants or other external people to take on the role of querdenker as a less expensive alternative to full-time employment. A companion strategy in this and other companies can be to seek diversity through external alliances.

Using Idea Generators

The last of the twelve search strategies observed among Innovation Lab companies is to use creativity tools and techniques to increase the flow of radical ideas. Participants sometimes find external agencies to help with the generation of ideas with discontinuous potential. They point out that these external agents are not necessarily required to produce detailed concepts or ideas but rather to act as early warning systems for weak signals about changing trends. A particularly interesting idea came from P&G; their P&G Encore program uses retirees to help act as gatekeepers and spotters.

Conclusion: Turning New Opportunities into Company Routines

Research by Andrew Hargadon and others suggests an emerging challenge at the level of skills and human resource policy. Given the growing emphasis on crossover between knowledge sets—whether internal or interorganizational—the nature of bridging and brokering skills becomes a central question. What skill set is needed to act as a broker and can this be trained or recruited? The evidence collected by Tom Kelley and Jonathan Littman (2001) is that in many cases firms are, at least temporarily, recognizing a skills gap and employing outsourcing approaches to a growing service sector with skills in design, creative concept generation, trend spotting, search, and the like.

To facilitate bridging to the mainstream of the organization, there is a need to codify and facilitate a scale up or transfer from fringe units currently engaged in the process. This highlights the role of what could be termed "tool making"—converting experimental approaches in, for example, futures work into robust and communicable methodologies so that successful experiments become regularly used and reinforced routines. Examples in the Innovation Lab research reported here include work on codifying and understanding lead user methods, prototyping, and co-evolution. The objective is to have a suite of responses (though any one firm is unlikely to use all of the ideas discussed in this chapter).

Idea for Innovative Leaders: Prepare Your Company to Absorb Outside Ideas

The importance of finding ways to embed search strategies for discontinuous innovation into an organization's fabric, as well as ensuring that the resulting findings and insights are not rejected by the corporate immune system, cannot be emphasized enough. Companies involved in Innovation Labs agree that it is very important to consider the degree to which mechanisms are in place to transfer insights into the mainstream organization. Routines for experimentation emerge only if they are regularly deployed and reinforced—and for many Innovation Lab organizations the sense was that the connections are so far weak. Similarly, unless mechanisms are deliberately and consciously put in place, new ideas are accessible to only a few, generally not the people able to decide whether or not to act on the information received.

These issues are closely related to another obstacle, a lack of connectedness inside the organization. Unless different strands of information and insight come together in one particular area and can be combined to create a more persuasive and convincing picture, insights about potential discontinuities will be ignored. For example, suggestions from hired idea scouts may receive little attention.

Another problem identified is a potential lack of buy-in. By its nature, discontinuous innovation challenges and often undermines existing skills and mindsets. Therefore those at the core of the organization are inclined to reject insights and discount them as unrealistic or label possible ways forward as "not feasible." This reflects the gap identified by Shaker Zahra and Gerry George between "cognitive absorptive capacity"—learning about what is going on—and "operational absorptive capacity"—essentially doing something about it.

In the end, it is not about doing any one of the things outlined in this chapter, or a combination of them, but rather about acting on the insights generated, and ensuring that they are integrated into the wider organization. Success is also about allocating people to the task of exploration, which tends to be an ongoing activity rather than a project.

References and Further Reading

Bessant, J., and B. von Stamm. 2008. Search strategies for discontinuous innovation. In J. Bessant and T. Venables, eds., *Creating Wealth from Knowledge: Meeting the Innovation Challenge*. Cheltenham, UK: Elgar, 203–226.

Bessant, J., B. von Stamm, K. Möslein, and A.-K. Neyer. 2010. Backing outsiders: Selection strategies for discontinuous innovation. *R&D Management* 40 (4): 345–56.

Birkinshaw, J., and C. Gibson. 2004. Building ambidexterity into an organization. *Sloan Management Review* 45 (4): 47–55.

Buckland, W., A. Hatcher, and J. Birkinshaw. 2003. *Inventuring: Why Big Companies Must Think Small*. London: McGraw Hill Business.

Dodgson, M., D. Gann, and A. Salter. 2005. *Think, Play, Do: Technology, Innovation, and Organization*. Oxford: Oxford University Press.

Gundling, E. 2000. *The 3M Way to Innovation: Balancing People and Profit*. New York: Kodansha International.

Hargadon, A. 2003. *How Breakthroughs Happen*. Boston: Harvard Business School Press.

Kelley, T., and J. Littman. 2001. *The Art of Innovation: Lessons in Creativity from Ideo, America's Leading Design Firm*. New York: Currency.

Leifer, R., C. M. McDermott, G. C. O'Connor, L. S. Peters, M. Rice, and R. W. Veryzer. 2000. *Radical Innovation: How Mature Companies Can Outsmart Upstarts*. Boston: Harvard Business School Press.

March, J. 1991. Exploration and exploitation in organizational learning. *Organization Science* 2 (1): 71–87.

McGrath, R. G. 2001. Exploratory learning, innovative capacity, and managerial oversight. *Academy of Management Journal* 44 (1): 118–131.

Pinchot, G., III. 1986. *Intrapreneuring in Action: Why You Don't Have to Leave a Corporation to Become an Entrepreneur*. New York: HarperCollins.

Schrage, M. 2000. *Serious Play: How the World's Best Companies Simulate to Innovate*. Boston: Harvard Business School Press.

Schroeder, A., and D. Robinson. 2004. *Ideas Are Free: How the Idea Revolution Is Liberating People and Transforming Organizations*. San Francisco: Barrett Koehler.

Schwartz, P. 1991. *The Art of the Long View*. New York: Currency Doubleday.

Thomke, S. H. 2003. *Experimentation Matters: Unlocking the Potential of New Technologies for Innovation*. Boston: Harvard Business School Press.

Tushman, M., and C. O'Reilly. 1996. Ambidextrous organizations: Managing evolutionary and revolutionary change. *California Management Review* 38 (4): 8–30.

von Stamm, B., and J. Bessant. 2007. Beyond the lamppost: Innovation search strategies for discontinuous conditions. Working paper. The Innovation Lab.

Zahra, S. A., and G. George. 2002. Absorptive capacity: A review, reconceptualization and extension. *Academy of Management Review* 27 (2): 185–94.

7 Cooperation for Innovation

Lynda Gratton

Introduction

"Hot spots" of energy and potential innovation can arise when people, often working across functional, national, and organizational boundaries, are able to work energetically and effectively together on critical tasks. I named my book *Hot Spots* after this phenomenon because it captures so well the transient and high-energy nature of these groups and communities. For innovators, the capacity to encourage hot spots to emerge by drawing on varied sources from both within and beyond the organization is crucial to the capacity of hot spots to create new sources of value.

Historically there have been a number of waves of value creation strategies. In the 1980s, for example, value often was created by taking costs out of often bloated businesses. From this the next wave of value creation came from mergers and other kinds of reorganizing as the ecosystems of an industry began to emerge. However, executives realized that once these two strategies had been accomplished—then value creation through innovation becomes central to high-performing companies. In this decade growth will increasingly depend on the capacity to innovate—from products and services to practices and processes.

One of the challenges of the second wave of value creation—mergers and restructuring—is that as executives pushed performance through reorganization they also created stand-alone business units and siloed functions. This was crucial to driving performance to the bottom line and increasing efficiency. However, this also led to the replication of activities and erected barriers to knowledge sharing across boundaries. So in this third, innovative wave of value creation, the challenge is to pull the organization back together again in order to gain the advantages of synergies and knowledge sharing. Clearly, hard structures are a way of achieving this, but what is also crucial is the capacity to build cooperative ties across functions, across businesses themselves, and of course across organizations.

Hot Spots

Given this need for re-integration, it is no surprise that cooperation is increasingly an issue on the organizational agenda. For the last three years I have directed a research consortium focusing on the future of work. We have collected data from fifty companies around the world, in a process that asks executives to consider how they believe their company has to develop in the future, and how well they are currently prepared for these future needs. It is no surprise that of the top ten areas they identify as risks, many of them refer to cooperation. Specifically, they are concerned about how they encourage cooperation within virtual teams, how they support cross-function collaboration, and how they build the capabilities to support open innovation.

Over the last decade my research team and I have specifically studied cooperation in over a hundred complex teams across the world. We looked closely at the organizational contexts that are most likely to support or act as barriers to cooperation and the emergence of hot spots of energy and innovation. It is clear that the heart of the innovative agenda has to be a commitment to the values and actions that encourage a cooperative mindset and indeed the opportunities for people to work across boundaries. However, while these two elements are necessary, more is needed to create the energy of a hot spot. The third and decisive element is an igniting purpose. All three elements have been identified before. It is less clear what practices, processes, and leadership capabilities put them into practice.

Identifying and Understanding Hot Spots

The research began more than a decade ago when my colleague Sumantra Ghoshal and I wrote case studies about what were then five successful multinational companies. Added to this, I built the Cooperative Consortium with many other companies including ABN Amro, BBC, British Petroleum, British Telecom, Citigroup, French Telecom, Lehman Brothers, Rogers Communication, PriceWaterhouseCoopers, Nokia, Marriott, Royal Bank of Scotland, Reuters, Siemens, Unilever, and XL CAPITAL. Since that time, with funding from the Singapore government, we have also worked with teams from across Asia and Europe in seeking to understand more deeply the basis of their cooperative endeavors.

The speed of organizational transformation in complex collaboration is such that we are seeing practice move ahead of theory in this area. It appears that theory is in a catch-up mode, while cooperative practices are even more complex than we realized. The groups we studies from around the world are drawing their members across time zones, working with strangers who don't know each other very well—participants who vary in many ways, including their skills.

It is obvious that the scope and scale of cooperation is becoming more complex. For example, our study found that the size of collaborating groups has dramatically increased. We anticipated that the groups we surveyed would be from 10 to 50 people. The companies sent back the names of many more—as many as 130 people on one team. We also saw the extent to which most knowledge-based teams operating across national boundaries and time zones must operate in a virtual environment. Finally, complexity has been increased by the sheer number of specialists involved in many teams, typically with their own competencies, technical language, and performance norms. Together, these characteristics of many contemporary teams and communities place enormous demands on their capacity to innovate and work effectively together.

As an overview of results from the quantitative analysis, I want to offer some insights on cooperation interpreted with the help of the case studies we also created. Our first interesting observation is that cooperation is not a stand-alone competency but is rather deeply embedded in a whole value set that often becomes a self-fulfilling prophecy. We discovered that for cooperation to occur, people in an organization need to feel that there is goodwill, trust, and generosity around them. The case studies provided some insight into the executive role of modeling, useful organizational practices, and managerial behavior that support this cycle.

However, while a cooperative mindset is essential, it simply creates the latent energy for innovation. It does not of itself ignite the energy that serves innovation. What are crucial are the insights and perspectives that people have about the task. We found that there are two elements that have to be in place before the hot spots that interest me emerge. One element is that people are adept at working across boundaries. At the heart of a community's capacity to work across boundaries are people whom we called "boundary spanners"—those individuals who introduce people to each other so that knowledge transfer can take place.

In addition the communities need an igniting purpose. This is the spark that ignites latent energy. I don't think my field of Human Resources adequately understands this. The spark that ignites latent energy can take a number of forms. An exciting task is the most obvious. We also found that the more complex the task, particularly the more ambiguous it is, the more people feel ignited and are willing to actively cooperate.

How Do Organizations Break away from Current Practice?

It is clear that many companies struggle with the cooperative element of innovation. What we have found is that those that have created a culture of cooperation often have done so by developing a cycle of practices and processes that encourage people to believe it is necessary to work together. This includes for example, the extent to which executives are seen to role-model cooperative behavior, promotion systems that identify cooperative behaviors, and cooperative practices such as coaching and mentoring.

Interestingly the factors that make a positive difference to cooperation do not include remuneration. We found no significant positive correlation between the type of remuneration and the extent of cooperation. It appears that organizations cannot simply change their remuneration practices and expect to make a significant difference in cooperation. More specifically, organizations cannot change remuneration practices from individual rewards to team-based rewards and expect that within a week everybody will start working cooperatively with each other. At best, team-based rewards seem to be neutral, rather than intrinsically positive, while individual rewards may act as a significant barrier to cooperative working. These are very interesting findings from an HR and a strategic point of view. The topic needs further research and further attention from those who design corporate management systems.

While remuneration may not play a central role in the emergence of hot spots of energy and innovation, psychological safety and trust seems to be crucial. We found this to be one of the strongest relationships with purposeful cooperation in our data set. Positive outcomes are found when people feel safe, they feel they are listened to, and they believe it is possible to take risks. It seems that people, and the innovations they can create among them, flourish in this environment. In addition we discovered that the experience of being mentored is highly related with purposeful cooperation. Role-modeling by senior executives who demonstrate cooperative values is a second important predictor. A third contributor is cooperative goals. There are no surprises from these three factors, but it is important to work with them when designing more collaborative organizations.

I am also convinced by an interesting and very strong negative relationship between cooperative working and competitive goals. What that means in practice is that if organizations set up task goals where people are expected to compete with each other, they establish an environment that has a very negative effect on the complex system that supports cooperation. Again, designers of organizational processes should care for alignment.

While cooperation plays a key role in the emergence of a hot spot of energy and innovation—we found that the depth and extent of networks was crucial to the way in which cooperation was practiced and knowledge transferred. To understand this better, we profiled the past and current networks of team members, specifically how much experience they had of working across boundaries, across countries, across sectors. We then created a boundary-spanning index for each member. We found that the extent of this index predicted to what extent individuals shared information with others, and indeed whether the team they are part of shares information with their stakeholders (suppliers and customers) outside of the team. It seems the past experience with boundary spanning that people bring to a team strongly determines subsequent knowledge sharing.

This insight has implications for how companies encourage people to move around functions and businesses. It also has specific ramifications for women. The teams we studied had almost equal numbers of men and women so we were able to look closely at their working styles. Contrary to popular belief, we found no significant differences between how men and women collaborate. However, when we looked at past experience, we discovered that in many cases, women tend to report less experience of working across boundaries than men, and therefore they are less likely to be currently involved in cooperative networking. What is clear is that if we are to encourage innovation and knowledge sharing, then the past experience of working across functions for both men and women is crucial.

Boundary spanning is indeed crucial to the innovative performance of the team. We found that a group's innovative capacity is significantly enhanced by their members' capacity to build strong, cooperative, and positive relationships with those outside the team. There is a clear and strong finding in our research that the more innovative groups clearly have stronger and more effective networks into their stakeholder communities.

In sum, I have come to believe that real knowledge creation comes less from individual cognitions—and more in the space between people—in their interactions, conversations, and shared tasks. I am not sure to what extent executives really understand that it is the building of high-performance relationships and in diverse networks that the path to innovation lies. It seems that too often little effort is focused on building communities. For example, organizations that rapidly promote a few stars actively negate the likelihood of creating knowledge in the space between people. It seems that most HR practices and processes remain resolutely individual—when the real value is in the relational.

The Need for Balance

A risk of cooperation and relational boundary spanning is the economic theory that asserts that people create networks as a form of personal arbitrage. In this model of human nature, "tit for tat" is the basis of when and why a person would share knowledge. I believe this is a significant risk to cooperation. Our data paint a picture that is closer to my own experience, that most networkers introduce people to each other because they think the association will create value, and not because they think they can personally appropriate that value. It seems that network theory field of research has focused too much on the appropriation of value, and not enough on the creation of value. In the highly collaborative and innovative teams we looked at, people seem to be saying "Hey, you guys should meet each other," not thinking "Hey, if I introduce Joan to Robert I will benefit."

Although relationships within and across teams are indeed crucial to innovation, we discovered interesting nuances in the type and extent of relationships required to really fuel innovation. For example, even when cooperative efforts are created with good intentions, it is important that leaders think about the kind of groups they are forming. Two specific questions are crucial. When should relationships be strong so that people stay together in their groups, get to know each other very well, and, by doing so, share deep and tacit knowledge? When should less strong relationships (weak ties) be created across groups? The choice is outlined in figure 7.1, which suggests there is some tension between the efficiency and speed of maintaining strong relationships between people who know each other well and therefore can easily share tacit knowledge and the potential innovation (but also lack of efficiency) generated when people work across boundaries with people they know less well.

These complications have big implications for HR practices such as career development. In the past a company like Shell moved people around on a very regular basis in order to develop broad networks—they moved to the right hand of figure 7.1. However, over time it became obvious that, by doing so, they were in danger of destroying the tacit knowledge that is so important to quality and speed. It's a complex balance. Clearly, it is not wise for a company to move everyone around all the time so that there

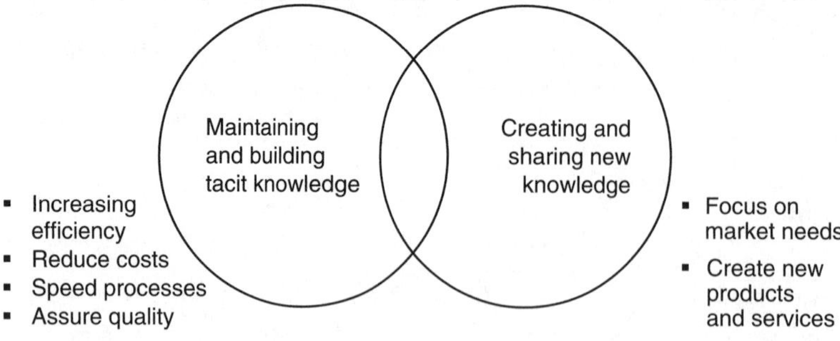

Figure 7.1
Balancing value creation strategies

is collaboration across boundaries, since that defuses the tacit knowledge base that gradually develops in the space between people working together. Of course, new connections are needed for vitality, especially when innovation is the goal. The challenge is to balance depth and breadth. How to creatively balance strong and weak network ties seems to me to be an important question for executives and for academic research.

Igniting Purpose

Creating a cooperative mindset and focusing on high-quality networks are crucial elements of hot spot energy and innovation. However, without a spark to ignite this latent energy, innovation rarely takes place. We have several ideas about how this happens from our research.

Vision about an exciting and engaging future is the first obvious spark. This is clear in communities such as the Linux community where Linus Torvalds's vision of an open source platform free to everyone created a spark that was able to catalyze the energy and imagination of thousands of people around the world. Visions like this can be a great rallying call to focus the energy and imagination of cooperative crowds.

However, many CEOs seem to struggle with clarity of vision. Faced with the demands for short-term performance returns, they are often more comfortable talking about ROCE than focusing on visions. So, if leaders can't or don't create a sharp vision for the future, does that mean they don't play a role in new innovations? It seems that there are other ways that successful leaders can push people's energy into the future. A particularly important tool is the Socratic method of asking important questions.

I saw this clearly in the behavior of a new CEO. Within a month of taking office, she called the senior group together, stood at the front and simply asked: "Why do we hate each other?" It was a difficult, Socratic question. It takes a very confident CEO to ask a question when people around them are thinking and saying "You should know the answer to that, why are you asking me?" The same courage of the Socratic question was seen when John Browne was halfway through his tenure as CEO of BP. His question was this: "How can BP be a force for good?" This was a very interesting challenge because BP is an oil company in an industry that is often accused of destroying the environment, and an industry that many graduates don't want to join. Yet Browne had the courage to ignite energy by asking the tough question—how in a sector known for its destruction could BP become a force for good. As we now know, this courage was to be tested to its limits when his successor was faced with a major environmental catastrophe in the Gulf of Mexico. Surely prior thinking about Browne's question was of some value.

The key implication of a Socratic question, however, is that the leader's role is not to provide an answer. I wonder if academics and the city have damaged senior leaders by always expecting them to have a clear vision that answers all questions. They are only human. How could they have more answers than we have collectively? Some leaders will be able to create visions—but many will not. What they can do is to ask really Socratic questions that those less familiar with the organization might not ask: questions that have the potential to act as points of ignition.

Making Signature Processes

When Sumantra Ghoshal and I researched a number of companies, we were fascinated by the similarities and differences among them. We knew that truly great companies use best practice that is available in their sector—and we saw many examples of how best practice around many management activities had been found and then embedded. However, one of the striking features of our five cases of high-performing companies is that beyond shared best practice, each of them in their own way also did something that nobody else did.

We called these unique features that seemed to contribute to high-performance "signature processes." These seemed to play an important role in creating a context in which hot spots of energy could emerge. The point is that large-scale organizational transformation is well-nigh impossible. Signature processes focus attention instead on one or two unique practices that the leader is prepared to champion. But we found that leaders where hot spots emerge are very adept at championing one or two critical practices that resonate with their own values and the history of their unique organization.

In an important sense signature processes are ways the senior team can influence the company that also is authentic to its employees. Some people say that the leader is the architect of the organization. I think this is implausible. How can any one person, even the CEO, truly be the architect of a huge company? It is unlikely that an established company will be completely redesigned, though in extreme circumstances you do occasionally see this effort. What leaders under less extreme conditions can do is work with the relatively few practices, processes, and routines that are unique to their companies. These signature processes are a way of bringing the "inside out" and demonstrating the CEO's values to the wider company.

In this sense signature processes contrast with best practices which are basically about bringing the "outside in." The combination is important to collaboration and innovation since, while best practices like Six Sigma create a level playing field for

	Best practice	Signature process
Provenance	"Bringing the outside in" external and internal search for best practice processes	"Bringing the inside out" a path dependent history
Development	Careful adaptation and alignment to the business goal and industry context	Championing by executives
Core	Shared knowledge from across the sector	Corporate values

Figure 7.2
Difference between best practice and signature processes

competition—it is the signatures that can potentially bring competitive advantage. The difference between the two is depicted in figure 7.2.

We saw very different collaborative signature across the three companies we studied in detail: the Royal Bank of Scotland, BP, and Nokia. Figure 7.3 showcases the three signature processes. At the Royal Bank of Scotland, for example, the CEO Fred Goodwin brought his team together every day for a morning meeting. Every day of the week except Saturday and Sunday, beginning at nine o'clock, people in the senior team met to talk with each other for more than an hour. When we asked Fred Goodwin where the idea of the morning meetings he championed came from, we found that morning meetings had existed since 1727. Goodwin started with a process that fit the culture and heritage of the company, but then made it his own. In particular, he used the morning meetings to speed up decision-making in the company.

At the time we studied it, the executive team at the Royal Bank was able to work in a very fast way. This was apparent in everyday language. We noticed at that time that people at RBS did not talk about months. They did not even talk about weeks. Every single project or intervention they talked about was measured in terms of days. Projects were 30-, 60-, or 90-day projects. The daily meetings helped people make mutual adjustments that supported this speed. Their ability to cooperate, plus task focus, was a unique source of value that propelled the bank to become one of the most profitable banks in the world. But, of course, the story of the morning meetings also had a downside. By speeding up decision-making and putting all the decisions into a small group, Goodwin was able to act quickly, but he was also able to act rashly. It was the rapid decision-making about the purchase of the Dutch bank ABN Amro that was the

	RBS morning meetings CEO Fred Goodwin	Nokia modular structure	BP peer assist
Provenance • Path dependent	Banking tradition dating back to 1727	Technology heritage from the 1980s: reusability through slicing and sequencing, standardization	Initially created in mid-1990s
Development • Executive champion	Shared training the senior team: • CEO a forensic accountant	Shared education of the senior team: • Technical focus • "Taste for complexity"	Philosophy of CEO J. Browne: • Small scale • Learning • Nonhierarchical
Core values	Respect and accountability	Renewal and respect	Learning and accountability

Figure 7.3
Anatomy of signature processes

downfall of the bank in 2010. A signature process that had been valuable had become a destroyer of value.

The key feature of signature processes is that they are not easily copied. They very much represent the history and culture of the place—with an overlay of the CEO's values and style, and as such they become unique, not so much in their description but in the way they are carried out. This was true in our study of Nokia. The modular structure at Nokia was as extraordinary and as unusual as RBS's morning meetings. In this unique organizational structure the balance between building tacit knowledge and boundary spanning was achieved by moving whole groups around and re-connecting them together.

The mindset behind the signature of team modularity at Nokia lay within the experience and training of the senior team. At that time most of the senior team had been trained as software engineers at the Helsinki School of Technology. The basic idioms of software engineers include modularity and the reusability of knowledge. This shared mental model had become the underlying theory and structural architecture of the company when we studied it and Nokia's signature process. It was very difficult for anybody else to replicate.

We found that BP also has its signature process—their "peer assist" program. During the development of the idea, CEO John Browne split the company into around a hundred and fifty business units and then horizontally pulled them back together into twelve groups with clear performance measures. What he did next was based on his personal belief that people learn more from peers than from bosses. The peer assist program that developed from Browne's core idea was one of intense collaboration between businesses. Each of the business leaders was obliged, as a citizen of BP, to assist their peers. This simple idea became a very powerful concept. Experience with peer assist was so strong that it was stretched to include "peer challenge," where groups review each other's requests for new funding before they are sent forward.

This is truly a signature idea. Over the years, information about the peer assist program has been widely disseminated. But even though many know about BP's processes, no other company that I know of has been able to replicate them. Why not? It is a signature process—John Browne's contribution to BP.

Conclusion: Priorities for Leaders and Researchers Interested in Creating Hot Spots

I would love to see three questions pursued by scholars and practitioners interested in leading collaborations that produce significant innovations:

1. How can we increase understanding of how to build the spirit of collaboration in organizations? It seems that many companies are simply tweaking the practices and processes they have been working on for some time. Often the HR function relies on reward structures, when in fact extrinsic reward does not seem to play a strong role in collaboration or innovation. It seems that some widely accepted ideas about how to create a collaborative setting are probably wrong for today's organizations. Other ideas probably hold: for example, our study reinforces the idea that role-modeling and mentoring are important. We need to know more. The question both managers and researchers have to answer is: *Of all the things that might contribute to a culture of collaboration, what really makes a difference?*

2. A number of studies show that innovation often takes place across boundaries. Here the challenge is one of degree. When is boundary spanning appropriate, when does it simply lead to the disintegration of teams? Some groups will need to stay together and build tacit knowledge over a longer period of time. We need more experience and more research to understand: *When are networks across boundaries critical for organizational benefit, when do they erode benefit?*

3. A third important issue involves the ignition of collaborative hot spots. We have found that this could be a vision, or it could be a great task. The challenge that executives and scholars face is: *How do we create tasks and projects that are sufficiently meaningful to ignite the latent energy within every organization into hot spots of innovation?*

Idea for Innovative Leaders: Organizational Structures Facilitate Cooperation

• Resist the urge to overly structure tasks when cooperation is desired, since research shows that people collaborate less when tasks are structured.

• Remunerate team-based outcomes, but do not expect remuneration to create a cooperative mindset. Research suggests that effective collaborators are not primarily motivated by personal gain.

• Eliminate individual competitive goals, as these are negatively associated with collaborative settings.

• Facilitate cross-boundary assignments for women in the organization to increase their future collaborative capacity.

References and Further Reading

Gratton, L., and S. Ghoshal. 2005. Beyond best practice. *Sloan Management Review* 46 (3):49–57.

Gratton, L. 2007. *Hot Spots: Why Some Teams, Workplaces, and Organizations Buzz with Energy—And Others Don't.* San Francisco: Berrett-Koehler.

Gratton, L., and T. Erickson. 2007. Eight ways to build collaborative teams. *Harvard Business Review* 85 (11): 101–109.

Kilduff, M., and W. Tsai. 2003. *Social Networks and Organizations.* London: Sage.

Nahapiet, J., and S. Ghoshal. 1998. Social capital, intellectual capital, and the organizational advantage. *Academy of Management Review* 23 (2): 242–66.

Nahapiet, J., L. Gratton, and H. Rocha. 2005. Knowledge and cooperative relationships: When cooperation is the norm. *European Management Review* 2 (1): 3–14.

8 User Innovation

Eric von Hippel

Open User Innovation

Ever since Schumpeter (1934) promulgated his theory of economic development, economists, policy makers, and business managers have assumed that the dominant mode of innovation is a "producer's model." That is, it has been assumed that most important innovations would originate from producers and be supplied to consumers via goods that were for sale.

This view seemed reasonable on the face of it—producers generally serve many users and so can profit from multiple copies of a single innovative design. Individual users in contrast, depend on benefits from in-house use of an innovation to recoup their investments. Presumably a producer who serves many customers can therefore afford to invest more in innovation than any single user. From this it follows logically that producer-developed designs should dominate user-developed designs in most parts of the economy.

However, the producers' model is only one mode of innovation. A second, increasingly important model is *open user innovation*. Under this second model economically important innovations are developed by users and other agents who divide up the tasks and costs of innovation development and then *freely reveal* their results. Users obtain direct use benefits from the collaborative effort. Other participants obtain diverse benefits such as enjoyment, learning, reputation, and an increased demand for complementary goods and services.

Open user innovation is an institution that competes with and, my colleagues and I argue, can displace producer innovation in many parts of the economy (Baldwin and von Hippel 2011). A growing body of empirical work clearly shows that users are the first to develop many, and perhaps most, new industrial and consumer products. In addition the importance of product and service development by users is increasing over time. This shift is being driven by two related technical trends: (1) the steadily improving *design capabilities* (innovation toolkits) that advances in computer hardware and software make possible for users and (2) the steadily improving ability of individual users to *combine and coordinate* their innovation-related efforts via new communication media such as the Internet.

The ongoing shift of innovation to users has some very attractive qualities. It is becoming progressively easier for many users to get precisely what they want by designing it for themselves. Innovation by users also provides a very necessary complement to and feedstock for manufacturer innovation. And innovation by users appears to increase social welfare. At the same time the ongoing shift of product-development activities from manufacturers to users is painful and difficult for many manufacturers. Open, distributed innovation is "attacking" a major structure of the social division of labor. Many firms and industries must make fundamental changes to long-held business models in order to adapt. Furthermore governmental policy and legislation sometimes preferentially supports innovation by manufacturers. Considerations of social welfare suggest that this must change. The workings of the intellectual property system are of special concern. But, despite the difficulties, a user-centered system of innovation appears well worth striving for.

Today a number of innovation process researchers are working to develop our understanding of open user-innovation processes. In this chapter I offer a review of some collective learning on this important topic to date.

Importance of Innovation by Users

Users, as I use the term, are firms or individual consumers that expect to benefit from *using* a product or a service. In contrast, manufacturers expect to benefit from *selling* a product or a service. A firm or an individual can have different relationships to different products or innovations. For example, Boeing is a manufacturer of airplanes, but it is also a user of machine tools. If one were examining innovations developed by Boeing for the airplanes it sells, Boeing would be a manufacturer-innovator in those cases. But, if one were considering innovations in metal-forming machinery developed by Boeing for in-house use in building airplanes, those would be categorized as user-developed innovations and Boeing would be a user-innovator in those cases.

Innovation user and innovation manufacturer are the two general "functional" relationships between innovator and innovation. Users are unique in that they alone benefit *directly* from innovations. All others (here lumped under the term "manufacturers") must sell innovation-related products or services to users, indirectly or directly, in order to profit from innovations. Thus, in order to profit, inventors must sell or license knowledge related to innovations, and manufacturers must sell products or services incorporating innovations. Similarly suppliers of innovation-related materials or services—unless they have direct use for the innovations—must sell the materials or services in order to profit from the innovations.

The user and manufacturer categorization of relationships between innovator and innovation can be extended to specific functions, attributes, or features of products and services. When this is done, it may turn out that different parties are associated with different attributes of a particular product or service. For example, householders are the users of the switching attribute of a household electric light switch—they use it to turn lights on and off. However, switches also have other attributes, such as "easy wiring" qualities, that may be used only by the electricians who install them. Therefore, if an electrician were to develop an improvement to the installation attributes of a switch, it would be considered a user-developed innovation.

Both qualitative observations and quantitative research in a number of fields clearly document the important role users play as first developers of products and services later sold by manufacturing firms. Adam Smith (1776) was an early observer of the phenomenon, pointing out the importance of "the invention of a great number of machines which facilitate and abridge labor, and enable one man to do the work of many." Smith went on to note that "a great part of the machines made use of in those manufactures in which labor is most subdivided, were originally the invention of common workmen, who, being each of them employed in some very simple operation, naturally turned their thoughts towards finding out easier and readier methods of performing it." Rosenberg (1976) explored the matter in terms of innovation by *user firms* rather than individual workers. He studied the history of the US machine tool industry, finding that important and basic machine types like lathes and milling machines were first developed and built by user firms having a strong need for them. Textile manufacturing firms, gun manufacturers, and sewing machine manufacturers were important early user-developers of machine tools.

Quantitative studies of user-innovation document that many of the most important and novel products and processes in a range of fields have been developed by user firms and by individual users. Thus, Enos (1962) reported that nearly all the most important innovations in oil refining were developed by user firms. Freeman (1968) found that the most widely licensed chemical production processes were developed by user firms. Von Hippel (1988) found that users were the developers of about 80 percent of the most important scientific instrument innovations, and also the developers of most of the major innovations in semiconductor processing. Pavitt (1984) found that a considerable fraction of invention by British firms was for in-house use. Shah (2000) found that the most commercially important equipment innovations in four sporting fields tended to be developed by individual users.

Empirical studies also show that *many* users—from 10 percent to nearly 40 percent—engage in developing or modifying products. This has been documented in the case of specific types of industrial products and consumer products, and in large, multi-industry studies of process innovation in Canada and the Netherlands as well (table 8.1). When taken together, the findings make it very clear that users are doing a *lot* of product development and product modification in many fields.

Studies of innovating users (both individuals and firms) show them to have the characteristics of "lead users" (Urban and von Hippel 1988; Herstatt and von Hippel 1992; Olson and Bakke 2001; Lilien et al. 2002). That is, they are ahead of the majority of users in their populations with respect to an important market trend, and they expect to gain relatively high benefits from a solution to the needs they have encountered there. The correlations found between innovation by users and lead-user status are highly significant, and the effects are very large (Franke and Shah 2003; Lüthje et al. 2002; Morrison et al. 2000).

Since lead users are at the leading edge of the market with respect to important market trends, one could guess that many of the novel products they develop for their own use would appeal to other users too and so provide the basis for products manufacturers would wish to commercialize. This turns out to be the case. A number of studies have shown that many of the innovations reported by lead users are judged to be commercially attractive and/or have actually been commercialized by manufacturers.

Research provides a firm grounding for these empirical findings. The two defining characteristics of lead users and the likelihood that they would develop new or modified products have been found to be highly correlated (Morrison et al. 2004). In addition it has been found that the higher the intensity of lead-user characteristics displayed by an innovator, the greater is the commercial attractiveness of the innovation that that lead user develops (Franke and von Hippel 2003a). In figure 8.1 the increased concentration of innovations toward the right indicates that the likelihood of innovating is higher for users having higher lead-user index values. The rise in average innovation attractiveness as one moves from left to right indicates that innovations developed by lead users tend to be more commercially attractive. (Innovation attractiveness is the sum of the novelty of the innovation and the expected future generality of market demand.)

Table 8.1
Studies of user innovation frequency

Innovation area	Number and type of users sampled	Percentage developing and building product for own use
Industrial products		
1. Printed circuit CAD software (a)	136 User-firm attendees at a PC-CAD conference	24.3
2. Pipe hanger hardware (b)	Employees in 74 pipe hanger installation firms	36.0
3. Library information systems (c)	Employees in 102 Australian libraries using computerized OPAC library information systems	26.0
4. Medical surgery equipment (d)	261 Surgeons working in university clinics in Germany	22.0
5. Apache OS server software security features (e)	131 Technically sophisticated Apache users (webmasters)	19.1
Consumer products		
6. Outdoor consumer products (f)	153 Recipients of mail-order catalogs for outdoor activity products for consumers	9.8
7. "Extreme" sporting equipment (g)	197 Members of 4 specialized sporting clubs in 4 "extreme" sports	37.8
8. Mountain biking equipment (h)	291 Mountain bikers in a geographic region known to be an "innovation hot spot."	19.2
Multi-industry process innovation surveys		
26 "Advanced manufacturing technologies" (i)	Canadian manufacturing plants in 9 manufacturing sectors (less food processing) in Canada, 1998 (population estimates based on a sample of 4,200)	28.0 Developed 26.0 Modified
39 "Advanced manufacturing technologies" (j)	16,590 Canadian manufacturing establishments that met the criteria of having at least $250,000 in revenues, and at least 20 employees.	22.0 Developed 21.0 Modified
Any type of process innovation or process modification (k)	Representative, cross-industry sample of 498 "high-tech" Netherlands SMEs	41.0 Developed only 34.0 Modified only 54.0 Developed and/or modified

Data sources: (a) Urban and von Hippel (1988); (b) Herstatt and von Hippel (1992); (c) Morrison et al. (2000); (d) Lüthje (2003); (e) Franke and von Hippel (2003b); (f) Lüthje (2004); (g) Franke and Shah (2003); (h) Lüthje et al. (2002); (i) Arundel and Sonntag (1999); (j) Gault and von Hippel (2009); (k) de Jong and von Hippel (2009).

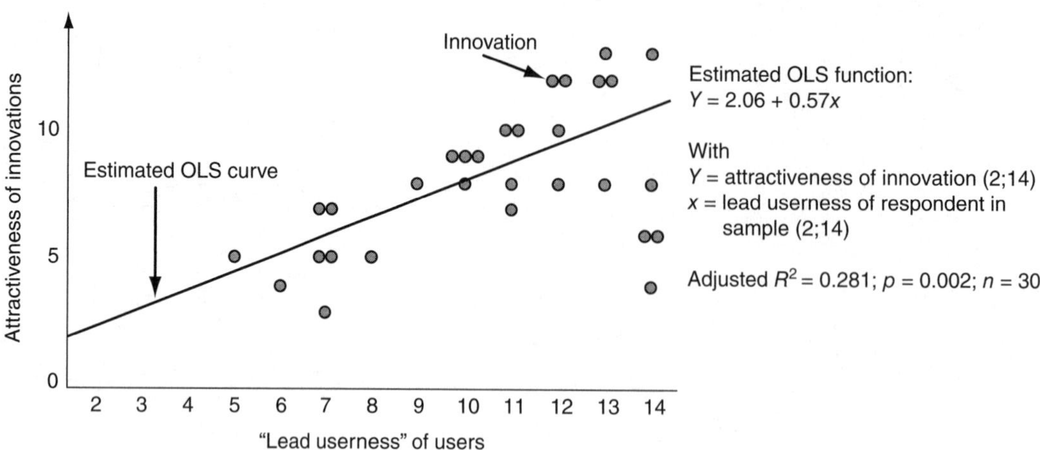

Figure 8.1
User-innovators with stronger lead-user characteristics develop innovations having higher appeal in the general marketplace
Data Source: Franke and von Hippel (2003a)

Why Many Users Want Custom Products

Why do so many users develop or modify products for their own use? Users may innovate if and as they want something that is not available on the market and are able and willing to pay for its development. It is likely that many users do not find what they want on the market. Meta-analysis of market-segmentation studies suggests that users' needs for products are highly heterogeneous in many fields (Franke and Reisinger 2003).

Mass producers tend to follow a strategy of developing products that are designed to meet the needs of a large market segment well enough to induce purchase from and capture significant profits from a large number of customers. When users' needs are heterogeneous, this strategy of "a few sizes fit all" will leave many users somewhat dissatisfied with the commercial products on offer and probably will leave some users seriously dissatisfied. In a study of a sample of users of the security features of Apache web server software, Franke and von Hippel (2003b) found that users had a very high heterogeneity of need, and that many had a high willingness to pay to get precisely what they wanted. Nineteen percent of the users sampled actually innovated to tailor Apache more closely to their needs. Those who did were found to be significantly more satisfied.

Users' Innovate-or-Buy Decisions

Even if many users want "exactly right products" and are willing and able to pay for their development, we must understand why users often do this for themselves rather than hire a custom producer to develop a special just-right product for them. After all, custom producers specialize in developing products for one or a few users. Since these firms are specialists, it is possible that they could design and build custom products for individual users or user firms faster, better, or cheaper than users could do this for themselves. Despite this possibility, several factors can drive users to innovate rather than buy. Both in the case of user firms and in the case of individual user-innovators, agency costs play a major role. In the case of individual user-innovators, enjoyment of the innovation process can also be important.

With respect to agency costs, consider that when a user develops its own custom product that user can be trusted to act in its own best interests. When a user hires a producer to develop a custom product, the situation is more complex. The user is then a principal that has hired the custom producer to act as its agent. If the interests of the principal and the agent are not the same, there will be agency costs. In general terms, agency costs are (1) costs incurred to monitor the agent to ensure that it (or he or she) follows the interests of the principal, (2) the cost incurred by the agent to commit itself not to act against the principal's interest (the "bonding cost"), and (3) costs associated with an outcome that does not fully serve the interests of the principal (Jensen and Meckling 1976). In the specific instance of product and service development, a major divergence of interests between user and custom producer does exist: the user wants to get precisely what it needs, to the extent that it can afford to do so. In contrast, the custom producer wants to lower its development costs by incorporating solution elements that it already has or that it predicts others will want in the future—even if, by doing so, it does not serve its present client's needs as well as it could.

A user wants to preserve its need specification because that specification is chosen to make *that user's* overall solution quality as high as possible at the desired price. For example, an individual user may specify a mountain-climbing boot that will precisely fit his unique climbing technique and allow him to climb Mount Everest more easily. Any deviations in boot design will require compensating modifications in the climber's carefully practiced and deeply ingrained climbing technique—a much more costly solution from the user's point of view. A custom boot producer, in contrast, will have a strong incentive to incorporate the materials and processes that it has in stock and expects to use in future even if this produces a boot that is not precisely right for the present customer. For example, the producer will not want to learn a new way to bond boot components together even if that would produce the best custom result for one client. The net result is that when one or a few users want something special, they will often get the best result by innovating for themselves.

A model of the innovate-or-buy decision (von Hippel 2005) shows in a quantitative way that user firms with unique needs (i.e., a market of one) will always be better off developing new products for themselves. It also shows that development by producers can be the most economical option when *n* or more user firms want the same thing. However, when the number of user firms wanting the same thing lies between 1 and *n*, producers may not find it profitable to develop a new product for just a few users. In that case more than one user may invest in developing the same thing independently, owing to market failure. This results in a waste of resources from the point of view of social welfare. The problem can be addressed by new institutional forms, such as the user-innovation communities that will be mentioned later.

It is important to note that an additional incentive can drive individual user-innovators to innovate rather than buy: they may value the *process* of innovating because of the enjoyment or learning that it brings them. On the one hand, it might seem strange that user-innovators can enjoy product development enough to want to do it themselves—after all, producers pay their product developers to do such work! On the other hand, it is clear that enjoyment of problem solving is a motivator for many individual problem solvers in at least some fields. Consider, for example, the millions of crossword-puzzle aficionados. Clearly, for these individuals enjoyment of the problem-solving process rather than the solution is the goal. One can easily test this by attempting to offer a puzzle solver a completed puzzle—the very output he or she is working so hard to create. The completed puzzle would likely be rejected with the rebuke that it would spoil the fun. Pleasure as a motivator can apply to the development of commercially useful innovations as well. Studies of the motivations of volunteer contributors of code to widely used software products have shown that these individuals too are often strongly motivated to innovate by the joy and learning they find in this work (Hertel et al. 2003; Lakhani and Wolf 2005).

Users' Low-Cost Innovation Niches

An exploration of the basic processes of product and service development shows that users and producers tend to develop different *types* of innovations. This is due in part to information asymmetries: users and producers tend to know different things. Product developers need two types of information in order to succeed at their work:

need and context-of-use information (generated by users) and generic solution information (often initially generated by producers specializing in a particular type of solution). Bringing these two types of information together is not easy. Both the need information and the solution information are often very "sticky"—that is, costly to move from the site where the information was generated to other sites (von Hippel 1994). It should be noted that the observation that information is often sticky contravenes a central tendency in economic theorizing. Much of the research on the special character of markets for information and the difficulty of appropriating benefit from invention and innovation has been based on the idea that information can be transferred at very low cost. Thus Arrow observes that "the cost of transmitting a given body of information is frequently very low. . . . In the absence of special legal protection, the owner cannot, however, simply sell information on the open market. Any one purchaser can destroy the monopoly, since he can reproduce the information at little or no cost" (1962: 614–15).

When information is sticky, innovators tend to rely largely on information they already have in stock. One consequence of the resulting typical asymmetry between users and producers is that users tend to develop innovations that are functionally novel, requiring a great deal of user-need information and use-context information for their development. In contrast, producers tend to develop innovations that are improvements on well-known needs and require a rich understanding of solution information for their development. Similarly users tend to have better information regarding ways to improve use-related activities such as maintenance than do producers: they "learn by using" (Rosenberg 1982).

This sticky information effect is quantitatively visible in studies of innovation. Riggs and von Hippel (1994) studied the types of innovations made by users and producers that improved the functioning of two major types of scientific instruments. They found that users are significantly more likely than producers to develop innovations that enabled the instruments to do qualitatively new types of things for the first time. In contrast, producers tended to develop innovations that enabled users to do the same things they had been doing, but to do them more conveniently or reliably (Table 8.2). For example, users were the first to modify the instruments to enable them to image and analyze magnetic domains at submicroscopic dimensions. In contrast, producers were the first to computerize instrument adjustments to improve ease of operation. Sensitivity, resolution, and accuracy improvements fall somewhere in the middle, as the data show. These types of improvements can be driven by users seeking to do specific new things, or by producers applying their technical expertise to improve the products along known general dimensions of merit, such as accuracy.

Table 8.2
Source of innovations by nature of improvement effected

Type of improvement provided by innovation	Innovation developed by:			
	Percentage of users	Users	Producers	Total
New functional capability	82	14	3	17
Sensitivity, resolution, or accuracy improvement	48	11	12	23
Convenience or reliability improvement	13	3	21	24
Total	64			

Source: Riggs and von Hippel (1994).

The sticky information effect is independent of Stigler's (1951) argument that the division of labor is limited by the extent of the market. When profit expectations are controlled for, the impact of sticky information on the locus of innovation is still strongly evident (Ogawa 1998).

If we extend the information-asymmetry argument one step further, we see that information stickiness implies that information on hand will also differ among *individual* users and producers. The information assets of some particular user (or some particular producer) will be closest to what is required to develop a particular innovation, and so the cost of developing that innovation will be relatively low for that user or producer. The net result is that user-innovation activities will be *distributed* across many users according to their information endowments. With respect to innovation, one user is by no means a perfect substitute for another.

Why Users Often Freely Reveal Their Innovations

The social efficiency of a system in which individual innovations are developed by individual users is increased if users somehow diffuse what they have developed to others. Producer-innovators *partially* achieve this when they sell a product or a service on the open market (partially because they diffuse the product incorporating the innovation, but often not all the information that others would need to fully understand and replicate it). If user-innovators do not somehow also diffuse what they have done, multiple users with very similar needs will have to independently develop very similar innovations—a poor use of resources from the viewpoint of social welfare. Empirical research shows that users often do achieve widespread diffusion by an unexpected means: they often "freely reveal" what they have developed. When we say that an innovator freely reveals information about a product or service it has developed, we mean that all intellectual property rights to that information are voluntarily given up by the innovator and all interested parties are given access to it—the information becomes a public good (Harhoff et al. 2003).

The empirical finding that users often freely reveal their innovations has been a major surprise to innovation researchers. On the face of it, if a user-innovator's proprietary information has value to others, one would think that the user would strive to prevent free diffusion rather than help others to free-ride on what it has developed at private cost. Nonetheless, it is now very clear that individual users and user firms—and sometimes producers—often freely reveal detailed information about their innovations.

The practices visible in "open source" software development were important in bringing this phenomenon to general awareness. In these projects it was clear *policy* that project contributors would routinely and systematically freely reveal code they had developed at private expense (Raymond 1999). However, free revealing of product innovations has a history that began long before the advent of open source software. Allen, in his 1983 study of the eighteenth-century iron industry, was probably the first to consider the phenomenon systematically. Later Nuvolari (2004) discussed free revealing in the early history of mine-pumping engines. Contemporary free revealing by users has been documented by von Hippel and Finkelstein (1979) for medical equipment, by Lim (2000) for semiconductor process equipment, by Morrison, Roberts, and von Hippel (2000) for library information systems, and by Franke and Shah (2003) for sporting equipment. Henkel (2003) has documented free revealing among producers in the case of embedded Linux software.

Innovators often freely reveal because it is often the best or the only practical option available to them. Hiding an innovation as a trade secret is unlikely to be successful for long: too many generally know similar things, and some holders of the "secret" information stand to lose little or nothing by freely revealing what they know. Studies find that innovators in many fields view patents as having only limited value (Harhoff et al. 2003). Copyright protection and copyright licensing are applicable only to "writings," such as books, graphic images, and computer software.

Active efforts by innovators to freely reveal—as opposed to sullen acceptance—are explicable because free revealing can provide innovators with significant private benefits as well as losses or risks of loss. Users who freely reveal what they have done often find that others then improve or suggest improvements to the innovation, to mutual benefit (Raymond 1999). Freely revealing users also may benefit from enhancement of reputation, from positive network effects due to increased diffusion of their innovation, and from other factors. Being the first to freely reveal a particular innovation can also enhance the benefits received, and so there can actually be a rush to reveal, much as scientists rush to publish in order to gain the benefits associated with being the first to have made a particular advancement.

Innovation Communities

Innovation by users tends to be widely distributed rather than concentrated among a very few very innovative user-developers (table 8.3). As a result it is important for user-innovators to find ways to combine and leverage their efforts. Users achieve this by engaging in many forms of cooperation. Direct, informal user-to-user cooperation (assisting others to innovate, answering questions, etc.) is common. Organized cooperation is also common, with users joining together in networks and communities that provide useful structures and tools for their interactions and for the distribution of innovations. Innovation communities can increase the speed and effectiveness with which users and also producers can develop and test and diffuse their innovations. They also can greatly increase the ease with which innovators can build larger systems from interlinkable modules created by community participants.

Free and open source software projects are a relatively well-developed and very successful form of Internet-based innovation community. However, innovation communities are by no means restricted to software or even to information products, and they can play a major role in the development of physical products. Franke and Shah

Table 8.3
User innovation widely distributed, but with few users developing more than one major commercialized innovation

	Number of innovations each user developed					
User samples	1	2	3	6	na	sample (n)
Scientific instrument users (a)	28	0	1	0	1	32
Scientific instrument users (b)	20	1	0	1	0	28
Process equipment users (c)	19	1	0	0	8	29
Sports equipment users (d)	7	0	0	0	0	7

Table source: von Hippel (2005), table 7–1.
Data sources: (a) von Hippel (1988, app.), GC, TEM, NMR Innovations; (b) Riggs and von Hippel (1994), Esca and AES; (c) von Hippel (1988, app.), semiconductor and pultrusion process equipment innovations; (d) Shah (2000, app. A), skateboarding, snowboarding, and windsurfing innovations developed by users.

(2003) have documented the value that user-innovation communities can provide to user-innovators developing physical products in the field of sporting equipment. The analogy to open source innovation communities is clear.

The collective or community effort to provide a public good—which is what freely revealed innovations are—has traditionally been explored in the literature on "collective action." However, behaviors seen in extant innovation communities fail to correspond to that literature at major points. In essence, innovation communities appear to be more robust with respect to recruiting and rewarding members than the literature would predict. The reason for this appears to be that innovation contributors obtain some private rewards that are not shared equally by free riders (those who take without contributing). For example, a product that a user-innovator develops and freely reveals might be perfectly suited to that user-innovator's requirements but less well suited to the requirements of free riders. Innovation communities thus illustrate a "private-collective" model of innovation incentive (von Hippel and von Krogh 2003).

Adapting Policy to User Innovation

Is innovation by users a "good thing?" Welfare economists answer such a question by studying how a phenomenon or a change affects social welfare. Henkel and von Hippel (2005) explored the social welfare implications of user innovation. They found that relative to a world in which only producers innovate, social welfare is very probably increased by the presence of innovations freely revealed by users. This finding implies that policy-making should support user innovation, or at least should ensure that legislation and regulations do not favor producers at the expense of user-innovators.

The transitions required of policy-making to achieve neutrality with respect to user innovation as opposed to producer innovation are significant. Consider the impact on open and distributed innovation of past and current policy decisions. Research done in the past thirty years has convinced many academics that intellectual property law is sometimes, or often, not having its intended effect. Intellectual property law was intended to increase the amount of innovation investment. It now appears instead that there are economies of scope in both patenting and copyright that allow firms to use these forms of intellectual property law in ways that are directly opposed to the intent of policy makers and to the public welfare (Foray 2004). Major firms can invest to develop large portfolios of patents. They can then use these to create "patent thickets"—dense networks of patent claims that give them plausible grounds for threatening to sue across a wide range of intellectual property. They may do this to prevent others from introducing a superior innovation and/or to demand licenses from weaker competitors on favorable terms (Shapiro 2001; Bessen 2003). Movie, publishing, and software firms can use large collections of copyrighted work to a similar purpose (Benkler 2002). In view of the distributed nature of innovation by users, with each tending to create a relatively small amount of intellectual property, users are likely to be disadvantaged by such strategies.

It is also important to note that users (and producers) tend to build prototypes of their innovations economically by modifying products already available on the market to serve a new purpose. Laws such as the (US) Digital Millennium Copyright Act, intended to prevent consumers from illegally copying protected works, also can have the unintended side effect of preventing users from modifying products that they purchase (Varian 2002). Both fairness and social welfare considerations suggest that innovation-related policies should be made neutral with respect to the sources of innovation.

It may be that current impediments to user innovation will be solved by legislation or by policy-making. However, beneficiaries of existing law and policy will predictably resist change. Fortunately, a way to get around some of these problems is in the hands of innovators themselves. Suppose that many innovators in a particular field decide to freely reveal what they have developed, as they often have reason to do. In that case, users can collectively create an information commons (a collection of information freely available to all) containing substitutes for some or a great deal of information now held as private intellectual property. Then user-innovators can work around the strictures of intellectual property law by simply using these freely revealed substitutes (Lessig 2001).

This pattern is happening in the field of software—and very visibly so. For many problems, user-innovators in that field now have a choice between proprietary, closed software provided by Microsoft and other firms, and open source software that they can legally download from the Internet and legally modify as they wish to serve their own specific needs. It is also happening, although less visibly, in the case of process equipment developed by users for in-house use. Data from both Canada and the Netherlands show that about 25 percent of such user-developed innovations get voluntarily transferred to producers. A significant fraction—about half—being transferred both unprotected by intellectual property and without charge (Gault and von Hippel 2009; de Jong and von Hippel 2009).

Policy-making that levels the playing field between users and producers will force more rapid change onto producers but will by no means destroy them. Experience in fields where open and distributed innovation processes are far advanced show how producers can and do adapt. Some, for example, learn to supply proprietary platform products that offer user-innovators a framework upon which to develop and use their improvements (Jeppesen 2004).

Diffusion of User-Developed Innovations

Products, services, and processes developed by users become more valuable to society if they are somehow diffused to others who can also benefit from them. If user innovations are not diffused, multiple users with very similar needs will have to invest to (re)develop very similar innovations that, as was noted earlier, would be a poor use of resources from the social welfare point of view. In the case of information products, users have the possibility of largely or completely doing without the services of producers. Open source software projects are object lessons that teach us that users can create, produce, diffuse, provide field support, update, and use complex products by and for themselves in the context of user innovation communities. In physical product fields the situation is different. Users can develop products. However, the economies of scale associated with manufacturing and distributing physical products give producers an advantage over "do-it-yourself" users in those activities.

How can, or should, user innovations of general interest be transferred to producers for large-scale diffusion? We propose that there are three general methods for accomplishing this. First, producers can actively seek innovations developed by lead users that can form the basis for a profitable commercial product. Second, producers can draw innovating users into joint design interactions by providing them with "toolkits for user innovation." Third, users can become producers in order to widely diffuse their innovations. We discuss each of these possibilities in turn.

To systematically find user-developed innovations, producers must redesign their product-development processes. Currently almost all producers think that their job is to find a need and fill it rather than to sometimes find and commercialize an innovation that lead users have already developed. Accordingly, producers have set up market-research departments to explore the needs of users in the target market, product-development groups to think up suitable products to address those needs, and so forth. In this type of product-development system, the needs and prototype solutions of lead users—if encountered at all—are typically rejected as outliers of no interest. Indeed, when lead users' innovations do enter a firm's product line, they typically arrive with a lag and by an unconventional and unsystematic route. For example, a producer may "discover" a lead-user innovation only when the innovating user firm contacts the producer with a proposal to produce its design in volume to supply its own in-house needs. Or sales or service people employed by a producer may spot a promising prototype during a visit to a customer's site.

Modification of firms' innovation processes to *systematically* search for and further develop innovations created by lead users can provide producers with a better interface to the innovation process as it actually works, and so provide better performance. A natural experiment conducted at 3M illustrates this possibility. Annual sales of lead-user product ideas generated by the average lead-user project at 3M were conservatively forecast by management to be more than eight times the sales forecast for new products developed in the traditional manner—$146 million versus $18 million per year. In addition lead-user projects were found to generate ideas for new product lines, while traditional market-research methods were found to produce ideas for incremental improvements to existing product lines. As a consequence 3M divisions funding lead-user project ideas experienced their highest rate of major product line generation in the past fifty years (Lilien et al. 2002).

Tool kits for user innovation custom design involve partitioning product-development and service-development projects into *solution*-information-intensive subtasks and *need*-information-intensive subtasks. Need-intensive subtasks are then assigned to users along with a kit of tools that enable them to effectively execute the tasks assigned to them. In the case of physical products, the designs that users create using a toolkit are then transferred to producers for production (von Hippel and Katz 2002). Toolkits make innovation cheaper for users and also lead to higher customer value. Thus Franke and Piller (2004), in a study of consumer wristwatches, found the willingness to pay for a self-designed products was 200 percent of the willingness to pay for the best-selling commercial product of the same technical quality. This increased willingness to pay was due to both the increased value provided by the self-developed product and the value of the toolkit process for consumers engaging in it (Schreier and Franke 2004).

Producers that offer toolkits to their customers can attract innovating users into a relationship with their firm and so get an advantage with respect to producing what the users develop. The custom semiconductor industry was an early adopter of toolkits. In 2003 more than $15 billion worth of semiconductors were produced that had been designed using this approach (Thomke and von Hippel 2002).

Innovations developed by users sometimes achieve widespread diffusion when those users become producers—setting up a firm to produce their innovative product(s) for sale. Shah (2000) showed this pattern in sporting goods fields. In the medical field, Lettl and Gemunden (2005) have shown a pattern in which innovating users take on many of the entrepreneurial functions needed to commercialize the new medical products they have developed without themselves abandoning their user roles. New work in this field is exploring the conditions under which users would become entrepreneurs rather than transfer their innovations to established firms (Hienerth 2004; Shah and Tripsas 2004).

Summary

I summarize this overview article by again saying that users' ability to innovate is advancing *radically* and *rapidly* due to the steadily improving quality of computer software and hardware, improved access to easy-to-use tools and components for innovation, and access to an increasingly rich innovation commons. Today user firms and even individual hobbyists have access to sophisticated programming tools for software and sophisticated computer-aided design (CAD) tools for hardware and electronics. These information-based tools can be run on a personal computer, and they are rapidly coming down in price. As a consequence innovation by users will continue to grow even if the degree of heterogeneity of need and willingness to invest in obtaining a precisely right product remains constant.

Equivalents of the innovation resources described above have long been available within corporations to a few.. Senior designers at firms have long been supplied with engineers and designers under their direct control, and with the resources needed to quickly construct and test prototype designs. The same is true in other fields, including automotive design and clothing design: just think of the staffs of engineers and model makers supplied so that top auto designers can quickly realize and test their designs.

But, if, as we have seen, the information needed to innovate in important ways is widely distributed, the traditional pattern of concentrating innovation-support resources on a few individuals is hugely inefficient. High-cost resources for innovation support cannot efficiently be allocated to "the right people with the right information": it is very difficult to know who these people may be before they develop an innovation that turns out to have general value. When the cost of high-quality resources for design and prototyping becomes very low (the trend we have described), these resources could be diffused very widely, and the allocation problem would diminish in significance. The net result would be a pattern where a development of product and service innovations isincreasingly shifting to users—a pattern that will involve significant changes for both users and producers.

Note

This chapter previously appeared as chapter 9 in *Handbook of Economics of Technological Change* (2010), Bronwyn H. Hall and Nathan Rosenberg, eds., Elsevier B.V. Press.

References and Further Reading

Allen, R. C. 1983. Collective invention. *Journal of Economic Behavior & Organization* 4 (1): 1–24.

Arrow, Kenneth J. 1962. Economic welfare and the allocation of resources of Invention. In *The Rate and Direction of Inventive Activity: Economic and Social Factors*. A Report of the National Bureau of Economic Research. Princeton: Princeton University Press, 609–25.

Baldwin, Carliss Y., and Eric von Hippel. 2011. Modeling a paradigm shift: From producer innovation to user and open collaborative innovation. *Organization Science* 22 (6): 1399–1417.

Benkler, Y. 2002. Intellectual property and the organization of information production. *International Review of Law and Economics* 22 (1): 81–107.

Bessen, J. 2003. Patent thickets: Strategic patenting of complex technologies. Research on Innovation working paper. Boston University School of Law.

de Jong, Jeroen P. J., and Eric von Hippel. 2009. Measuring user innovation in Dutch high tech SMEs: Frequency, nature and transfer to producers. *Research Policy* 38 (7): 1181–91.

Enos, J. L. 1962. *Petroleum Progress and Profits: A History of Process Innovation*. Cambridge: MIT Press.

Foray, D. 2004. *Economics of Knowledge*. Cambridge: MIT Press.

Franke, N., and H. Reisinger. 2003. Remaining within cluster variance: A meta analysis of the "dark" side of cluster analysis. Working paper. Vienna Business University.

Franke, N., and S. Shah. 2003. How communities support innovative activities: An exploration of assistance and sharing among end-users. *Research Policy* 32 (1): 157–78.

Franke, N., and F. Piller. 2004. Value creation by toolkits for user innovation and design: The case of the watch market. *Journal of Product Innovation Management* 21 (6): 401–15.

Franke, N., and E. von Hippel. 2003a. Finding commercially attractive user innovations. Working paper 4402–03. MIT Sloan School of Management.

Franke, N., and E. von Hippel. 2003b. Satisfying heterogeneous user needs via innovation toolkits: The case of Apache Security software. *Research Policy* 32 (7): 1199–1215.

Freeman, C. 1968. Chemical process plant: Innovation and the world market. *National Institute Economic Review* 45 (August): 29–57.

Gault, F., and E. von Hippel. 2009. The prevalence of user innovation and free innovation transfers: Implications for statistical indicators and innovation policy. Working paper 4722–09. MIT Sloan School of Management. Available at: http://papers.ssrn.com/sol3/papers.cfm?abstract_id=1337232.

Harhoff, D., J. Henkel, and E. von Hippel. 2003. Profiting from voluntary information spillovers: How users benefit by freely revealing their innovations. *Research Policy* 32 (10): 1753–69.

Henkel, J. 2003. Software development in embedded Linux: Informal collaboration of competing firms. In W. Uhr, W. Esswein, and E. Schoop, eds., *Proceedings der 6. Internationalen Tagung Wirtschaftsinformatik,* vol. 2. Heidelberg: Physica, 81–99.

Henkel, J., and E. von Hippel. 2005. Welfare implications of user innovation. *Business and Economics Essays in Honor of Edwin Mansfield,* Part 2: 45–59.

Herstatt, C., and E. von Hippel. 1992. From experience: Developing new product concepts via the lead user method: A case study in a "low tech" field. *Journal of Product Innovation Management* 9 (3): 213–22.

Hertel, G., S. Niedner, and S. Herrmann. 2003. Motivation of software developers in open source projects: An Internet-based survey of contributors to the Linux kernel. *Research Policy* 32 (7): 1159–77.

Hienerth, C. 2006. The commercialization of user innovations: The development of the rodeo kayak industry. *R&D Management* 36 (3): 273–94.

Jensen, M. C., and W. H. Meckling. 1976. Theory of the firm: Managerial behavior, agency costs, and ownership structure. *Journal of Financial Economics* 3 (4): 305–60.

Jeppesen, L. B. 2004. Profiting from innovative user communities: How firms organize the production of user modifications in the computer games industry. Working paper WP-04. Department of Industrial Economics and Strategy, Copenhagen Business School.

Lakhani, K. R., and B. Wolf. 2005. Why hackers do what they do: Understanding motivation and effort in free/open source software projects. In J. Feller, B. Fitzgerald, S. Hissam, and K. R. Lakhani, eds., *Perspectives on Free and Open Source Software,* Cambridge: MIT Press.

Lessig, L. 2001. *The Future of Ideas: The Fate of the Commons in a Connected World.* New York: Random House.

Lettl, C., and H. G. Gemnden.2005. The entrepreneurial role of innovative users. *Journal of Business and Industrial Marketing* 20 (7): 339–46.

Lilien, G. L., P. D. Morrison, K. Searls, M. Sonnack, and E. von Hippel. 2002. Performance assessment of the lead user idea generation process. *Management Science* 48 (8): 1042–59.

Lim, K. 2009. The many faces of absorptive capacity: Spillovers of copper interconnect technology for semiconductor chips. *Industrial and Corporate Change* 18 (6): 1249–84.

Lüthje, C. 2003. Customers as co-inventors: An empirical analysis of the antecedents of customer-driven innovations in the field of medical equipment. *Proceedings from the 32th EMAC Conference* 2003, Glasgow.

Lüthje, C. 2004. Characteristics of innovating users in a consumer goods field: An empirical study of sport-related product consumers. *Technovation,* forthcoming.

Lüthje, C., C. Herstatt, and E. von Hippel. 2005. User-innovators and "local" information: The case of mountain biking. *Research Policy* 34 (6): 951–65.

Morrison, P. D., J. H. Roberts, and D. F. Midgley. 2004. The nature of lead users and measurement of leading edge status. *Research Policy* 33 (2): 351–62.

Morrison, P. D., J. H. Roberts, and E. von Hippel. 2000. Determinants of user innovation and innovation sharing in a local market. *Management Science* 46 (12): 1513–27.

Nuvolari, A. 2004. Collective invention during the British industrial revolution: The case of the Cornish pumping engine. *Cambridge Journal of Economics* 28 (3): 347–63.

Ogawa, S. 1998. Does sticky information affect the locus of innovation? Evidence from the Japanese convenience-store industry. *Research Policy* 26 (7–8): 777–90.

Olson, Erik L., and Geir Bakke. 2001. Implementing the lead user method in a high technology firm: A longitudinal study of intentions versus actions. *Journal of Product Innovation Management* 18 (2): 388–95.

Pavitt, K. 1984. Sectoral patterns of technical change: Towards a taxonomy and a theory. *Research Policy* 13 (6): 343–73.

Raymond, E. 1999. *The Cathedral and the Bazaar: Musings on Linux and Open Source by an Accidental Revolutionary*. Sebastopol, CA: O'Reilly.

Riggs, W., and E. von Hippel. 1994. The impact of scientific and commercial values on the sources of scientific instrument innovation. *Research Policy* 23 (July): 459–69.

Rosenberg, N. 1976. *Perspectives on Technology*. New York: Cambridge University Press.

Rosenberg, N. 1982. *Inside the Black Box: Technology and Economics*. New York: Cambridge University Press.

Schreier, M., and N. Franke. 2004. Tom Sawyer's great law in action: Why users are willing to pay to design their own products via toolkits for user innovation and design. Working paper. Vienna University of Economics and Business Administration.

Schumpeter, J. A. 1934. *The Theory of Economic Development*. New York: Oxford University Press.

Shah, S. 2000. Sources and patterns of innovation in a consumer products field: Innovations in sporting equipment. Working paper 4105. MIT Sloan School of Management.

Shah, S., and M. Tripsas. 2004. When do user-innovators start firms? Towards a theory of user entrepreneurship. Working paper 04–0106. University of Illinois.

Shah, S. K., and M. Tripsas. 2007. The accidental entrepreneur: The emergent and collective process of user entrepreneurship. *Strategic Entrepreneurship Journal* 1 (1–2): 123–40.

Shapiro, C. 2001. Navigating the patent thicket: Cross licenses, patent pools, and standard setting. In A. Jaffe, J. Lerner, and S. Stern, eds., *Innovation Policy and the Economy*, vol. 1. Cambridge: MIT Press, 119–50.

Stigler, George J. 1951. The division of labor is determined by the extent of the market. *Journal of Political Economy* 59 (3): 185–93.

Thomke, S. H., and E. von Hippel. 2002. Customers as innovators: A new way to create value. *Harvard Business Review* 80 (4): 74–81.

Urban, G. L., and E. von Hippel. 1988. Lead user analyses for the development of new industrial products. *Management Science* 34 (5): 569–82.

Varian, H. R. 2002. New chips can keep a tight rein on consumers. *New York Times,* July 4.

von Hippel, E. 1994. Sticky information and the locus of problem solving: Implications for innovation. *Management Science* 40 (4): 429–39.

von Hippel, Eric. 2005. *Democratizing Innovation.* Cambridge: MIT Press.

von Hippel, E. 1988. *The Sources of Innovation.* New York: Oxford University Press.

von Hippel, E., and S. N. Finkelstein. 1979. Analysis of innovation in automated clinical chemistry analyzers. *Science and Public Policy* 6 (1): 24–37.

von Hippel, E., and R. Katz. 2002. Shifting innovation to users via toolkits. *Management Science* 48 (7): 821–33.

von Hippel, E., and G. von Krogh. 2003. Open source software and the "private-collective" innovation model: Issues for organization science. *Organization Science* 14 (2): 209–23.

9 Co-creation with Customers

Frank Piller and Christoph Ihl

Introduction

The main objective of a company engaging in co-creation is to enlarge its base of information about needs, applications, and solution technologies that resides in the domain of customers and users creation (Piller and Ihl 2009; Ramaswamy and Gouillart 2010). The methods used to achieve this objective include but go beyond tools described in chapter 5: user idea contests (Ebner et al. 2008; Piller and Walcher 2006; Füller 2010), consumer opinion platforms (Hennig-Thurau et al. 2004; Sawhney, Verona, and Prandelli 2005), toolkits for user innovation (von Hippel and Katz 2002; Franke and Piller 2004), and communities for customer co-creation (Franke and Shah 2003; Füller, Matzler, and Hoppe 2008).

The difference between customer co-creation and the lead-user concept as introduced by Eric von Hippel (1988) and summarized in chapter 8 is often fuzzy in practice, but distinct from a conceptual point of view. Lead users are intrinsically motivated to innovate, performing the innovation process autonomously and without any interaction with a manufacturer. It then is the task of the interested firm to identify and capture the resulting inventions. Our understanding of customer co-creation, in contrast, is built on a firm-driven strategy that facilitates interaction with its customers and users. Instead of just screening the user base to detect any existing prototypes created by lead users, the firm provides instruments and tools to a broader group of customers and potential customers to actively co-create a solution together (Ramirez 1999).

Consider as a typical example of co-creation—the case of *Threadless*, a Chicago-based fashion company. Its innovative business model allows the company to follow the concept of "fast fashion" with a vast assortment of styles and designs without the typical forecasting risk and without heavy investments into many designs or into

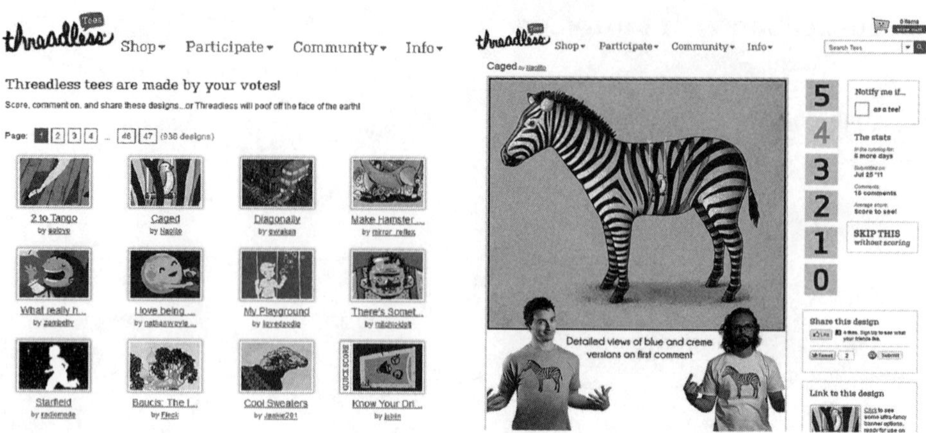

Figure 9.1
Evaluating T-shirt ideas at Threadless.com: Overview (left) and score sheet (right)
Source: Screenshots from Threadless.com

flexible manufacturing and distribution. Yet, the company is able to offer its customers a new assortment of styles and variants every week (Ogawa and Piller 2006).

Started in 2000 by designers Jake Nickell and Jacob DeHart, Threadless focuses on a hot fashion item: T-shirts with colorful graphics. This is a typical hit-or-miss product. Its success is defined by fast changing trends, peer recognition, and finding the right distribution outlets for specific designs. Despite these challenges, none of the company's many product variants has ever flopped. Examples of Threadless products appear on their website, www.threadless.com. The screen shot shown in figure 9.1 gives a good idea of the range of ideas submitted that are then ranked by the community.

All products sold by Threadless are approved by user consensus before any larger investment is made into a new product. The garment is produced only after a sufficient number of customers have expressed their explicit willingness to buy the design. If commitment is missing, a potential design concept is dismissed. But, if enough customers pledge to purchase the product, the design is finalized and goes into production. In this way relatively small market research expenditures are turned into early sales. New designs regularly sell out fast, and are reproduced only if a large enough number of additional customers commit to purchase a reprint.

The company exploits a large pool of talent and ideas to get new designs—much larger than it could afford if the design process were internalized. On average, 1,500 designs compete in any given week. Each week the staff selects about ten designs based primarily on an algorithm that gives priority to community response but also considers production and other factors. The selected designers receive $2,000 in cash, a $500 gift certificate (which they may trade in for $200 in cash), and an additional $500 for every reprint. When shirts are sold out, customers can request a reprint. However, reprinting occurs only when there is enough demand, and the decision to reprint is ultimately up to company.

Together with 51 employees, in 2010 the company's founders sold about 160,000 to 170,000 T-shirts per month for between $18 and $24 apiece with a 30 percent profit margin on sales. Total sales hit $30 million—with profits of roughly $9 million (Burkitt 2010). Since 2006, annual growth continued at more than 150 percent, with similar margins. Threadless has 1.5 million followers on Twitter and more than 100,000 fans on Facebook. The company's website logged 2.5 million unique visitors in August 2010, a 50 percent increase over the same month the previous year (Saadi 2010).

But Threadless is only one of many other examples of customer co-creation. Consider these additional examples:

- *Fujitsu Computers (FSC)*, a large IT hardware and infrastructure provider, organized an online idea contest for webmasters and IT professionals to get their ideas about how data centers will work in the future, what services will be required by users, and which topics will be of strategic importance. Participants were asked not just to provide needs but conceptual ideas for possible solutions. Participants became members of an innovation community, commenting on the ideas of others, developing ideas further, and providing suggestions for technological realization. Despite a rather low monetary incentive (the best idea was rewarded 5,000 euros) and a high level of required technological expertise, more than 200 active users contributed to the contest—most of them during work time and with permission of their employer.
- *Emporia Telecom*, an Austrian mobile phone manufacturer, demonstrated in a recent co-creation contest that the user base for this kind of engagement is not just young web-savvy people but also a much larger community of senior citizens. The task they identified was to develop age-specific mobile phones in terms of functionality and design. Using an online platform, users could submit ideas for both functional hardware features and innovative services. Contrary to the beliefs of many, Emporia learned that senior customers are very willing to engage in an online co-creation project. Overall, more than 6,000 users visited the contest site, spending more than 800 hours there, and generated more than 200 highly elaborated ideas. Several ideas from the contest made it into prototyping and further development in the company (Leyhausen and Vossen 2011).

• *Muji* is a Japanese specialty retail chain, selling all kinds of consumer commodities, furniture, apparel, and food items (Ogawa and Piller 2006). The company is famous in Europe for its powerful internal design practice; it continuously involves customers in product development. In its Japanese home market, the company receives more than 8,000 suggestions for product improvements or new product ideas each month. Suggestions are sent on postcards attached to catalogs, as e-mails, or via feedback forms on the company's website. On the sales floor, sales associates are encouraged to collect notes on customer behavior and short quotes from sales dialogues. But the most important means of interaction with its customers is its online community, Muji.net, with approximately 410,000 members. For evaluating new concepts and proposals, the company asks the opinion of its product managers, but it also hosts a broad evaluation and collaborative decision process, asking its community to vote on the products that should be introduced next. Recent data show that products that went through the screening of the crowd perform on average three times better than products that were selected by an internal steering committee.

What do have these examples in common? Despite a range of industries, different cultural contexts, and various target age groups, these examples show how firms can create value with large groups of customers and users, moving beyond workshops with selected lead users. We also see very different tasks, ranging from designing a T-shirt to creating functional technological concepts.

Structuring Customer Co-Creation

We propose the framework shown in figure 9.2 to differentiate various forms of co-creation. Drawing on our research in the field (Diener and Piller 2010), two characteristics provide the conceptual dimensions of a typology of co-creation with customers:

• *Degree of collaboration* refers to the structure of the underlying relationships in an open innovation setting. Whether there is, on the one hand, a dyadic collaboration between a firm and a group of customers who are not connected among each other, or on the other, there are networks of customers who collaborate among themselves more or less independent from the firm.

• *Degree of freedom* refers to the nature of the task that has been assigned to customers; this could be a narrow and predefined task with only a few degrees of freedom or an open and creative task for which a solution is hardly foreseeable because of many degrees of freedom.

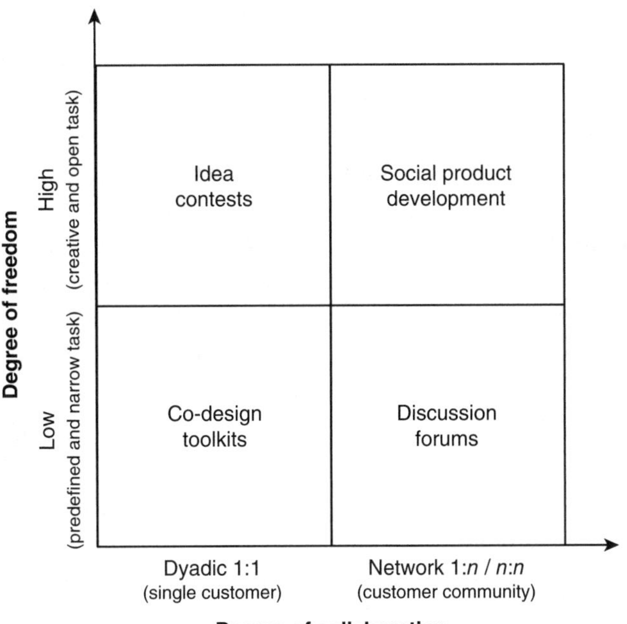

Figure 9.2
Defining co-creation activities

This framework yields four kinds of co-creation. These are discussed in detail below.

Two Dyadic (Individual) Based Co-creation Methods: Idea Contests and Co-design Toolkits

Dyadic co-creation starts when a company provides an opportunity for individual customers to engage in its innovation process. While the company may involve many different customers, there is little interaction among these actors and all activities are facilitated by the firm. The typical methods behind this form of co-creation are idea contests and co-design toolkits.

The starting point of the development process centers on two essential activities: (1) generating novel concepts and ideas and (2) selecting specific concepts and ideas to be pursued further (O'Hern and Rindfleisch 2009). Both of these tasks have successfully been handed over to customers by the means of an *idea contest* (Ebner et al. 2008; Ebner, Leimeister, and Krcmar 2009; Piller and Walcher 2006; Leimeister et al. 2009; Bullinger et al. 2010). In an idea contest a firm seeking innovation-related information posts a request to a population of independent, competing agents (e.g., customers), asking for solutions to a given task within a given time frame. The firm then provides an award to the participant that generates the best solution. Idea contests thus address a core challenge for firms when opening the innovation process, which is how to incentivize participants to transfer their innovative ideas. A solution reward is important in the early stages of the innovation process because customers are unlikely to benefit directly from their contributions through new product availability within a short time frame, as often occurs in later stages of the innovation process.

Some companies promise cash rewards or licensing contracts for innovative ideas; others build on nonmonetary acknowledgments—promising peer or company (brand) recognition that facilitates a pride-of-authorship effect. Obviously rewards or recognitions are not given to everyone submitting an idea, but only to those with the "best" submissions. This competitive mechanism is an explicit strategy to foster customer innovation. It should encourage more or better customers to participate, should inspire their creativity, and increase the quality of the submissions. For instance, over 120,000 individuals around the world served as voluntary members of Boeing's World Design Team, contributing input to the design of its new 787 Dreamliner airplane (www.newairplane.com).

Today we find a broad range of idea contests in practice. A good starting point to explore this field is www.innovation-community.de, a site listing more than 80 idea contests. These are differentiated according to the degree of problem specification, that is, by whether the problem clearly specifies the requirements for the sought solution or whether it is more or less an open call for solutions to a vaguely specified problem.

The example of *Threadless.com*, a company built entirely on a continuous idea contest and user voting process, shows how broadly this kind of co-creation can be used. This company and many others use customers for *idea screening and evaluation*, that is, customers select submissions with the highest potential. In a successful idea contest a firm might easily end up with hundreds or thousands of ideas generated by customers. They might be evaluated by a panel of experts from the solution-seeking firm—ranked according to a set of evaluation criteria—but we believe that without the integration of users in the idea screening process, large-scale idea contests are not possible. However, Toubia and Florès (2007) propose that in light of a potentially very large number of ideas it is unreasonable to ask each consumer to evaluate more than a few ideas. This raises the challenge of efficiently selecting the ideas to be evaluated by each consumer. Chapter 14, by Füller, Hutter, and Hautz, provides detail on one promising software solution that unites participants into interactive innovation workshops.

A very different method, *toolkits for customer co-design* (Franke and Piller 2003, 2004; von Hippel and Katz 2002; Franke, Schreier, and Kaiser 2010; Franke and Schreier 2010), is found in the southwest corner of figure 9.2. In this form of co-creation, a toolkit provides a development environment that enables customers to transfer their needs iteratively into a concrete solution—often without coming into personal contact with the manufacturer. The manufacturer provides users with an interaction platform where they can design a solution according to their needs in the solution space the toolkit makes available. Toolkits resemble, in principle, a chemistry set. Their solution space is theoretically boundless. Toolkit users not only combine the manufacturer's standard modules and components to create the best possible product for themselves, they can also expend a tremendous amount of effort in experimenting through trial and error processes on new and previously unknown solutions to their needs.

Chapter 13, by van Delden and Wünderlich, provides examples of kits offered for the development of a mustard dip that would appeal to students and could be manipulated with scissors and paste. A contest aimed at a more professional group of users was developed by BAA, an international developer of flavors for food (Thomke and von Hippel 2002). The company established a new form of cooperation by providing toolkits to chefs interested in innovating. Each toolkit has a collection of flavors the company produces. For a new Mexican sauce, for example, the kit contained 25 flavors in little plastic bags with instructions on how to use them correctly. Though BAA's flavorings are somewhat different from traditional raw ingredients, they save a great deal of effort, and chefs can discover how to use them through trial and error. The key insight from studying the results of this and similar kits, however, is that when a successful recipe is created, it can be immediately produced in the company's factory because the user and the producer are using the same language. In BAA's case the time to develop new ideas for flavor was reduced from around 26 weeks to around 3 weeks. The main effect behind this impressive improvement has been that the costly and demanding iteration between customers setting their specifications and the manufacturing unit turning these preferences into product specifications is replaced by customers themselves turning their ideas into a new product via the toolkit. It should be noted that some toolkits provide very complicated solution information that requires using programming languages or drawing software.

A final type of toolkit targets consumers for development of custom variants within an existing solution space. This can be compared to a set of Lego bricks. Toolkits for user co-design offer users a choice of individual building blocks (modules, components, parameters) that can be configured to make a product according to the user's individual requirements. These building blocks lie within the range of a manufacturer's economic and technological capability. Configuration toolkits are often integrated into a mass customization strategy (Salvador et al. 2009). Well-known examples of this kind of toolkit include Dell's product configurator and configurators found, for example, in the automobile industry. Clothing and other consumer products can also be ordered to customer specification—a recent video describing the appeal of this option can be found at http://vimeo.com/25132966.

Two Network (Community) Based Co-creation Methods: Discussion Forums and Social Product Development

Two other types of co-creation methods shown on the right side of figure 9.2 build on facilitating collaboration among customers. These efforts have shown that user communities can be an important locus of innovation as they can operate entirely independent of firms. Chapter 8 indicates that Franke and Shah (2003) analyzed four firm-independent sports communities, showing that on average one-third of the community members improved or even designed their own product innovations for sports equipment. It is important to note that these innovations do not emerge solely from individual efforts but are driven to a significant extent by collaborations with other community members.

In our understanding of customer co-creation, however, a focal company is needed to organize and facilitate a large, open network of participants in joint value creation. In these networks, tasks are broadcasted by individual users or a focal coordinating body; participants self-select whether or not they will contribute to a task, to what extent they will contribute, and with what resources. Those who respond to an open call for contributions are motivated by various incentives but not by (market) prices, salaries, or hierarchical commands (Füller et al. 2008; Prandelli, Verona, and Raccagni 2006; Sawhney and Prandelli 2000; Franke and Shah 2003).

Starting with a rather low degree of freedom, product-related *discussion forums* at the bottom right of the figure offer a platform in which customers primarily exchange usage experiences and support each other. A good example of this form of firm-organized community is offered by Stata Corporation. The company is a manufacturer of statistical software, as further described by von Hippel (2005). Their customers are typically scientists or developers who use the software for a large number of statistical tests. In cases where the applications provided within the software cannot solve a certain task, or solve it elegantly enough for the customer, customers can program new tests. To facilitate that process, Stata has divided its software into two parts. One part contains basic features developed by the company and protected by proprietary rights. This functionality is sold through a traditional software license. The second part of the software is open. The user community contributes new statistical algorithms and tests and Stata supports these expert users by providing a development environment and a forum on the Internet where users trade tests, ask other users questions, and expand upon the developments of others.

Since not all users are well-versed in programming, Stata also has developed a procedure in which the "best" or most popular developments taken from the user community are regularly selected by the company and made a part of their next commercial release. This decision is made entirely by Stata's software developers, who take and improve applications by users and integrate them smoothly into the standard software. The additional value created by Strata is also an incentive for users to make their personal developments available to the company, usually without monetary return, simply because their motives for developing a new application are to use it in their own scientific work.

In contrast, the concept of *social product development* in so-called communities of creation (Sawhney and Prandelli 2000) generate novel ideas and concepts. Consider as an example *Quirky.com*, a company that makes community-based innovation the core of its business model. Similar to Threadless, the community suggests new concepts, votes on the best ideas, and collectively commits to purchasing a product before it goes into production. These products include electronic gadgets, travel goods, and household items. Figure 9.3 provides a screenshot of *Quirky.com* with a few products on sale.

Quirky goes much further than Threadless by engaging the community in many more activities along the entire span of the innovation process, including its financing. A project starts when a user pays a fee to suggest a new product idea (currently $99). The Quirky community then votes on the ideas that should enter the next stage of development, where ideas are jointly turned into a more developed product by the community and by Quirky's own developers. This development is followed by another evaluation. If passed, the staff works with manufacturers and suppliers to specify a price and the concept is out for community financing. If the product receives enough (discounted) online preorders, it goes into production (The process is outlined at http://www.quirky.com/learn).

Quirky currently is one of the best examples of co-creation in a firm-organized community. The site provides a platform for products originating from deep user insights and offering anyone the platform of turning great ideas into real products. Also an inventor whose idea does not make it to a final stage gets plenty of feedback from others on the idea. Quirky is a great model of "hybrid" co-creation between openness

Figure 9.3
Products on sale on Quirky.com
Source: Screenshot from Quirky.com

and closeness. Most activities are performed by the community and are freely revealed on the platform, but Quirky provides (hierarchical) coordination and takes over the more complicated developing activities, like partitioning the development task into chunks, assigning these subtasks to the community, integrating the granular solutions, and finalizing the design and manufacturing of the products. But still the community has a much larger work span and creative freedom compared to an idea contest. Finally, Quirky really takes external contributors seriously. According to its founder, the core challenge when launching the company was developing an algorithm that provides a fair distribution of 30 percent of all revenues to the community members

Switch Your Tool, Your Way

Switch is the ultimate modular pocketknife, with 18 different attachments so you can mix and match your most frequently used tools.

Ventu Strain and Serve

Prep, strain, serve, and store, all in one elegant solution. Just pivot the handle to easily switch between straining and serving functions.

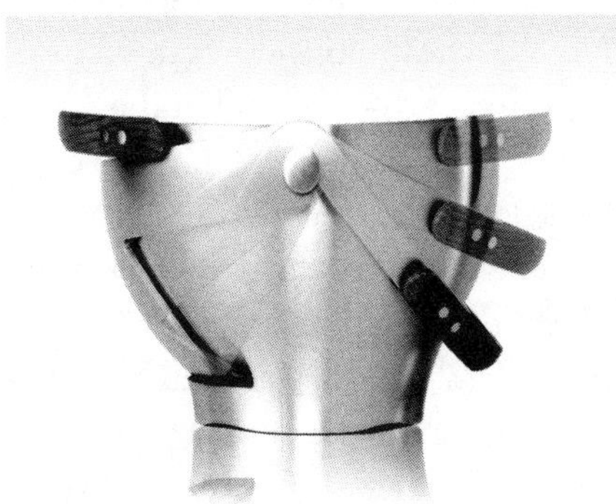

Figure 9.4
Two examples of the Quirky co-creation process
Source: Quirky.com

who contributed to a particular project (Piller 2010). In average, 1,200 to 1,500 contributors are paid per product! Such a large-scale contribution scheme still is very rare in for-profit industries—but could become a role model for the co-creation economy. Two examples of successful products that have come out of the Quirky co-creation process are shown in figure 9.4.

Conclusion: Next Tasks for Co-Creation

The objective of this chapter was to describe different methods of customer co-creation. But, in the end, all methods of customer co-creation follow a common principle. The underlying idea is that of an active, creative, and social collaboration process between producers and their customers (users). Co-creation involves customers in a company's innovation process. Companies intending to profit from co-creation need to know which of the different methods are most suited to their organization and how to best use these tools (Diener and Piller 2010). To answer questions about co-creation, coordinated practical experience in companies and detailed research are needed.

First, firms need to assess whether a particular innovation task is suited for customer co-creation. This could include answers to questions like how do innovation projects have to be reorganized for co-creation, what kinds of projects are suited for customer integration, and how do internal development processes have to be adjusted in order to allow optimal customer integration. More research is required that provides some "simple rules" to managers to cope with these questions.

Second, much previous research has focused on successful examples of the application of co-creation. These examples are valuable evidence and are generating attention for customer co-creation, but they lack a differentiated perspective. To take the discussion of co-creation to the next level, more research on specific design components is needed in order to understand how the method can be best used. For example, while the motives of customers participating in an idea contest have recently become the subject of research (e.g., see Füller 2010; Füller, Matzler, and Hoppe 2008), the ways to best design an idea contest remain relatively vague. Which design factors, for instance, attract the desired participants or evoke the preferred behavior? How can a company influence the output of the co-creation activities? How can interaction and sharing among community members being facilitated?

Idea for Innovative Leaders: Recognize the Power of NIH (Not Invented Here)

Leaders of organizations who want to use co-creation need a clear picture of their organizations capabilities. They must also recognize organizational barriers and hurdles when implementing co-creation. An important challenge of applying co-creation (and other ideas from open innovation) involves the difficulties of integrating ideas and solutions created in the firm's periphery into the corporate context. Internal (proprietary) knowledge has to be connected with externally generated knowledge. This process appears to be one of the most challenging tasks for firms that want to utilize gains from open innovation.

Even as companies manage to search for and extract innovative inputs--perhaps investing in the installation of appropriate innovation-focused online platforms that collect customer inputs--the desired transfer of knowledge frequently fails due to the "not-invented-here" (NIH) problem. Katz and Allen (1982: 7) define the NIH syndrome as "the tendency of a project group of stable composition to believe that it possesses a monopoly of knowledge in its field, which leads it to reject new ideas from outsiders to the detriment of its performance." Interestingly the NIH phenomenon was originally found between two different domains within one enterprise; for example, resistance on the part of the R&D engineers to innovations suggested by the marketing department. But resistance against external knowledge is often even greater than resistance against the knowledge of one's own colleagues. We still have very little knowledge about the drivers of NIH and feasible ways of how to overcome it in a firm context.

But, if the transfer and transformation of customer input generated by co-creation fails, investments in customer innovation initiatives only turn into additional costs.

References and Further Reading

Bullinger, A. C., A. K. Neyer, M. Rass, and K. M. Moeslein. 2010. Community-based innovation contests: Where competition meets cooperation. *Creativity and Innovation Management* 19 (3): 290–303.

Burkitt, L. 2010. Need to build a community? Learn from Threadless. *Forbes*, January (01.07.10). Available at: http://www.forbes.com/2010/01/06/threadless-t-shirt-community-crowdsourcing-cmo-network-threadless.html

Diener, K., and F. T. Piller. 2010. *The Market for Open Innovation.* Raleigh, NC: Lulu.

Ebner, W., J. M. Leimeister, and H. Krcmar. 2009. Community engineering for innovations: The ideas competition as a method to nurture a virtual community for innovations. *R&D Management* 39 (4): 342–56.

Ebner, W., M. Leimeister, U. Bretschneider, and H. Krcmar. 2008. Leveraging the wisdom of crowds: Designing an IT-supported ideas competition for an ERP software company. In *Proceedings of the 41st Annual Hawaii International Conference on System Sciences (HICSS 2008)*, January 7–10, Waikoloa, Big Island, Hawaii.

Franke, N., and F. T. Piller. 2003. Key research issues in user interaction with user toolkits in a mass customization system. *International Journal of Technology Management* 26 (5): 578–99.

Franke, N., and F. T. Piller. 2004. Toolkits for user innovation and design: An exploration of user interaction and value creation. *Journal of Product Innovation Management* 21 (6): 401–15.

Franke, N., and S. Shah. 2003. How communities support innovative activities: An exploration of assistance and sharing among end-users. *Research Policy* 32 (1): 157–78.

Franke, N., and M. Schreier. 2010. Why customers value self-designed products: The importance of process effort and enjoyment. *Journal of Product Innovation Management* 27 (7): 1020–31.

Franke, N., M. Schreier, and U. Kaiser. 2010. The "I designed it myself" effect in mass customization. *Management Science* 56 (1): 125–40.

Füller, J. 2010. Refining virtual co-creation from a consumer perspective. *California Management Review* 52 (2): 98–122.

Füller, J., K. Matzler, and M. Hoppe. 2008. Brand community members as a source of innovation. *Journal of Product Innovation Management* 25 (6): 608–19.

Hennig-Thurau, T., K. P. Gwinner, G. Walsh, and D. D. Gremler. 2004. Electronic word-of-mouth via consumer-opinion platforms: What motivates consumers to articulate themselves on the internet? *Journal of Interactive Marketing* 18 (1): 38–52.

Katz, R., and T. Allen. 1982. Investigating the not invented here (NIH) syndrome. *R&D Management* 12 (1): 7–19.

Leimeister, J. M., M. Huber, U. Bretschneider, and H. Krcmar. 2009. Leveraging crowdsourcing: Activation-supporting components for IT-based ideas competition. *Journal of Management Information Systems* 26 (1): 197–224.

Leyhausen, F., and A. Vossen. 2011. We could have known better—Consumer-oriented marketing in Germany's ageing market. In M. Boppel, S. Boehm, and S. Kunisch, eds., *From Grey to Silver.* Berlin, Heidelberg: Springer, 175–84.

O'Hern, M. S., and A. Rindfleisch. 2009. Customer co-creation: a typology and research agenda. In K. M. Naresh, ed., *Review of Marketing Research*, vol. 6. Armonk, NY: Sharpe, 84–106.

Ogawa, S., and F. T. Piller. 2006. Reducing the risks of new product development. *Sloan Management Review* 47 (2): 65–72.

Piller, F. T. 2010. Ten reasons why I consider Quirky.com as best in crowdsourcing and open innovation. MC&OI News (Web Blog), October. Available at: http://mass-customization.blogs.com/mass_customization_open_i/2010/10/.

Piller, F. T., and C. Ihl. 2009. *Open Innovation with Customers: Foundations, Competences and International Trends.* Expert study commissioned by the European Union, The German Federal Ministry of Research, and the European Social Fund. Published as part of the project "International Monitoring.". Aachen: RWTH ZLW-IMA.

Piller, F. T., and D. Walcher. 2006. Toolkits for idea competitions: A novel method to integrate users in new product development. *R&D Management* 36 (3): 307–18.

Prandelli, E., M. S. Sawhney, and G. Verona. 2008. *Collaborating with Customers to Innovate: Conceiving and Marketing Products in the Networking Age.* Cheltenham, UK: Elgar.

Prandelli, E., G. Verona, and D. Raccagni. 2006. Diffusion of web-based product innovation. *California Management Review* 48 (4): 109–36.

Ramaswamy, V., and F. Gouillart. 2010. *The Power of Co-Creation.* New York: Free Press.

Ramirez, R. 1999. Value co-production: intellectual origins and implications for practice and research. *Strategic Management Journal* 20 (1): 49–65.

Saadi, S. 2010. T-Shirts are just the start for Threadless, *Bloomberg Businessweek*, September 20, issue: 24–26.

Salvador, F., M. de Holan, and F. T. Piller. 2009. Cracking the code of mass customization. *MIT Sloan Management Review* 50 (3): 71–78.

Sawhney, M., and E. Prandelli. 2000. Communities of creation: Managing distributed innovation in turbulent markets. *California Management Review* 42 (4): 24–54.

Sawhney, M., G. Verona, and E. Prandelli. 2005. Collaborating to create: The internet as a platform for customer engagement in product innovation. *Journal of Interactive Marketing* 19 (4): 4–17.

Thomke, S., and E. von Hippel. 2002. Customers as innovators: A new way to create value. *Harvard Business Review* 80 (4): 74–81.

Toubia, O., and L. Florès. 2007. Adaptive idea screening using consumers. *Marketing Science* 26 (3): 342–60.

von Hippel, E., and R. Katz. 2002. Shifting innovation to users via toolkits. *Management Science* 48 (7): 821–33.

von Hippel, E. 1988. *The Sources of Innovation*. Cambridge: MIT Press.

von Hippel, E. 2005. *Democratizing innovation*. Cambridge: MIT Press.

10 Contributions by Developers

Karim R. Lakhani

Introduction

If fifteen years ago you had gone to SAP, Microsoft, or Oracle and said that a bunch of strangers on the Internet will get together somehow and start creating software without any direct monetary incentives, without traditional managerial controls, and without any long-term plans, they would have just laughed at you, saying there is no way that would happen. But today we see that open source software communities have become a legitimate and important component in the way software gets developed. It has surprised us all to see this new form of organization appear and do so well.

It is even more surprising that the biggest companies in the world, like IBM, are now participating in these communities and releasing code, their own property, back to the community. Economists didn't anticipate that. Sociologists didn't anticipate that.

My interest in this phenomenon comes from my experience working with GE. You may remember GE's slogan: "We bring good things to life." In the medical systems division where I worked we certainly thought that we brought good things to life. But we had a few clients who were basically two years ahead of our engineering schedule. They were innovating in communities that we knew almost nothing about. This reality never fit my model of how research or innovation gets done and it did not fit anyone else's model either.

The Revolution Changing the Way We Can Think about Innovation

I tried to solve the puzzle of how and why innovation happens outside of organizations when I went back to school to get my doctorate. To describe a way of innovating that has been almost invisible until recently, let me distinguish two leadership models for organizing innovation. One will be very familiar to you, one not so familiar.

The familiar model is exemplified by Bill Gates, who in 1976 wrote this letter to the hobbyist (or hacker) community that was using/creating new software.

> Will quality software be written for the [hacker] market? . . . [M]ost of you steal your software. . . . What [hacker] can put 3-man years into programming, finding all bugs, documenting his product and distribute for free? . . . Most directly the thing you do is theft.
>
> Nothing would please me more than being able to hire ten programmers and deluge the [hacker] market with good software.
>
> —Bill Gates, 1976

Gates achieved near dominance in the software industry by understanding network economics and creating a firm that was highly disciplined and motivated to win. But this centralized view is not the only model for software development or dominance. About sixteen years later Linus Torvalds articulated a different, distributed vision. Writing to a user network on the Internet, to no one in particular, he starts off:

> Hello Netlanders, do you pine for the nice days of minix-1.1, when men were men and wrote their own device drivers? Are you without a nice project and just dying to cut your teeth on an OS you can try to modify for your needs? . . . I'm doing a free operating system, just a hobby, won't be big and professional. I´d like any feedback on things people like/dislike. This is a program for hackers by a hacker. I´ve enjoyed doing it, and somebody might enjoy looking at it and even modifying it for their own needs. Drop me a line if you are willing to let me use your code.
>
> —Linus Torvalds

Two very different perspectives: one about "you steal my software (and) I'm going to hire ten programmers and deluge the marketplace" another about "write your own code and send it to me; it's a hobby; won't be big and professional." Both models have been extremely successful. Microsoft is one of the most successful organizations in the world. But what Linus Torvalds did as a young software developer is quite revolutionary. He changed how people think about software development. More generally, Torvalds fundamentally changed how people can think about innovation.

I think Torvalds' impact will be as lasting as Bill Gate's. However, we can already see how these two really different perspectives can coexist as well as be competitive, even though they are two very different logics about how innovation gets done. Over time Microsoft has actually embraced open source, pushed in part by the European Union, which is trying to raise understanding of the potential of free and open source software (F/OSS).

For a picture of this change, consider Jim Allchin, Group Vice President at Microsoft for the Platforms Group—the group responsible for Vista and Windows XP among many other things. In February 2001 Allchin actually said:

> Open Source is an intellectual property destroyer. I can´t imagine something that could be worse for the software business and the IT business. . . .
>
> I worry if government encourages Open Source. I don´t think we have done enough education of policy makers to understand the threat.
> —Jim Allchin, Microsoft, 2001

While this statement makes it very clear what Allchin thought about the threat from open source and what that would mean to Microsoft and their business in 2001, three years later he had changed his mind completely:

> This is a rant, I'm sorry, I am not sure how . . . [Microsoft] lost sight of what matters to our customers (both business and home), but in my view we lost our way. . . . I would buy a Mac today if I was not working at Microsoft. . . . Apple did not lose their way.
> —Jim Allchin, 2004

This is an acknowledgment from within Microsoft that open source is a model of knowledge development that has the potential to change the way we think about innovation. What's interesting is that the core operation of the Mac is BSD, a free and open source operating system. I have an iPhone with me. If you check, you will find ten pages devoted to the Open Source licenses the iPhone uses as well. So even proprietary products use open source code. No wonder Allchin said in 2004 "if we are to rise to the challenge of Linux and Apple, we need to start taking lessons."

The Principles of Open Source Innovation

What are the principles of open source innovation? You can get a sense of some open source principles, extracted from a lot of work that many people have done in the field, in figure 10.1.

Starting on the left, this is a development paradigm that encourages engagement. Its behavioral norms ask people to participate. Modularity is also very important because it allows large projects to be disaggregated and enables many people to work on smaller tasks. Underneath both modularity and participation are a lot of collective practices that create a network and make it effective.

In terms of the resource model, intrinsic motivation is the biggest driver of open source development. People write code for fun, for enjoyment. I was never a good

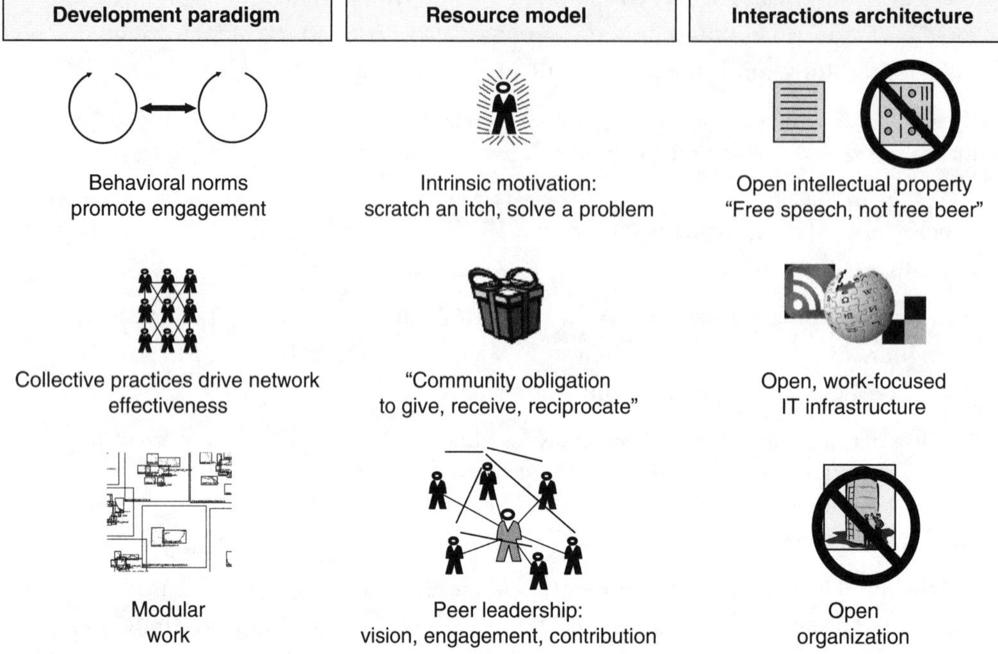

Figure 10.1
Open source principles

coder as an electrical engineer; I did not think coding was fun. But there are many people in the world who enjoy and even love coding. Part of that emotion is a sense of community. To belong means the obligation to give and to receive. Coders reciprocate. That connects them to each other.

Peer leadership is equally important. Leaders have to do the work in open source development. They can´t sit on the mountain and direct the staff and tell people what to do as they do in the traditional model. Leaders actually have to engage and contribute to the work themselves. In the process a common vision of the work emerges.

The interactive architecture of open source is also very important. It requires open intellectual property. People say "it's about free speech and not free beer." Free beer might be the outcome, but free speech is the core of what is going on. Further, the infrastructure is such that the conversations, the e-mails, and so on, are all focused on the work itself. Finally, there is an open organization, not one characterized by silos. These highly interconnected principles are the driving factors that allow open source communities to make innovative contributions.

Why Contribute?

Many observers ask why hackers participate in distributed innovation. They want to know why people are working for free with no guarantee of reward. The studies that I have done show that contributors often focus on the highly creative nature of the work, as shown in figure 10.2. This is significant, of course, because creativity is what organizations seeking innovative inputs need as well.

When asked what motivates them to participate in open source projects, the answers are basically: "I enjoy it. I am building skills. I have freedom to do what I want to do. And by the way, sometimes I have a real need for the software. I can´t get it anywhere else, so I do it myself." In addition to fun, increasing knowledge is the

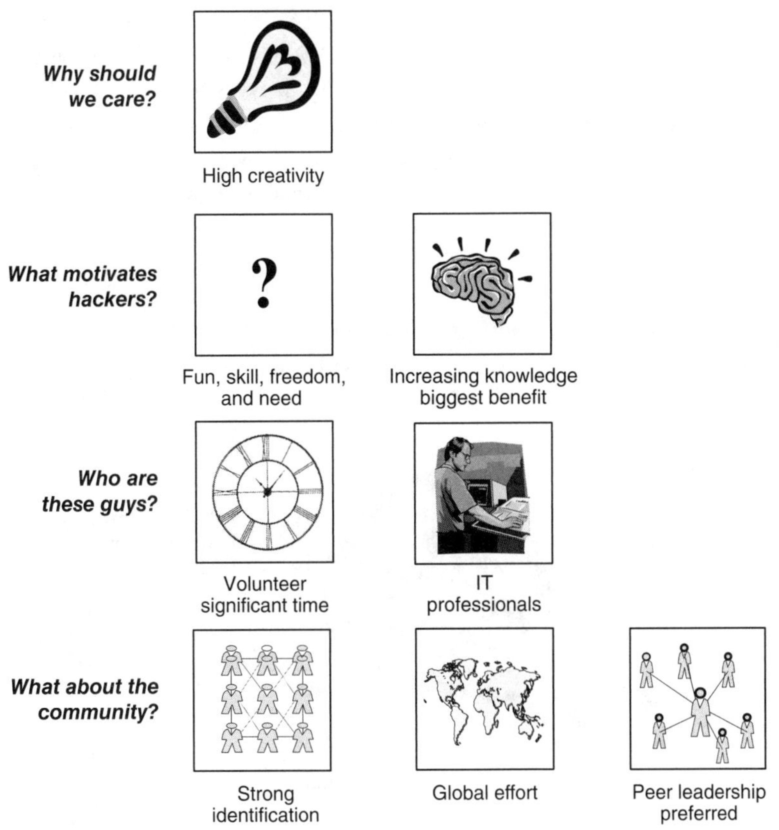

Figure 10.2
Why do people participate in distributed innovation?

biggest benefit they see for themselves, while the biggest cost that occurs to them is lack of sleep.

Central members of a successful open source community voluntarily spend a significant amount of time on projects, on average about 15 to 20 hours a week. Most of them are not freshmen studying at MIT or some other technical college. They are not working in their basements. They are actually IT professionals who have a lot of experience writing code. They participate for pleasure and because they have an actual need for the projects they work on.

The Community's Role in Motivating Input

The compelling nature of open source involvement is summarized in figure 10.3. When I ask people about the projects they work on, about 62 percent say this project is as creative as, or the most creative thing, I have ever worked on my life. For some of us programming may not be so creative, but for many hackers this seems to be a great outlet. To provide a platform to do that is highly important. It is the same thing as Sudoku. Many people just love to do Sudoku. I am terrible at it, but for other people it is a creative outlet. So imagine open source as Sudoku being done on a very large scale.

People also say:

- When I program I lose track of time (72.6 percent).
- With one more hour in the day I would spend it programming (60 percent).
- Almost half of them say it's like composing music or poetry (48.4 percent).

Figure 10.3
Participation is highly engaging

This high engagement is a key factor driving participation. Somehow the community creates an energizing setting that is rarely available in the more traditional model of work outlined at the beginning of these remarks.

What Leaders of Distributed Innovation Do

The role of leaders is very different in the two models of innovation and development we are discussing. The new leadership model can be introduced with an e-mail posting by Rik van Riel, who is a core member of the Linux community and also a developer at high-tech firms:

> It seems like Linux really isn´t going anywhere in particular and seems to make progress through sheer luck.
>
> —Rik van Riel

He's saying "I don't know what's happening — we're just lucky it's going on." But Linus Torvalds, the one person who might be considered the leader of open source, responds (in several e-mails in a longer thread):

> Hey that's not a problem, that's a FEATURE! [his emphasis]
>
> —Linus Torvalds

Torvalds says that sheer luck is the mechanism that ensures the Linux system survives. Just think how contrary that is. If you were to ask a leader at Microsoft or SAP: "Are you making progress because of luck or because of your big vision?" they would almost certainly say "It´s my vision that drives me."

Linus, in contrast, is very honest about how the alternative leadership system works. He says:

> Do I direct some stuff? Yes. But, quite frankly, so do many others. . . . And a lot of companies are part of the evolution whether they realize it or not. And all the users end up being part of the "fitness testing" . . . A strong vision and a sure hand sound good on paper. It´s just that I have never met a technical person (including me) whom I would trust to know what is really the right thing to do in the long run.
>
> —Linus Torvalds

Talk about being honest, right? Torvalds says "too strong a vision can kill you—you´ll walk right over the edge with confidence about the path in front of you . . . ." He is being totally honest about his own limitations, the limitations of those around him, and the implications of that reality for what's going on.

Again, this is someone who has won many awards, who is at the forefront of this movement, and he´s saying:

I'd much rather have "Brownian motion" where a lot of microscopic directed improvements end up pushing the system slowly in a direction that none of the individual developers really had the vision to see on their own.

—Linus Torvalds

What Business Can Learn from Open Source Development

We don't teach "Brownian motion management" at the Harvard Business School; we don´t know what that means. But, by thinking about and studying what is going on, we might be able to start making some progress. Certainly we see (as in many other situations) that practice actually leads theory. By studying open source communities, we should be able to make some progress in describing a new model, a new logic of innovation.

One thing that is being used to explain why distributed innovation succeeds is "Joy´s law." Bill Joy, co-founder of Sun Microsystems and key contributor to many innovative projects, famously said:

No matter who you are, most of the smartest people work for someone else.

—Bill Joy, Sun Microsystems

This is anathema to most executives. Let me show you what this looks like using data that I collected while working at BCG. Figure 10.4 shows a network of scientific papers, published in one field of neuroscience. We simply went into Pubmed, which is a database for all sorts of biological publications, and retrieved all articles that were related to that field of expertise via key words. We found 6,000 articles by 10,000 people in a two-year time period (see figure 10.4).

We were working with people in a company who thought they were at the core of the scientific area they worked in. They thought they were leading the field. When we put the data together, we saw that they were in the small cluster at the right of the figure. You can see the rest of the world in this figure—illustrating Bill Joy's notion that most of the smart people work for someone else.

What is the explanation for this? One important observation (in 1945) comes from an economist:

Knowledge is unevenly distributed.

—Frederick Hayek

Hayek's core insight made him push for a market-based economy without a centralized plan. His notion was that society can in no way aggregate all the knowledge that is out there. Self-selection, people deciding what knowledge they need, making their own decisions, is what happens.

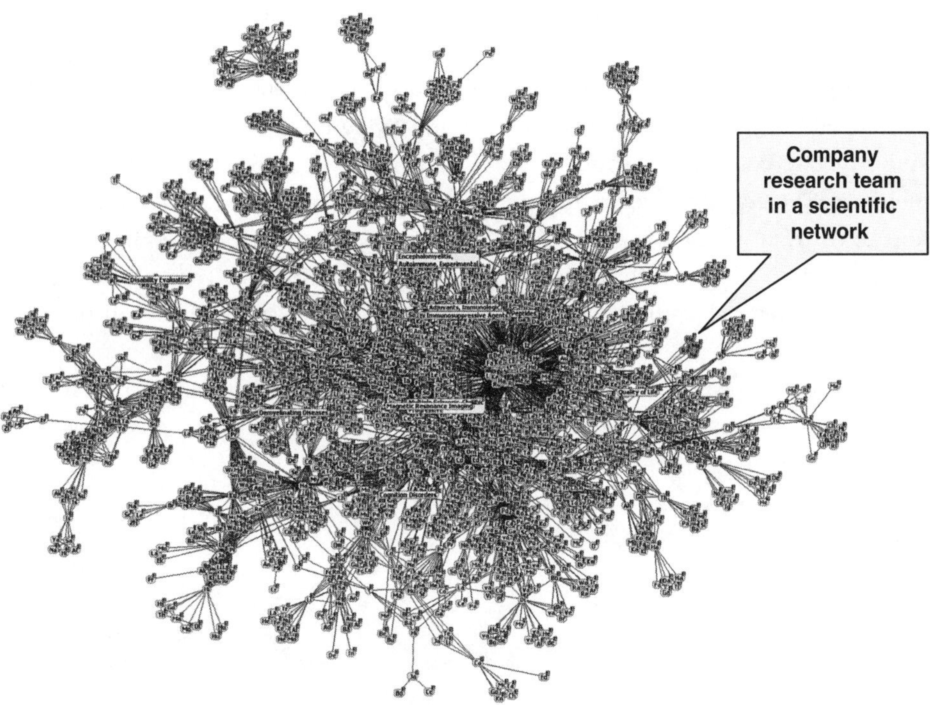

Figure 10.4
Joy's law in life sciences research

Further, as Eric von Hippel's work has shown:

Knowledge is sticky.

It is hard to move knowledge from one place to another place, and thus the locus of innovation shifts to where knowledge is the stickiest. Knowledge held at one point, which might be very relevant to someone at another point, can be very hard to access or even identify. That helps us understand the importance of Joy´s law. When Joy says that most of the smart people work for someone else, it is not because companies are hiring dumb people. It is not because employees in any given firm are not smart. It is because of the nature of knowledge—getting hold of it is tough. It is unevenly distributed and sticky.

Examples of Open Source Development

One contribution of the open source model of knowledge management is to reveal the benefits of problem broadcasting: reveal to the outside world the problems you are working on and invite external individuals to help you solve the problem. In other words: embrace transparency!

In figure 10.5 we see an open source network. Over 8,000 e-mail messages were exchanged in this community over one month. Every message went to everyone else and anybody could participate. The plot of what took place uses dots to identify members. The gray dots are pretty active, the lighter gray a little farther out, the dark dots to the right of the figure even more peripheral. The people starred in the center participated the most, but the network was open and transparent. That enabled people to solve problems that they didn´t know about before receiving an e-mail message. They contributed to the knowledge base as it was produced.

Figure 10.4, shown previously, is ex post; it shows what happens in a traditional knowledge development effort after information is exchanged. If the people publish-

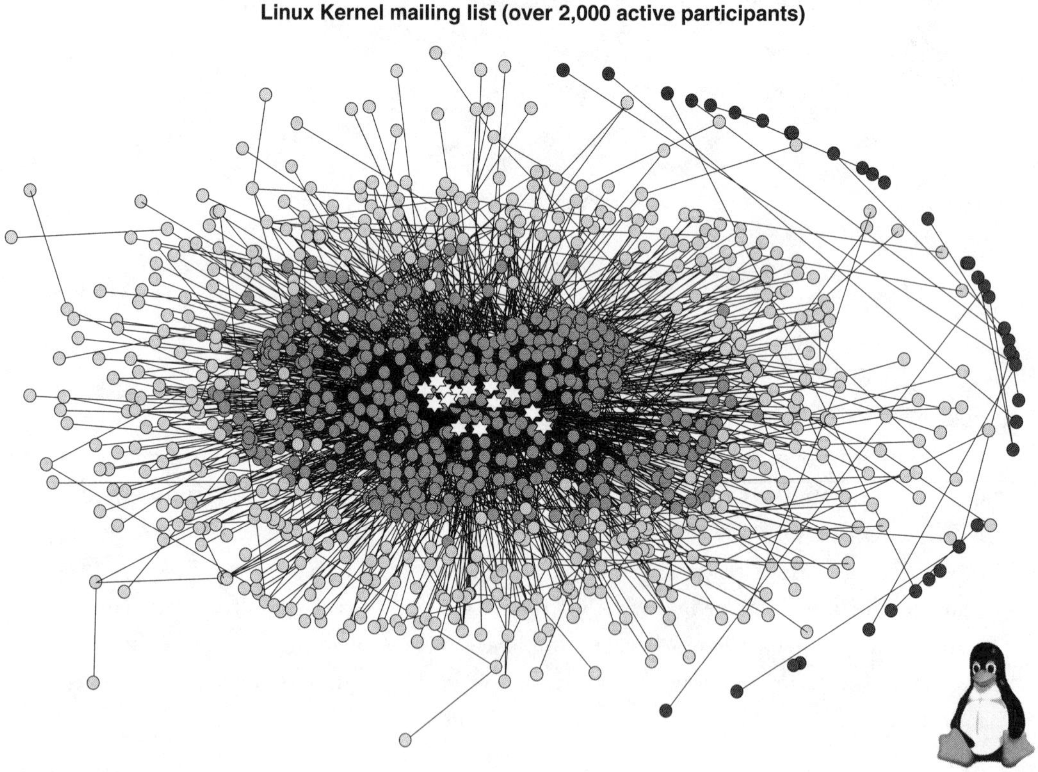

Linux Kernel mailing list (over 2,000 active participants)

Figure 10.5
Problem broadcasting and transparency key to open source success

ing the work shown in figure 10.4 had been communicating in the way we see in figure 10.5, if people had broadcasted their interests before papers were published and shared knowledge beforehand, as it is in open source communities, we might see very different outcomes from academic research.

I've described how well-distributed innovation works in software development. We are seeing similar things happen in Wikipedia. Once again, if you had asked somebody in 2001 about the idea of a free encyclopedia to which anybody could contribute, nobody would have agreed that idea would succeed. Now we know this is one of the most frequently searched sites on the Internet.

Another interesting example of open development is the Myelin Repair Foundation. This is a nonprofit drug discovery foundation. Their vision is to create a treatment for multiple sclerosis and they compete against the pharma companies as a nonprofit. Their idea is to force early collaboration across entire scientific teams, and they are making quick progress.

A fourth example is InnoCentive. Basically this company takes one portion of the open source idea, the public broadcasting of knowledge, and has made it into a business. InnoCentive is a knowledge broker. They work with companies to post scientific problems and say now much an answer would be worth. They often shield the identity of the company broadcasting requests because there may be a problem of intellectual property.

Figure 10.6 shows a sample problem from InnoCentive posted in June 2001 with a solution deadline of November 2001. The seeker offered $25,000 as reward. The company also posted these solution criteria:

- Synthesize the chemical in two steps or fewer
- 80 percent overall yield
- 95 percent purity
- At a cost of less than $100/kilogram
- Submit as proof of solution two grams of off-white solvent.

What happened in response to this posting is that 221 individuals expressed an interest in solving the problem and created "project rooms." You cannot imagine any company, even a very large global corporation, assigning over 200 independent people to look at a micro-problem like this internally, so that is the first leveraging effect of the distributed innovation model. For the problem we're discussing, more than ten independent trials from seven countries were submitted for analysis.

A retired scientist, Dr. Werner Mueller, who had set up a wet lab in his backyard came up with the answer. He solved the posted problem because he already knew how

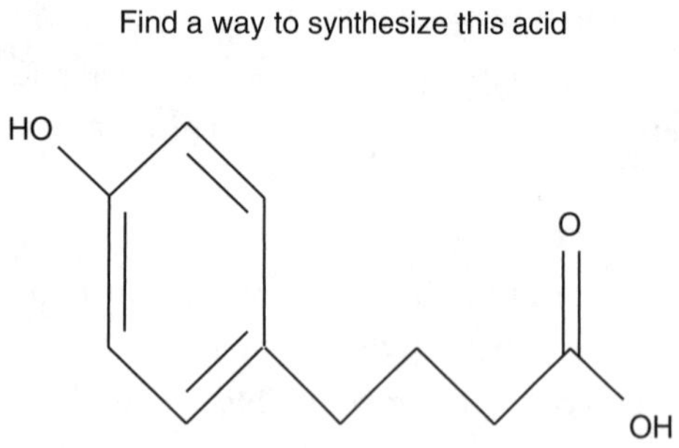

Find a way to synthesize this acid

HO

O

OH

Figure 10.6
Sample problem from InnoCentive

to solve it. He had been in the R&D department of his company, but found that as he went up the corporate hierarchy, he did less and less chemistry; thus he had been doing chemistry as a hobby.

So how well does the InnoCentive model work in aggregate? In my study

- Firms had typically spent between six months and two years trying to solve the problem internally.
- They offered on average of $30,000 for a solution.
- Solutions were either "reduction to practice," as in the case above where solvers were asked to send the chemical solution, or a paper solution.
- Typically solvers needed to submit a solution about six months after initial posting.

Research I have done with colleagues shows that about 30 percent of the problems that could not be solved in company labs were solved by the broader community InnoCentive has created. Here is a second interesting observation: many times the seeking company discovers that there are multiple pathways to solving a problem, and they want to own all these solutions so they give out multiple awards to a posted problem. Other patterns shown by my research on InnoCentive includes these interesting observations:

- On average, 240 individuals examine a problem statement.
- Ten solutions are submitted per problem.
- The winner spends about two weeks or 74 hours of time to come up with the solution.
- Only two-thirds of the people submitting successful solutions have PhDs in a scientific discipline.

My data also suggest that the more heterogeneous the population of scientists that is attacking a problem, the more likely the problem is solved. Diversity of intellectual ability matters a lot. You just don´t get that very often in the traditional model of knowledge development. On their own, people are specialists. What you see at InnoCentive is that you have a computer scientist, for example, thinking about a chemistry problem; a biologist might submit a winning solution to an engineering problem. People are all deeply specialized, but in open development projects they are much more likely to try solving problems outside of their field. That's a major change from the traditional model.

The Characteristics of Winning Problem Solvers

Enjoying problem solving and the challenge of learning drives participation in open development, as I have already said. As hinted above, when people were asked, "Is the problem you solved inside of your expertise, at the boundary of your expertise, or outside of your expertise?" the solvers who said the problem was further from their field of expertise were more likely to be the winning solvers.

Money also matters. But what's interesting is that the money component and the intrinsic motivation are negatively correlated in our data. One set of actors is in it for the money and another set of actors is in it for the fun of it. Most open source communities don´t care; you come for whatever reason you want, they just want your talent.

Let me give another example. InnoCentive received a question about a puzzling toxicology result in a new drug development program. Toxicology experts from the firm could not make sense of it. The outside toxicology experts they called in could not solve the puzzle. When the problem was posted on InnoCentive, a protein crystallographer provided an answer. She had no background in toxicology. Her PhD in crystallography led her to interpret the problem on the basis of crystallography principles and she solved it on that basis. The toxicologists never thought that this was a crystallography problem. She saw the problem and said: "Ah, in one week I can have an answer for your apparently intractable problem."

In short, crossing fields of knowledge is often key to innovation. Of course, the puzzled toxicologists could have said to their neighbors in a lab next door, who might have been crystallographers, "We have this problem; please have a look." If that had happened, they might have stumbled on the solution that InnoCentive provided. But that never happens. Internal broadcasting of problems is very, very rare.

Conclusion: The Importance of Collaboration

Let me end with a picture of distributed collaboration. In InnoCentive, independent people are competing for a prize and one (or perhaps several) winners are selected at the end of a contest. But some recent analysis in other settings shows that when you have massive collaboration, you get an even greater improvement in performance.

For example, a company called MathWorks, which creates mathematical simulation software, runs a fun contest every six months where coding is required to solve a relatively hard mathematical optimization problem. The interesting feature of the contest is that anybody can look at any previous entry, modify it, and then resubmit it. It's a Wiki-like programming contest. You look at a programming entry and say: "That's very interesting, let me take that code; let me add a bit of my own, and then submit a new solution."

In this contest it was observed that over a one-week time period more than 100 individuals participated by submitting code. The contest received over 3,000 entries and the collective performance of the code improved by two orders of magnitude (which is extremely high). Yi Cao, the winner, lives in the United Kingdom. His code included contributions from 32 other people.

This is the future. This is what we see so clearly in open source. I think it is the future for many innovation activities —where we will see collaboration among many individuals and organizations to help solve some of the toughest challenges facing our societies. One of my driving questions is how can we enable transparency inside organizations and across organizations so that they can get this kind of benefit?

Ideas for Innovative Leaders: Learn to Post Problems and Consider Providing More Information to Open Communities

Being a leader in open development means being willing to post problems for unknown others to solve. It is not easy to do that if you are used to taking an active role in problem solving yourself.

In addition to relinquishing that central role, it is necessary to learn how to post a compelling problem. But there is obvious learning by the posting firm. Over time firms learn to post problems that get solved. In other words, this is a new way of working. You don't know how to post a problem to the outside world at the beginning. But firms do get better at it, and then reap larger rewards.

Finally, companies, like academic institutions, need to understand how to share knowledge more effectively. The way science works today, there is a lot of secrecy, no sharing, and we all compete for a big prize—the Nobel Prize or some other prize. That's the first model I described at the beginning of this chapter, and it has done well for itself. However, we are now seeing an alternative model where cooperation and collaboration are key drivers—this model is in its infancy but is showing significant potential. The challenge for leaders is to enable knowledge sharing and create mechanisms and institutions that foster collaboration. The open source community has figured it out—maybe other settings can learn from them.

References and Further Reading

Boudreau, K. J., N. Lacetera, and K. R. Lakhani.2011. Incentives and problem uncertainty in innovation contests: An empirical analysis. *Management Science* 57 (5): 843–63.

Feller, J., B. Fitzgerald, S. Hissam, and K. R. Lakhani, eds. 2005. *Perspectives on Free and Open Source Software*. Cambridge: MIT Press.

Hayek, F. A. 1945. The use of knowledge in society. *American Economic Review* 35 (4): 519–30.

von Hippel, E. 1994. "Sticky information" and the locus of problem solving: Implications for innovation. *Management Science* 40 (4): 429–39.

Jeppesen, L. B., and K. R. Lakhani. 2010. Marginality and problem-solving effectiveness in broadcast search. *Organization Science* 21 (5): 1016–33.

Lakhani, K. R., and K. J. Boudreau. 2009. How to manage outside Innovation. *MIT Sloan Management Review* 50 (4): 69–76.

Lakhani, K. R., and J. A. Panetta. 2007. The principles of distributed innovation. *Innovations: Technology, Governance, Globalization* 2 (3): 97–112.

West, J., and K. R. Lakhani. 2008. Getting clear about communities in open innovation. *Industry and Innovation* 15 (2): 223–31.

11 Strategic Crowdsourcing: The Emergence of Online Distributed Innovation

J. Andrei Villarroel

The Rise of Crowdsourcing

Back in year 2000 few people would envision that a valuable project could be successfully developed by individuals spread around the world without any contractual ties or physical offices, and for free or almost for free. What seemed a far-fetched idea only a decade ago has fueled the creation of humanity's largest knowledge repository, Wikipedia, the most extensive multilingual social network site, Facebook, and the first general-purpose human computer, Amazon Mechanical Turk.

The value created through these and other online platforms is undeniable, as two *Time* magazine's Person of the Year awards now attest.[1] One was granted to "You" in 2006—to all the individuals who contributed to such platforms on a truly global scale never seen before; and the second one to Facebook's founder Mark Zuckerberg in 2010—for creating a new platform to interconnect us all as one global social network. Yet the organizing principles surrounding these platforms are radically different from those traditionally studied in business school curricula.

Online platforms of this kind enable the rapid assembly of distributed resources held by individuals who are geographically dispersed throughout the world. Endeavors built around these platforms have been referred to as "crowdsourcing" (Howe 2006) initiatives. They source knowledge, money, services, and so on, from a large and undefined group of people (the "crowd") through an open call. Thousands of such initiatives have been created over the last decade,[2] which we are now studying systematically.[3]

As more such platforms become available, our ability to design organizations as globally distributed systems is greatly enhanced. In this chapter, I provide evidence of the nature and effectiveness of crowdsourcing from an organizational point of view, and introduce concepts and frameworks that explain how crowdsourcing extends the industrial era concept of the firm. Managers should find value in understanding the concepts and frameworks in this chapter to guide their decisions about engaging in crowdsourcing endeavors. Researchers may find new ideas for further study.

The Encyclopedia Revolution: When Excellence Meets Digitization and Crowdsourcing

For a few years now, I have been telling the story of the double revolution faced by Encyclopedia Britannica to illustrate the point of how first digitization and then crowdsourcing are leading us toward more effective organizational designs. Every time I tell the story, I am thrilled to find out who in the audience has actually used Encyclopedia Britannica. With the notable exception of senior academic audiences, where about one-third have used it, I found that less than one-tenth of young college graduates have, and it is rare to find current college students who have even heard of it. By contrast, everyone knows Wikipedia, the encyclopedia written by a crowd.

Encyclopedias provide a compelling story of how excellence in organization has been revolutionized by digitization, and then revolutionized again by crowdsourcing. It illustrates a progression toward more effective forms of knowledge sourcing, production and distribution that challenge our traditional understanding of organization. Why start with organizational excellence? Because as firms "organize" or reorganize to achieve excellence, they achieve efficiencies. First digitization and then crowdsourcing are transforming how we organize for excellence on a global scale. They bring unprecedented new efficiencies by extending the traditional firm to work in concert with a globally interconnected crowd. They bring to life the realization that as one global society, "together we create more."

When It Came to Encyclopedias, Excellence Had a Name—Britannica

Encyclopedia Britannica embodies a bicentennial example of excellence in organization. The company introduced its first encyclopedia in 1768 and has since continued to develop what was long regarded as "the gold standard of human knowledge." Its compendium of printed books, which in its 2010 edition contained 32 volumes with about 65,000 articles in total, was written by over 4,300 expert contributors including more Nobel Prize winners than any other encyclopedia.[4] In April 2011 this fine compendium was priced[5] at £1,195, weighing just about 140 pounds.

In the summer of 1985 Britannica was approached by Microsoft —a young company back then. Microsoft offered Britannica a deal to digitize their content to sell with PC software. Britannica's president refused the offer citing how an alternate sales channel would alienate the company's most important asset, their sales force.[6] In such an organization sales people are numerous and core to the business.[7] Britannica, in particular, had a sales hierarchy where all levels earned a commission on each sale, which indirectly incentivized senior managers to hire even more sales people.[8]

After many a hurdle in the quest for content, Microsoft licensed the text from Funk & Wagnalls, a second tier encyclopedia. The resulting product became the *Encarta* digital encyclopedia, enriched with video and audio content, and educational interactive tools. Launched in 1993, Encarta was not the first digital encyclopedia in the market. Both The World Book—the most popular encyclopedia at the time—and Britannica-owned Compton's already had a CD version. However, these leading encyclopedias relied heavily on their large sales force for the distribution of their products.

Digitization Changed the Game, Enabling the Dematerialization of Information Products

Microsoft distributed Encarta on CDs bundled with new PC computers. This wholesale approach helped the product reach a young mass market effectively.[9] Microsoft became a pioneer in selling digital encyclopedias at the relatively low price of $99.[10] This was unlike Britannica, whose CD version cost $1,500[11] and whose copies were sold through its own sales force. From an organizational standpoint, Microsoft had effectively introduced a disintermediation of the encyclopedia sales force. Two years later, by February 1995, Bill Gates claimed Encarta to be the most widely sold encyclopedia in the world.[12]

Encarta's position grew stronger over the next few years, while Britannica struggled. In just five years Encyclopedia Britannica saw its revenues sliced in half from a peak of $650 million in 1991, to a mere $325 million in 1996.[13] This fall in revenue was associated with a fall in sales volume of the printed collection: from 117,000 hard copies sold in 1993, down to only 55,000 hard copies sold in 1996. Financially distressed, the company was sold to a private investor. By then, Microsoft had recruited more editors than any other encyclopedia, thereby improving the quality of their content and making it available in languages other than English.[14]

Crowdsourcing Changed the Game, Once Again Enabling the Dematerialization of Knowledge Organizations

On January 15, 2001, at a time when Encarta had established a clear market leadership over Britannica and its competitors, a new encyclopedia was born: Wikipedia. Not one that would be distributed on a physical CD, rather only available electronically over the Internet. Wikipedia was not first in this space, however. Britannica Online had been launched in 1994 and Britannica.com had been in existence since 1999.[15] In addition, Microsoft Encarta had a strong online presence.

Ten years later, however, Wikipedia had over 3.5 *million* articles in the English language alone. This is 55 times more articles than Encyclopedia Britannica,[16] and 83 times more articles than the last version of Encarta —which had 42,000 articles.[17] Furthermore, while Britannica was available only in English and Encarta was available in 8 languages, Wikipedia was available in 36 language editions, each with more than 100,000 articles.[18]

Crowdsourcing as Organizational Design

From a traditional perspective, Wikipedia faced three seemingly insurmountable organizational challenges at its launch: (1) how to produce its content, (2) how to distribute it effectively, and—not the least—(3) how to involve the right talent. First, Wikipedia had no content available, which had been the single most difficult challenge Microsoft faced in launching Encarta. Second, its sole focus on online distribution represented only one of several distribution channels already mastered by both Encarta and Britannica. Third, contrary to what was then the norm in the encyclopedia industry, a formal staff of editors and paid expert contributors was notably absent.

Granted, Wikipedia's rise relied on the use of new technology, the wiki.[19] However, technology alone was not sufficient. A key enabler was the organizational innovation we call "crowdsourcing": a radical new way of organizing distributed resources for the synchronous collective creation of value via the Internet. This involved a simple set of rules of engagement governing how self-selected individuals[20] could participate in the process of creation of a common good, and an attractive policy stating that the good be "free" to access, use, and repurpose. These basic organizing principles were at odds with those upon which both Britannica and Encarta were conceived.

A New Approach to Organization: Open Policy, Distributed Process, and Flat Structure

From Wikipedia's inception, any person—regardless of expertise, even anonymously—could contribute new content and edit any of the existing content, while a single-layer distributed bureaucracy of volunteer administrators governed the editorial process.[21] People were inherently motivated by the idea of having a "free" encyclopedia. Wikipedia's open and distributed approach to organization and the associated choices of policy (free, open, collaborative), process (distributed, asynchronous, cumulative) and organizational structure (flat, distributed, democratic) contributed to its success.

All things combined, the change in the organization of knowledge sourcing, production, and distribution illustrated by the recent history of the encyclopedia industry is radical. A once prevalent organizational model that started with sourcing and production relying on the formal hiring of thousands of professional staff and a distribution

Table 11.1
Organizational differences between traditional work and crowdsourcing work

Characteristics	Traditional work	Crowdsourcing work
Project staffing	Assigned teams of employees	Self-selected online communities
Scale of participants	Small predefined	Large undefined
Geographic scope	Local	Global
Focus of responsibility	Central product	Distributed tasks
Intellectual property	Tight or exclusive	"Loose" or nonexclusive
Labor relationship	Formal legal contracts	Informal relational contracts
Work environment	Physical	Virtual
Interactions	Personal and synchronous	Impersonal and asynchronous
Incentives	Monetary, power	Altruistic, fun, monetary

channel comprising tens of thousands of sales people had been outcompeted by an online distributed organizational model where sourcing and production relied on volunteer self-selected editor-contributors and an efficient distribution channel that reduced the sales force to nil.

The Principles of Traditional Work and Crowdsourcing Work Differ Dramatically

By virtue of having the bulk of the actual work performed by individuals outside the formal boundaries of the firm, crowdsourcing is a new way of thinking about work that requires new rules of engagement. This open approach requires that the work be accessible to occasional contributors, offering a win-win exchange, thereby fostering an informal yet durable relationship. In table 11.1, I contrast the differences between a traditional approach to work and crowdsourcing work.

The Competitive Advantage of Crowdsourcing

In retrospect, Wikipedia enjoyed three important organizational advantages. First, regarding content, the unique wiki technology allowed the effective sourcing of dispersed bits of knowledge held by individuals all across society.[22] Second, regarding distribution the Internet was a cost-effective means to instantly provide up-to-date content to the largest number of people, free of the costs and production constraints of a CD or book. And, third, by virtue of being open to all, Wikipedia could reach out to even the rarest of talents lying outside the boundaries of the formal organization. Google Trends data shown in figure 11.1 provides information on the relative dominance in people's minds of the three encyclopedias over a critical three-year period, from 2004 through 2006.

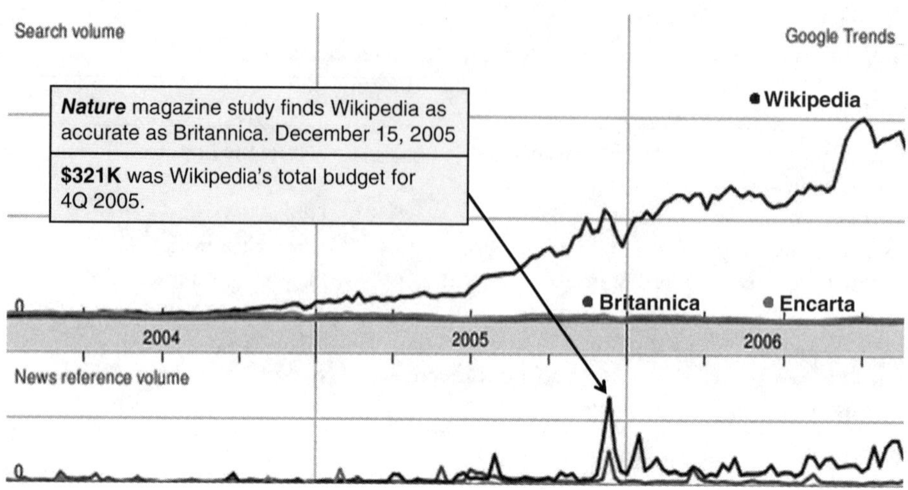

Figure 11.1
Competitive advantage of Wikipedia over time, 2004 to 2006

Crowdsourcing as a new form of organization quickly outperformed traditional organizations in various ways.

Market Advantage

The top half of figure 11.1 compares the three companies in terms of "search volume" (how many times people entered the word "Britannica," "Encarta," or "Wikipedia" in their web browser's Google search box). Before 2004, Wikipedia was not even visible on Google's radar. Over that period, Encarta was the dominant player among online encyclopedias, particularly since it was available as part of Microsoft's www.msn.com site, one of the top websites in the world at the time.[23] However, between 2004 and 2006, Wikipedia rapidly rose to become the world's dominant online encyclopedia.

Quality Advantage

The bottom half of the figure compares the three encyclopedias in terms of "news reference volume" (how many times news articles cited "Britannica," "Encarta," or "Wikipedia"). Over the three-year period, Wikipedia clearly became dominant. Note that a peak occurred at the end of 2005, after which Wikipedia consistently remained the dominant reference. The peak corresponds to the publication of the results of a study conducted by *Nature*—a prominent scientific journal—comparing the quality of Wikipedia to that of Britannica (Giles 2005). The study found no significant differences in quality between the two.

Speed Advantage

Britannica reacted strongly to the *Nature* article, stating that the study was "fatally flawed" and asking *Nature* to completely retract their conclusions.[24] *Nature* did not retract. Instead, it published a point-by-point rebuttal stating how the study was conducted and arguing that each aspect of the study was rigorous.[25] An important fact that is not captured in this exchange is that while Wikipedia articles did contain more errors, as a whole, all of the errors identified in Wikipedia had been fixed by the time *Nature*'s rebuttal was published.[26]

Cost Advantage

At the time of *Nature*'s study in December 2005, Wikipedia operated on a $321,000 budget per quarter, two-thirds of which related to hardware and Internet hosting. In addition, the formal organization behind Wikipedia was extremely lean--only two full-time and two part-time paid employees in 2005.[27] By 2010, about 4,000 volunteer administrators oversaw the entire encyclopedia, just as many expert editors as Britannica relied on in 2005 except that Wikipedia's workers were not on a payroll.

Online Distributed Organization: The End of One Era, the Beginning of Another

At this point you may rightfully wonder what happened to Encarta, the flagship encyclopedia of one of the world's most valuable technology companies, Microsoft Corporation, as well as the bicentennial trusted source of human knowledge, Encyclopedia Britannica. Albeit widely successful in their own ways, both encyclopedias went out of business in the formats upon which the organizations that owned them built their great reputations. On December 31, 2009, after sixteen years of existence, Microsoft Encarta had completely shut down its operations worldwide. At that time Wikipedia accounted for 97 percent of the US traffic for online encyclopedias, while Encarta was second with 1.27 percent. The announcement of the closing stated that "the category of traditional encyclopedias and reference material has changed" and that "people today seek and consume information in considerably different ways than in years past."[28]

As for Britannica, by 2009 it realized that its "closed" process was too slow to keep up with changes in the business landscape. On January 22, 2009, the company opened its process and invited users (after some screening) to edit its content. It was not enough. On March 14, 2012, Britannica announced that it would stop its print edition entirely—after 244 years. By mid-2011, Wikipedia was the sixth most visited Internet site in the world, sharing the top charts with Google, Yahoo and Baidu (Chinese). Like Wikipedia, other *younger* crowdsourcing endeavors such as YouTube, Facebook, and Twitter had also joined the world's top ten.

Valuing Online Distributed Organizations

The value of these new forms of online organizations is apparent when the "companies" behind them are traded. YouTube, third in global traffic rankings for 2012, was acquired by Google for $1.6 billion in October 2006.[29] Facebook, second in global traffic rankings, was already valued at $15 billion when Microsoft paid $240 million for a 1.6 percent stake in the company in October 2007.[30] Twitter, ninth on the list, was valued at $3.7 billion upon raising venture capital in December 2010. But wait, web traffic is not just web content generated by people!

Successful crowdsourcing initiatives typically have very large numbers of contributors distributed around the world, engaged in value-creating activities involving relatively small tasks. Most important, the vast majority of these people devote their know-how, time, and energy to these initiatives for free, or for very little monetary reward. For example, Facebook Translations (see Mini Case A at the end of the chapter) attracts 300,000 people from 190 countries around the world to translate Facebook's webpages into over 100 languages and dialects for free.

This evidence shows how individual users, not company employees, are the primary source of value in the emergent paradigm of online distributed organization. But it is not their sheer numbers that matter the most. Their diversity as well as their level of engagement are among the key factors determining the value they bring to the initiative (Villarroel 2008, ch. 4). This is what *Time* magazine was referring to when they awarded the 2006 Person of the Year to "You" (actually all of us) who had created more value together than any organization in such a short period.

From the evidence collected, it appears that knowledge intensive firms are the ones that may benefit the most from strategic crowdsourcing initiatives. A list of examples in various industries can be found in table 11.2.

A Product Complexity Model of Online Distributed Innovation

I here define online distributed innovation (ODI) as a new dynamic capability of the firm that enables the online sourcing and assembly of distributed knowledge resources held by a large and diverse pool of self-selected contributors beyond the formal boundaries of the organization. The product-complexity model of ODI that I present here builds on an adaptation of a base organization model proposed by Baldwin and von Hippel (2009). The base organization model involves two main dimensions: *communications costs* and *design costs*. As shown in figure 11.2, all combinations of design costs (horizontal axis) and communications costs (vertical axis) define the innovation space. Within this innovation space three innovation modes cover specific areas: (1) *individual user* innovation depicted on the left (vertical rectangle), (2) *group collaborative*

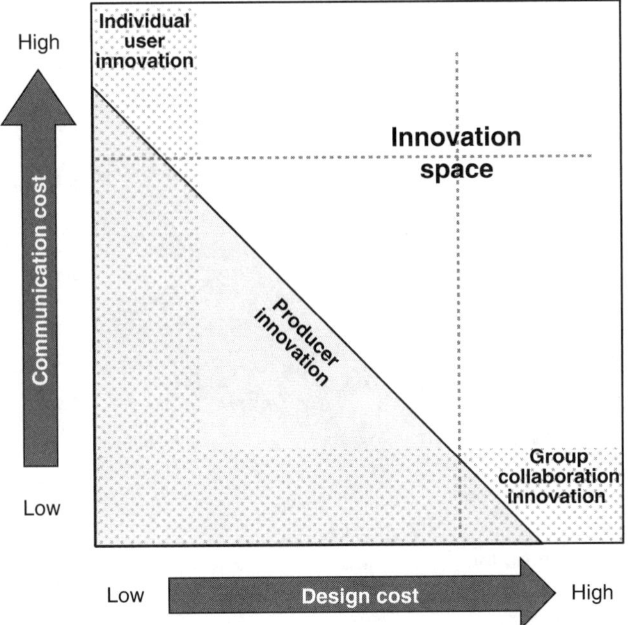

Figure 11.2
Base model describing the innovation space
Source: Adapted from Baldwin and von Hippel (2009)

innovation, depicted on the bottom (horizontal rectangle), and (3) *producer* firm innovation, shown in the middle (triangle).

For low design costs, the base model suggests that "individual" innovation can occur regardless of communications costs, since each individual is assumed to have the necessary resources and not need interact with others to innovate (i.e., what any one individual can create alone). For low communications costs, the base model suggests that "group" innovation can occur regardless of the design costs. The costs are assumed to be shared among the members of a community (i.e., what a community can create together). Finally, "producer" innovation covers a segment of the innovation space beyond what the low-cost subset of individual or collaborative innovation modes can cover (i.e., what a firm can create through coordination). These three innovation modes define the subset of realizable innovation within the broader innovation space.

Product Complexity

The innovation space covered by "product complexity" (circular segment at the bottom left corner of figure 11.3) corresponds to the amount of innovation required

Table 11.2
Examples of companies implementing ODI

Originating company	ODI initiative	Year	Target industry	Community size	Countries spanned	Self-organized
Amazon	Mechanical Turk	2005	General purpose	200,000 est.	100	
CDD	CDD	2004	Chemical and pharmaceuticals	70 firms	UD	
CNN	CNN iReport	2008	News reporting	763,920	212	
Eli Lilly	InnoCentive	2001	Scientific R&D	250,000	200	
Facebook	Translations—Spanish	2007	Language translation	7,254	25*	
Google	Image Labeler	2006	Image labeling	UD	UD	
Hubert Burda Media	BurdaStyle	2007	Fashion design	537,495	46**	
Netflix	Netflix prize	2006	Machine learning	51,051	186	
oDesk	oDesk	2004	Professional services	1,436,005	156	
Project Gutenberg	Distributed proofreaders	2000	Proofreading	104,585	27*	Y
TopCoder	Top coder	2001	Software development	301,406	200	
World Bank Institute	Evoke	2010	Social innovation	19,827	150	

Source: Company websites.
Note: Numbers in this table were updated on January 13, 2011. UD = undisclosed. *Actual numbers from our survey administered between March and April 2008.**From our survey administered between October and November 2009.

Firm-sponsored	Mediated market	Collaborative	Competitive	Participant compensation	Description of what an individual contributor can do
	Y		Y	Pay per task	Compete to work on tasks proposed by individual requesters
Y		Y		Access to information	Scientists can archive, mine, and collaborate around pre-clinical chemical and biological drug discovery data
Y			Y	No pay, leaderboard	Send a news report to CNN for a chance to get published
	Y		Y	Prize, leaderboard	Compete to provide solutions to problems held by seeker companies
Y		Y		No pay, leaderboard	Translate Facebook into Spanish, and vote on existing translations
Y		Y		Points, leaderboard	Labeling images to improve Google's image search results
Y		Y		No pay, open source	Contribute a design, pattern, or, technique for a chance to get published.
Y			Y	Prize, leaderboard	Compete to submit a better recommendation algorithm to Netflix
	Y		Y	Paid hourly	Compete to work on projects proposed by individual requesters/firms (online work)
		Y		No pay	Transcription of old manuscripts and books into e-books, proofreading of scanned texts
	Y		Y	Prize, leaderboard	Compete for code development to solve programming problems typically proposed by firms
Y		Y		Prizes	Submit creative solutions to tackle real life problems

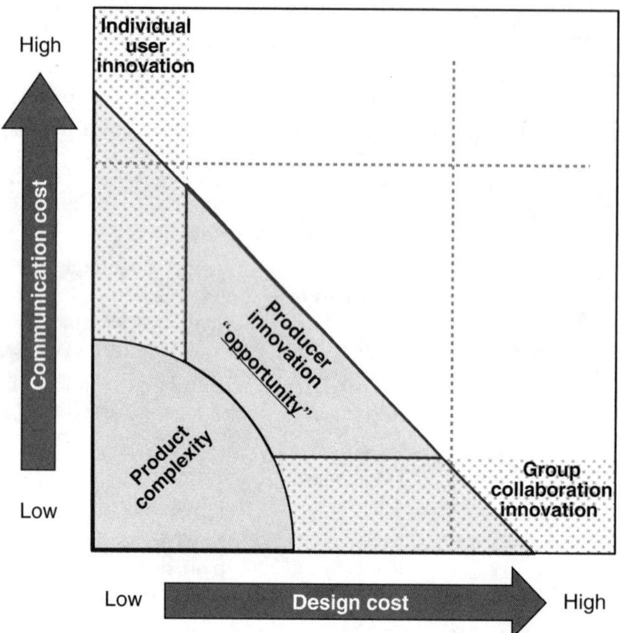

Figure 11.3
Base model with complexity

by a product to be put in the market. In the example of online encyclopedias, the market currently demands the level of product complexity of Wikipedia, covering a very broad range of topics, speedy corrections, multimedia content, up-to-date links to other Internet resources, an array of languages in which the encyclopedia is available, and so forth.

Product complexity is thus defined as the subset of the innovation space that needs to be covered in order to successfully produce what the market demands. Figure 11.3 suggests that while the individual innovation mode can cover some product complexity (e.g., designing new product ideas), and the group collaborative innovation mode can address another part of it (e.g., prototyping alternative products), there is some product complexity that neither of these modes can address (e.g., supporting a product through its life cycle).

This model suggests that one reason the producer firm is needed is to address the product complexity gap left by the other two innovation modes. The model does not imply that this gap always exists. If the scope of product complexity were small enough to be covered by either (or both) of the base modes, there would be no gap to be filled, and hence no reason a priori for the firm to exist. If the scope of product complexity were larger than what it is possible to cover by all three innovation modes considered here, the product could not be brought to market via these modes.

In other words, I argue that for there to be a business opportunity, product complexity must exceed what individuals and groups alone can achieve. In order for a business to be viable in this kind of innovation space, firms must gather resources from both individuals and communities playing a coordination role across them, until the firm covers an innovation space in excess of the product complexity demanded by the market. The innovation spectrum covered by the firm mode that is in excess of product complexity translates in turn into a busines "opportunity." At the same time some spectrum of innovation remains attainable solely by individuals or groups of individuals that the firm is not able to hire.

Dynamics of Communication Costs, Design Costs, and Product Complexity

Figure 11.4 considers the temporal dynamics of the proposed framework in order to explain the emergence of online distributed innovation. Communication costs among

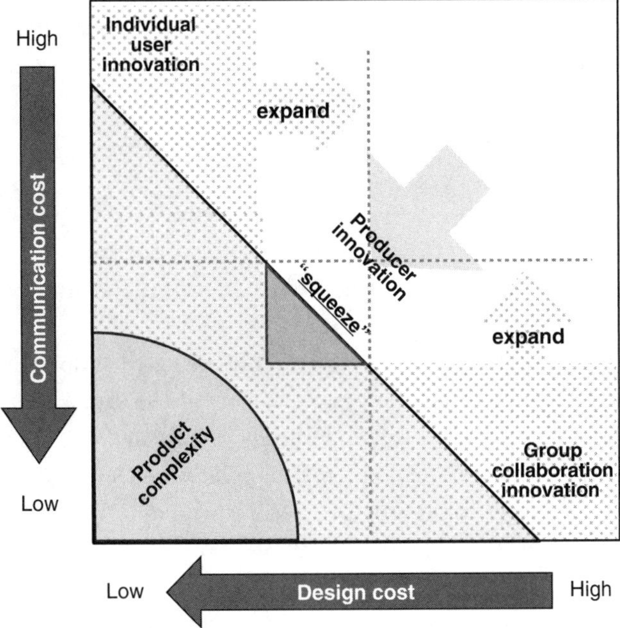

Figure 11.4
Producer squeeze problem

remote individuals and design costs for information-based goods are closely linked and dependent on the evolution of information and communications technology (ICT). Considered over time: (1) communications costs are decreasing as a result of Moore's law, Metcalfe's law, and Reed's Law;[31] (2) design costs are decreasing thanks to modularity (Ethiraj and Levinthal 2004) and greater availability of reusable toolkits (von Hippel and Katz 2002); finally, (3) product complexity demanded by the market is ever increasing.

At the same time, (1) *individuals* around the world are rapidly becoming more educated (*S&E Indicators* 2010) and—given access to the right tools—more of the innovation space can be covered by individual innovation. Similarly, (2) *collaborative groups* embracing more advanced communications platforms are better able to coordinate their otherwise informal innovation efforts and hence conquer a larger part of the innovation space. These temporal dynamics have the combined effect of *squeezing* the innovation spectrum covered by the firm. Over time, the firm faces ever greater competition from both individual and group innovation, and the viability of the firm depends increasingly on its ability to overcome growing product complexity. I call this the "producer innovation squeeze," as explicated in figure 11.4.

Both Britannica and Encarta suffered from the "producer innovation squeeze" as Wikipedia's community was able to quickly develop an increasingly more complex product, while savvy Internet users were able to find better information elsewhere, thanks to search engines (e.g., Google search). The market expected the product characteristics offered by Wikipedia (ease of access, up-to-date, free) and Google search. Britannica and Encarta were unable to offer any of these, failing to add significant value through coordination.

Online Distributed Innovation as a Solution to Producer Innovation Squeeze

ODI, in both competitive and collaborative approaches, offers solutions to the problem of producer innovation squeeze. This is depicted in figure 11.5.

First, in order to tap into the growing global pool of highly educated individual innovators (*S&E Indicators* 2010), the firm has the option to extend the scope of its business operations via an *online open competition*. This opportunity is illustrated by Netflix in a case found at the end of this chapter. The company launched the Netflix Prize challenge offering $1 million to whoever could provide a recommendation algorithm that would perform 10 percent better than Netflix's. Over 50,000 participants from around the world submitted more than 44,000 valid solutions. The goal was achieved less than three years later (for details, see Mini Case A at the end of this chapter).

Second, in order for the firm to tap into the increasing ability to globally coordinate work over the Internet, the firm has the option to extend its activities by launching an online *open mass collaboration* initiative. This is portrayed by Facebook. The company

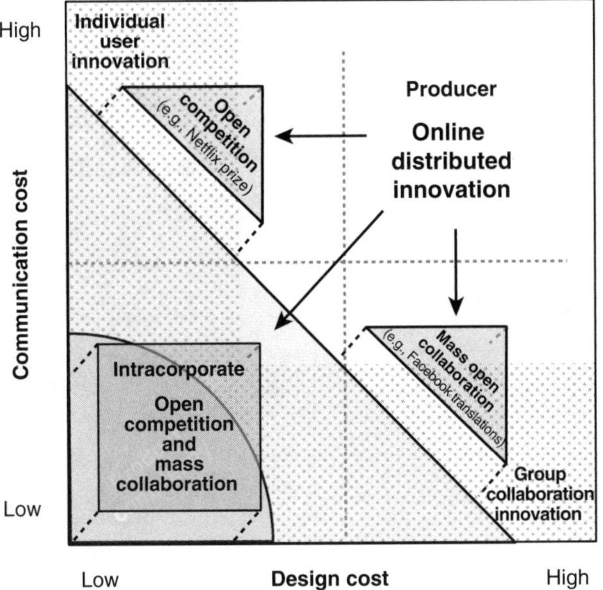

Figure 11.5
ODI as a solution to the producer squeeze problem

launched the Facebook Translations initiative by issuing a call to a community of translators. In about one year, 300,000 participants from around the world dedicated their time and effort to cumulatively create over 100 language and dialect versions of the Facebook website (for details, see Mini Case B at the end of this chapter).

Third, and equally important, large firms can choose to internally implement open competitions and open mass collaborations, which should help address product complexity. This is the case of client firms of Exago Markets, a corporate crowdsourcing platform provider. The company provides an innovation platform with a stock market for innovation component (for group collaboration) tied to a reward auctions market component where individuals bid for prizes (for individual competition). This intracorporate crowdsourcing solution effectively leverages the innovative ability of all the workforce (Villarroel and Reis 2010b, 2012).

Online Distributed Innovation as an Extension to the Firm

The framework I now present builds on the previous discussions, with a view to setting the foundations of ODI as an integral part of the firm. It makes an attempt at reconciling the theories of the resource-based view (Barney 1991) and activities-based view

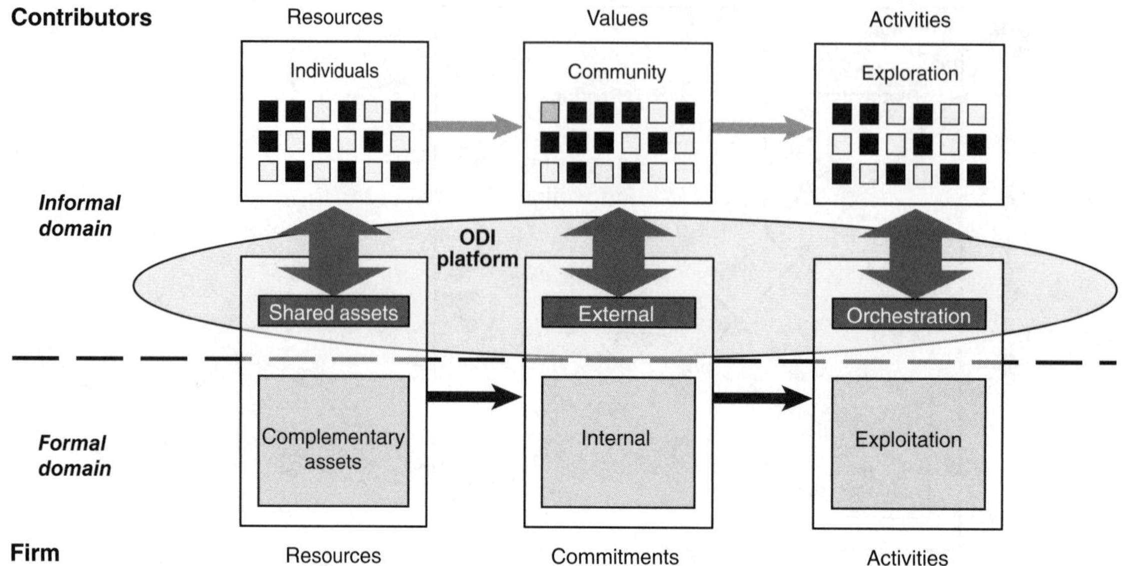

Figure 11.6
ODI as an extension to the firm
Source: Adapted from Villarroel (2008) and Ghemawat (2001)

(Porter 1979) with the understanding that there are open sources of competitive advantage for the firm in the public domain (Villarroel 2008). The framework depicted in figure 11.6 offers a complementary argument that extends the formal domain of the firm (involving formal contractual engagements) into the formal domain of the crowd by incorporating coordinated exchanges with community contributors (involving the nuturing of relational contracts as discussed by Gibbons and Henderson 2011).

The New Organization's Formal Domain: Resources, Commitments, and Activities Extended beyond Traditional Boundaries

Building on the dynamic view of the firm proposed by Ghemawat (2001: 120), this framework acknowledges the importance of commitment (Ghemawat 1991) as a link between the resources (Barney 1991) available to the firm and the activities (Porter 1979) that it undertakes. The bottom part of figure 11.6 depicts the traditional configuration of resources, commitments, and activities of the firm. The middle part of figure 11.6 depicts the extension of the firm at the boundaries between the formal and informal domains.

Implementing ODI implies a radically different approach, however. It necessitates an important and irreversible decision altering the existing business model of the firm and affecting its core resources, commitments, and activities. This is commitment to (1) knowing the value of the resources held by firm, openly sharing a fraction of them in the public or informal domain; (2) knowing the importance of the firm's activities, orchestrating some of them in the public domain or informal domain, and (3) knowing the need to appropriate rents, maintain control on a complementary system of closely held resources, focal commitments, and exploitation activities from which economic value is derived.

ODI implies engaging some of the private firm's resources and activities with some of the crowd's resources and activities in a mutually beneficial interaction. This is the result of the firm making external (environmental) commitments that are both a "fit" with its own internal (focal) commitments and with the values pursued by the external community contributors it seeks to attract and work with.

In the case of Netflix, described in Mini Case B below, the firm released a very large private data set to the public, engaged in an online forum with contest participants, and did so in conferences with academics. All the while Netflix kept the most recent (and more complete) data set private.

The Informal Domain of the Crowd: Contributor's Resources, Values, and Activities as an Extension of the Firm

Complementing the firm's formal set of resources, commitments, and activities, are the crowd's own set of resources, values, and activities. Situated entirely in the informal domain, the resources available to the crowd are individually owned by each contributor, and the activities that they engage in as a community are dependent on the shared values of its individual members. I argue that the *values* shared by those individuals constitute the defining link between the types of resources shared by the crowd, and the types of activities that the crowd engages in.

ODI draws from the collective action of large numbers of community members who self-select to contribute, hence necessitating an important common motivation—here referred to as values that the firm should be clearly aware of. Knowing the private interest behind an initiative, the firms motivate individuals to contribute their scarce resources to it. Knowing the social repercussions associated with participation in a for-profit initiative, they may motivate individuals to engage in related activities.

In the case of Facebook Translations, the company realized its private interest was to reach out to more people, and it could link that interest to the crowd's interest to have the platform available in their local language. Facebook does not charge anything for the use of its platform; users perceive that by engaging in translations they can also enlarge their social network, so they pay in kind by contributing to the effort. By articulating a clear call to "Join a community of translators to make Facebook available to everyone everywhere, in all languages," Facebook could tap the synergies within its community and benefit from their "translation potential."

Finally, the success of ODI lies in the strategic fit between the firm and the crowd, based on the alignment of resources and activities between the two and on the alignment of firm commitments and community values.

The ODI Platform: A Strategic Dynamic Capability of the Firm

At the boundaries between the aforementioned domains—private or formal, and public or informal—lies a sociotechnical platform. The ODI platform supports a bundle of relational contracts between the focal firm and the associated community of contributors by means of an IT infrastructure and a simple set of engagement rules. The ODI platform actively links the formal and informal domains surrounding the new organization, channeling resources, commitments, and activities shared by actors across the two domains.

The successful implementation of an ODI platform necessitates the articulation of a triple fitness:

1. Fit of shared assets, which the firm gives away to the crowd for it to work with. They should match the resources that individual contributors have at their disposal, while being complementary to the assets that the firm controls internally and extracts rents from.
2. Fit of external commitments that the focal firm makes to the community, which must be aligned with community values shared by the crowd while simultaneously being compatible with the internal commitments of the firm toward its employees.
3. Fit of orchestration activities, which must be aligned with the explorative activities of the crowd while feeding the results of such activities into the exploitation routines of the firm.

Combining formal and informal resources can create the basis for a new dynamic capability of the firm (Eisenhardt and Martin 2000), which is of strategic importance for new value creation. As a result of the interactions between value creation activities of the formal organization and the oftentimes significantly larger crowd, the firm has the possibility of continuously exploring a larger universe of innovative possibilities.

Online Distributed Organization (ODO) benefits come primarily from activities taking place beyond the formal boundaries of the firm from an informal crowd of individuals. In an ODO, organizational resistance may be reduced or be possibly irrelevant;[32] the pool of potential talent can be as vast as the reach of the Internet allows it to be.[33]

Knowledge Leverage through Positive Externalities

ODO benefits from operating in an environment of lower inertial resistance to novelty and greater abundance of talent than found in the traditional firm. The "free-revealing"[34] of information assets of the firm implementing ODI compounds positively with its ability to share resources and activities with online contributors on a global scale. In this context the firm has the potential to lower costs and create new value through online communities and the associated network effects.

Differentiation through Cultural Transformation

As the firm effectively reorganizes itself—implementing open policies, distributed processes, and flat organizational structures—to successfully operate in the unconventional way reguired by ODI, the cultural shift that results offers the firm a strong source of differentiation relative to its competitors, thereby gaining a strategic competitive advantage from organization.

Sustaining Advantage through Idiosyncratic Value Generation

The competitive advantage attained by the firm strategically implementing ODI is sustainable when the firm can manage and grow a trusted and lasting relationship with its external crowd of self-selected contributors. Trusted contributors continually enhance existing value and create new idiosyncratic value around the "freely revealed" assets of the firm and the "shared assets" of the community involved.

Indeed, although externally orchestrated communities are not under the direct control of the firm and their creations are not the exclusive property of the firm, the fact that new value is created around a core asset of the firm makes the communities—and the value they create—tightly linked to the firm originating the "freely revealed" assets.

Conclusion: Implications of Crowdsourcing for Innovation

In this chapter I show how crowdsourcing is contributing to a significant evolution of the concept of open innovation (Chesbrough 2003). Originally, Chesbrough identified value-generating potential from trading *strong* intellectual property (e.g., patents). Later, recognizing the simultaneous surge of *weak* intellectual property (e.g., open source), he advised firms to "construct business models that incorporate both trends in their logic" (2006: 48). For firms, this created a policy dilemma regarding intellectual property, and an organizational gap regarding its implementation.

The evidence and frameworks I present address the organizational gap, while suggesting that a "nonexclusive" intellectual property policy may be beneficial. Through cases I highlight the important knowledge-generating potential that firms have found in strategically working with crowds on the Internet, which I call online distributed innovation (ODI). The frameworks describe ODI as a platform extension of the firm into the public domain. ODI hence allows the firm to assemble distributed resources lying beyond its formal boundaries to gain leverage for its own value creating resources.

Facebook Translations (see Mini Case A) illustrates how an ODI implementation allowed 300,000 individuals to perform a massive online translation project efficiently—working remotely, yet collaboratively. The Netflix prize case (Mini Case B) illustrates another ODI implementation, where individuals came up with better solutions than a company could. This cases show, on the one hand, that given the right platform, collaborative groups can reach global scale and cumulatively create unprecedentedly large value. On the other hand, individuals are able to make more complex designs on their own when they are given access to the tools.

Crowdsourcing is establishing itself as an approach to organizational excellence that—besides the unprecedented scale factor and its inherent global reach—calls for knowledge-intensive firms to embrace a whole new organizational design (Villarroel and Gorbatai 2011a, b). At their core, ODI implementations are based on open policies, distributed processes, and a flat structure. Through the story of the encyclopedia revolution, I showed how this new organizational model can prove advantageous over traditional organizations, in terms of market reach, product quality, service responsiveness, and cost effectiveness, to the eventual demise of incumbents.

Traditional firms with strong cultures of centralized R&D would be wise to feel at risk of being shouldered out of competition as Microsoft Encarta was. Yet moving toward ODI is a frightening leap for many firms, and understandably so. The advantages of crowdsourcing come at a cost: less privacy and less appropriability of intellectual property. Without some level of transparency, without sharing, and without openness, there is no effective implementation of crowdsourcing. It is a fundamental change in how the production of knowledge is organized, and it cannot flourish with a small group of centralized, official, commanding leaders followed by a limited number of obedient employees.

Firms who can find a way to balance their internal controls with a loosening of the reins will be the most successful at leveraging the benefits of this new paradigm of knowledge production. Yet, if you look at the history of InnoCentive and similar companies described in this book by Frank Piller and Karim Lakhani, you will find many so-called open innovation companies that are very hesitant to let people collaborate, largely because of privacy and appropriability issues. The cases presented in this book suggest that more can be done to achieve the promise of open distributed innovation. Online distributed processes for collaborating and exchanging knowledge can help improve excellence in organization.

In the most profound sense, the new paradigm of crowdsourcing for innovation is about moving the locus of innovation outside the formal knowledge silos of the firm, by implementing new organizational processes that go beyond all boundaries—beyond the hierarchical, legal, and geographic boundaries that managers are accustomed to, and beyond the comfort zone for traditional executives. In today's increasingly virtualized world there is a competitive knowledge advantage to be gained from breaking away from the traditional knowledge silos of the firm. Online distributed organization offers a means to capture that advantage.

Mini Case A—Facebook Translations

In December 2007 Facebook launched an initiative where a subset of their users was invited to "join a community of translators to make Facebook available to everyone, everywhere, in all languages" (excerpt from Facebook's official open call). To support the effort, it posted 28,078 translations tasks, which together represented the actual corpus powering the Facebook website. The initiative was supported by a Facebook app featuring a dedicated community platform, translations.facebook.com.

In one year more than 300,000 people from the Facebook community had translated the Facebook platform into more than 70 different languages.[35] As a result Facebook is now available in over 100 "languages and dialects" including different language variants (e.g., Chilean Spanish, Venezuelan Spanish, Mexican Spanish). It is noteworthy that the Spanish community was among the first to be invited, and the fastest to complete the translation of the website—just about three weeks.

What is truly interesting about this crowdsourcing initiative is the iterative distributed process behind it (see figure 11.7). Some people are translating the content for the first time. Others are suggesting alternative translations, adding to the ones already received. Other people are voting on the existing alternative translations. The result is a "living translation" that is continuously updated. The key idea behind this initiative is what computer scientists are calling "distributed human computation" (Gentry et al. 2005).

The Translations initiative required that Facebook reveal the inner-coding of its website. Conversely, Facebook users involved in the initiative gave away all rights on their contributions to the firm. This two-way exchange enabled the rapid development of new language versions of the Facebook website, which benefited both the firm and its users. By tapping into the distributed intelligence latent in its community Facebook grew from 60 million to over 500 million just three years after the launch of the initiative.[36]

One could argue that to the extent that this translations initiative made Facebook accessible to a much broader global audience in their local language, it might have

Facebook translations iterative distributed process

1. **Break work W into manageable simple tasks T**
   Setup: Codify W, modularize into T's
2. **For each T, give it to random N individuals (N >> 1)**
   Goal: Get a set of R redundant raw inputs for each T (R << N)
3. **From each set R, choose subset of high-frequency ones O**
   Goal: Get the most likely raw output set O
4. **For each set O, give it to random M individuals to vote on them (M > N)**
   Goal: Select the most credible output F to use
5. **Repeat from 2.**

Figure 11.7
Iterative distributed process

been a key factor explaining why it overtook its top competitor, MySpace. Armed with a translation tool Facebook managed to get "the crowd" to do a much larger job than any formal company could do for them, essentially for free. Not just once, but perpetually. It created a living translation system that continues to serve them well.

Mini Case B—Netflix Prize

On October 2, 2006, online movie rental company Netflix launched a one million dollar challenge to improve upon its movie recommendation system by 10 percent. To support the company's open call for submissions, it offered 100 million entries of its customers' movie ratings database free for download. Additionally it put in place a dedicated website, www.netflixprize.com, featuring a community platform to encourage contestants to exchange ideas and submit their solutions electronically.

In one year, over 30,000 contestants from over 160 countries submitted more than 20,000 solutions that achieved 8.43 percent[37] improvement over the company's algorithm. On November 13, 2007, the company obtained a nonexclusive license to the then-best solution by awarding a progress prize of $50,000. Figure 11.8 depicts the 7,533 submissions that outperformed the company's own algorithm and reached the contest's official "Leaderboard" (http://www.netflixprize.com/leaderboard) during the first year of the competition.

The one million dollar prize was awarded on July 26, 2009, to a team composed of several previously competing smaller teams that joined forces to achieve a 10.6 percent improvement. We surveyed a sample of contest participants after the challenge was over.[38] A leading contestant testified: "An extremely well-organized competition. It

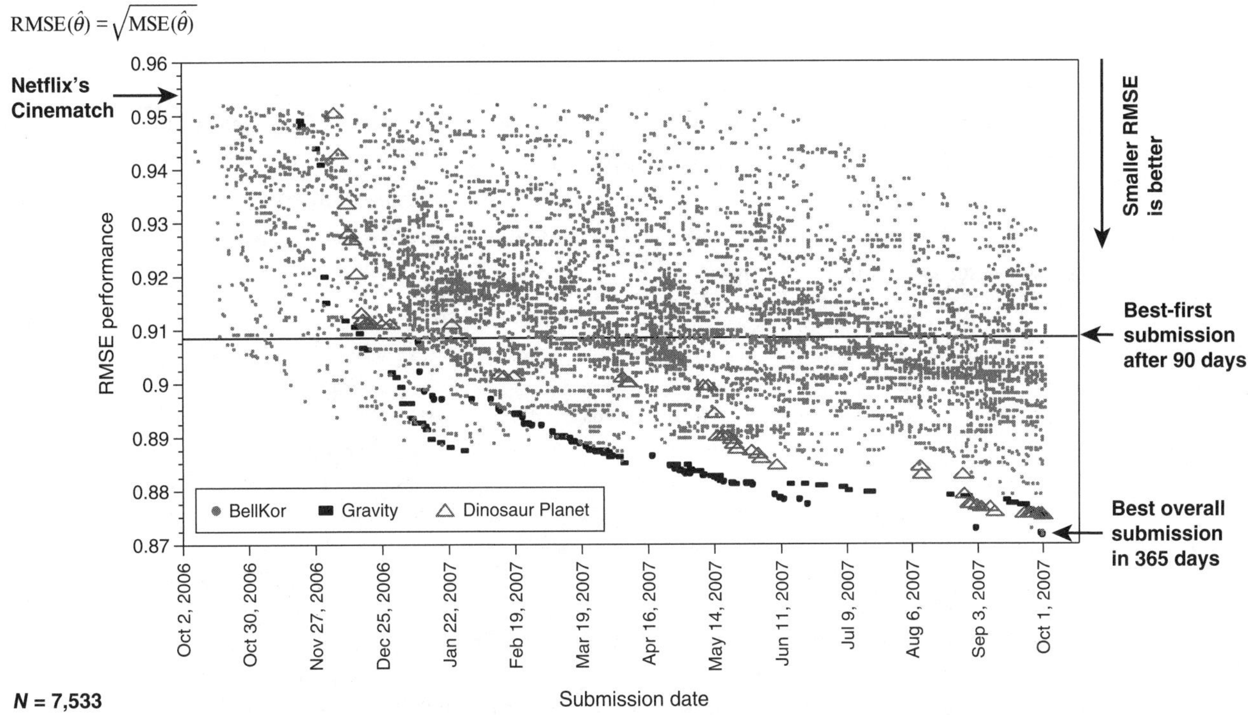

Figure 11.8
Scatter plot of Netflix leaderboard entries reveal a learning pattern over time

has advanced the field of machine learning considerably." This comment speaks to the "public" value yielded by this crowdsourcing initiative.

The "private value" for the company goes beyond that of having a better recommendation algorithm. It saved money, got involved with the best talent worldwide, and received lots of positive media attention in the process. Imagine the cost of recruiting across 186 countries, and hiring—even part-time— 5,169 teams of experts. Stated another way, how many years would it take for the highly capable employees of the firm to generate the 44,014 valid solutions the contest generated?

A close look at the evolution of the submissions to the Netflix Prize as a whole reveals that, on average, all contestants in the Netflix Prize learned from participating in the process. A look at the volatility in the submissions reveals convergence toward the end of the one-year period depicted on figure 11.8. Research revealed that these learning patterns result from a combination of knowledge-brokering and open sourcing activity in this multi-step repeat-submission process.[39]

From our survey we found that about 13 percent of participants open sourced their code, 19 percent of participants published at least part of their algorithms, and a very large 44 percent incorporated source code from other people. As a result 51 percent discovered something completely new, a completely new field or new computational technique from other people involved in the contest, and 55 percent incorporated completely new techniques into their work. The results of this research speak to the importance of enabling and managing the knowledge recombination process to achieve better innovation outcomes.

Notes

My deepest appreciation goes to Anne Huff, Ralf Reichwald, and Kathrin Möslein for believing in my work and inviting me to prepare this chapter. I appreciated your encouragement and endless patience. The ideas in this work date back to 2006 when I envisioned a symposium for the Academy of Management entitled "Open source corporate strategy (aka crowdsourcing): Reaching outside the firm's boundaries to tap upon global talent." For that endeavor, I was fortunate to work with Paul David, David Hsu, Lars Bo Jeppesen, Karim Lakhani, and my then doctoral advisor, Chris Tucci. Thanks to the ten anonymous reviewers whose extremely positive feedback helped validate the research topic. I developed my dissertation around a topic that gave life to everything that came next. In this sense, I also wish to recognize the invaluable exchanges I had on crowdsourcing with Eric von Hippel who mentored me during my postdoc at MIT Sloan; Tom Malone who hosted me as visiting scholar at MIT CCI; Larry Starr who hosted me as visiting scholar at Organizational Dynamics, University of Pennsylvania. Thanks also to Elaine Backman, Joshua Introne, Ted Benson, Andreea Gorbatai, and the Crowdfoo reading group. The preparation of this manuscript benefited from Filipa Reis's invaluable assistance and the financial support of the International Faculty Fellows Program at MIT Sloan. Any omissions are unintentional. Above all, I dedicate this piece to my wife Elisabeth and my son Yahnis whose immense love illuminates my every day.

1. See http://www.time.com/time/interactive/0,31813,1681791,00.html. "Time's Person of the Year" for 2006 and 2010. Accessed June 25, 2011.

2. A list of over 1,200 crowdsourcing initiatives can be found at http://www.crowdsourcing.org/directory. Accessed on June 25, 2011.

3. See Villarroel (2008), Malone et al. (2010), and Quinn and Bederson (2011). A good overview of various taxonomies of the field of crowdsourcing can be found in Geiger et al. (2011).

4. See Britannica's own product description at http://www.britannica.co.uk/ebproducts/EBSet.asp, and http://www.britannicastore.com/the-encyclop+aeligdia-britannica-2010-copyright/invt/printset10/. Accessed on June 3, 2012.

5. See http://www.britannica.co.uk/ebproducts/EBSet.asp. Accessed on April 9, 2011.

6. Stross (1996: 80). In his own testimony, Britannica's former Editor in Chief (1992–1997) Robert McHenry emphasizes that the Sales Operation at Britannica was the strongest area of the company, not just because it brought revenues for the company but also because many of the company's senior executives originated there. See "The Building of Britannica Online (Corporate Background)" at http://www.howtoknow.com/BOL2.html. Accessed June 25, 2011.

7. In 1989, during similar negotiations between Microsoft and the president of The World Book encyclopedia, Peter Mollman. Mollman noted that his commissioned sales force was 25,000 people strong. Mollman also refused to work with Microsoft, expressing a similar organizational concern to that of Britannica's president (Stross 1996: 82).

8. According to Robert McHenry's testimony, "The salesman, his district manager, that manager's regional manager, and the sales vice president next up the line all collected a commission on the sale." In "The Building of Britannica Online (Corporate Background)" at http://www.howtoknow.com/BOL2.html. Accessed June 25, 2011.

9. See http://www.britannica.com/blogs/2009/04/encarta-rip-cont-a-reply-from-tom-corddry. Accessed on April 7, 2011.

10. Greenstein and Devereux (2006, p. 13).

11. Read the testimony of Britannica's former editor in chief (1992–1997): Robert Dale McHenry, "The Building of Britannica Online (Part II)," available at http://www.howtoknow.com/BOL6.html. Accessed June 25, 2011.

12. See transcript of Bill Gates's speech at Lakeside High School's Anniversary on February 3, 1995: http://www.krsaborio.net/microsoft/research/1995/0203.htm. Accessed on April 7, 2011.

13. Greenstein and Devereux (2006: 17).

14. Ibid.

15. See http://www.britannica.com/EBchecked/topic/186603/encyclopaedia/32027/Online-encyclopaedias. Accessed on April 7, 2011.

16. See http://store.britannica.com/. Accessed on June 3, 2012.

17. See http://encarta.msn.com/artcenter_0/Encyclopedia_Articles.html. Accessed April 4, 2009. The reader may find a copy of this page from the Internet Archive: www.archive.org.

18. See http://meta.wikimedia.org/wiki/List_of_Wikipedias#100_000.2B_articles. Accessed on January 14, 2011.

19. "Wiki" technology is software for creating collaborative content via a web browser. Wikipedia first used UseModWiki a single-file web server perl plugin developed by Clifford Adams, based on the original wiki engine called Wiki Base, which was developed by Ward Cunningham for his WikiWikiWeb project. The origin of the word comes from Hawaiian *wiki*, which means "quick." For more, see http://en.wikipedia.org/wiki/Wiki.

20. Up until December 2007 there were over 1.8 million registered users in the English Wikipedia, and many more anonymous contributors. See Ortega (2009: 44).

21. Wikipedia administrators—also referred to as "sysops"—can block other users and delete entire pages. See more at http://en.wikipedia.org/wiki/Community_of_Wikipedia#Expansion_of_administrator_authority. Accessed April 29, 2011.

22. In his seminal work, Hayek (1945) argued that "data" are distributed among individuals in society, and there are no means for the whole society to "give" these data to a single mind. While Hayek's argument is still applicable, wiki technology was a giant step toward changing this claim.

23. According to Alexa.com rankings of Internet traffic, MSN.com ranked second in the world after Yahoo.com. For a snapshot of the global top websites on February 2, 2004, see the Internet archive: http://web.archive.org/web/20040202000309/http://www.alexa.com/site/ds/top_sites?ts_mode=global&lang=none.

24. See "Fatally Flawed—Refuting the recent study on encyclopedic accuracy by the journal Nature." Encyclopædia Britannica, Inc., March 2006. Available at http://corporate.britannica.com/britannica_nature_response.pdf . Accessed June 26, 2011.

25. See http://www.nature.com/nature/britannica/eb_advert_response_final.pdf. Accessed June 26, 2011.

26. The correction effort of the Wikipedia entries began within hours of the publication of the *Nature* study, and it was considered complete on January 25, 2006. For details on the correction effort, see http://en.wikipedia.org/wiki/Wikipedia:External_peer_review#Correction_progress. Accessed June 26, 2011.

27. See http://wikimediafoundation.org/wiki/Budget/2005. Wikipedia Budget for 4Q'05. Last accessed March 1, 2011.

28. See http://bits.blogs.nytimes.com/2009/03/30/microsoft-encarta-dies-after-long-battle-with-wikipedia. March 30, 2009. Last accessed February 28, 2011.

29. See http://www.nytimes.com/2006/10/09/business/09cnd-deal.html. October 9, 2006. Last accessed February 28, 2011.

30. See http://www.nytimes.com/2007/10/25/technology/25facebook.html. October 24, 2007. Last accessed February 28, 2011.

31. Moore's law states that computing capacity doubles about every eighteen months for the same cost (Moore 1965). This is the value you perceive when you see more powerful computers that are also more affordable every year. Metcalfe's law states that the value of a communication system is proportional to the square of the number of interconnected nodes in the system (Metcalfe 1996). This is the value you perceive when connecting your computer to the Internet. Reed's law states that the value of social networks grows exponentially with the size of the network (Reed 1999). This is the value you perceive from joining various "online communities" such as those found on Facebook.

32. Relative to organizational resistance or inertia found within the boundaries of the formal organization (Hannan and Freeman 1984).

33. With acknowledged limitations related to language, the law in different countries, the participant's own interest to participate, and so forth.

34. See Harhoff et al. (2003) and Henkel (2006).

35. See: http://www.facebook.com/press/info.php?statistics. Accessed on June 27, 2011.

36. Facebook officially announced the size of its user base to be 50 million in October 2007, and then 500 million in July 2010. See Facebook timeline at http://www.facebook.com/press/info.php?timeline. Accessed on June 27, 2011.

37. Netflix Prize: www.netflixprize.com. Statistics downloaded on April 21, 2008.

38. See Villarroel, Taylor, and Tucci (2010).

39. Villarroel (2008, ch. 13) and Villarroel and Taylor (2007, 2008).

References and Further Reading

Baldwin, C., and E. von Hippel. 2009. Modeling a paradigm shift: From producer innovation to user and open collaborative innovation. Working paper 4764–09. MIT Sloan School of Management.

Barney, J. 1991. Firm resources and sustained competitive advantage. *Journal of Management* 17 (1): 99–120.

Briscoe, B., A. Odlyzko, and B. Tilly. 2006. Metcalfe's law is wrong: Communications networks increase in value as they add members, but by how much? *Spectrum, IEEE* 43 (7): 34–39.

Chesbrough, H. 2003. *Open innovation: The new imperative for creating and profiting from technology*. Boston: Harvard Business School Press.

Chesbrough, H. 2006. *Open Business Models: How to Thrive in the New Innovation Landscape*. Boston: Harvard Business School Press.

Eisenhardt, K., and J. A. Martin. 2000. Dynamic capabilities: What are they? *Strategic Management Journal* 21 (10–11): 1105–1121.

Ethiraj, S. K., and D. Levinthal. 2004. Modularity and innovation in complex systems. *Management Science* 50 (2): 159–73.

Geiger, D., S. Seedorf, T. Schulze, R. Nickerson, and M. Schader. 2011. Managing the crowd: Towards a taxonomy of crowdsourcing processes. In *Proceedings of the Seventeenth Americas Conference on Information Systems (AMCIS)*, August 4–7, 2011. Detroit, MI.

Gentry, C., Z. Ramzan, and S. Stubblebine. 2005. Secure distributed human computation. In *Proceedings of the 6th ACM Conference on Electronic Commerce (EC '05)*, June 5–8, 2005, Vancouver.

Ghemawat, P. 1991. *Commitment: The Dynamic of Strategy*. New York: Free press.

Ghemawat, P. 2001. *Strategy and the Business Landscape*. New York: Prentice Hall.

Gibbons R., and R. Henderson. 2011. Relational contracts and organizational capabilities. *Organization Science*, forthcoming.

Giles, J. 2005. Encyclopedias go head to head. *Nature* 438 (7070): 900–901.

Greenstein, S., and M. Devereux. 2006. The crisis at encyclopedia Britannica. Case study 5-306-504. Kellogg School of Management. Northwestern University, Evanston.

Hannan, M., and J. Freeman. 1984. Structural inertia and organizational change. *American Sociological Review* 49 (2): 149–64.

Hayek, F. A. 1945. The use of knowledge in society. *American Economic Review* 35 (4): 519–30.

Hobday, M. 1998. Product complexity, innovation and industrial organization. *Research Policy* 26 (6): 689–710.

Howe, J. 2006. The rise of crowdsourcing. *Wired Magazine*, 14 (6).

Lakhani, K., and J. Panetta. 2007. The principles of distributed innovation. *Innovations: Technology, Governance, Globalization* 2 (3): 97–112.

Malone, T., R. Laubacher, and C. Dellarocas. 2010. The collective intelligence genome. *MIT Sloan Management Review* 51 (3): 21–31.

Metcalfe, R. 1996. There oughta be a law. *New York Times,* July 15.

Moore, G. E. 1965. Cramming more components onto integrated circuits. *Electronics* 38 (8): 114–17.

Nature. 2005. Supplementary information to accompany Nature news article. Internet encyclopaedias go head to head. *Nature* (438): 900–901. Available at: http://www.nature.com/nature/journal/v438/n7070/extref/438900a-s1.doc. Retrived on June 26, 2011.

Ortega, J. F. 2009. Wikipedia: A quantitative analysis. Unpublished PhD dissertation. Escuela Técnica Superior de Ingeniería de Telecomunicación, Madrid.

Porter, M. E. 1979. The structure within industries and companie's performance. *Review of Economics and Statistics* 61 (2): 214–27.

Quinn, A. J., and B. B. Bederson. 2011. Human computation: A survey and taxonomy of a growing field. *Human–Computer Interaction* 27: 1403–12.

Raymond, E. 1999. The cathedral and the bazaar. *Knowledge, Technology, and Policy* 12 (3): 23–49.

Reed, D.P. 1999. That sneaky exponential: Beyond Metcalfe's law to the power of community building. *Context Magazine* (spring).

S&E Indicators. 2010. Science and Engineering Indicators 2010. Available at: http://www.nsf.gov/statistics/seind10/pdfstart.htm. Accessed on September 2010.

Sorkin, A. R., and J. W. Peters. 2006. Google to acquire YouTube for $1.65 billion. *New York Times,* October 9. Available at: http://www.nytimes.com/2006/10/09/business/09cnd-deal.html.

Stone, B. 2007. Microsoft buys stake in Facebook. *New York Times,* October 25. Available at: http://www.nytimes.com/2007/10/25/technology/25facebook.html.

Stross, R. E. 1996. *The Microsoft Way: The Real Story of How the Company Outsmarts Its Competition.* New York: Perseus Books.

Van den Ende, J., J. A. Villarroel, and C. L. Tucci. 2009. Strategic crowdsourcing: Orchestrating innovation through the cream of the crowd. Symposium. In *Proceedings of Academy of Management Annual Meeting,* August 11, Chicago.

Villarroel, J. A. 2008. Open source corporate strategy (OSCS): Unveiling the firm's open sources of competitive advantage. Doctoral dissertation 4173, EPFL, Switzerland, August 28. Available at: http://library.epfl.ch/theses/?nr=4173.

Villarroel, J. A., and A. Gorbatai, eds. 2011a. The global ecology of crowdsourcing. In *Proceedings of Academy of Management Annual Meeting,* August 15, San Antonio, TX.

Villarroel, J. A., and A. Gorbatai, eds. 2011b. Online distributed organization. In *Proceedings of Academy of Management Annual Meeting,* August 16, San Antonio, TX.

Villarroel, J. A., and Reis, F. 2010a. A stock-market for innovation (SMI): Unveilling the efffects of gambling behavior on innovation performance. *Proceedings of Informatik 2010: Services Science—Neue perspektiven fur die Informatik*. Leipzig.

Villarroel, J. A., and Reis, F. 2010b. Intra-corporate crowdsourcing (ICC): Leveraging upon rank and site marginality for innovation. In *Proceedings of Crowdconf 2010: The World's First Conference on the Future of Distributed Work*. October 4, San Francisco. Accepted papers: http://www.crowdconf2010.com/papers.html

Villarroel, J. A., and Reis, F. 2012. Crowdsourcing corporate innovation: Bridging the remote knowledge silos of the multi-business firm. Proceedings of the Academy of Management Annual Meeting, August 7. Boston.

Villarroel, J. A., and Taylor, J. E. 2007. Managing competing communities of practice: The impact of open source and knowledge bridging on system-level learning. In *Proceedings of the North American Association for Computational Social and Organization Sciences* (NAACSOS), June 7–9, Atlanta. Winner, Best Paper Award.

Villarroel, J. A., and Taylor, J. E. 2008. Performance implications of knowledge brokering in open source communities of practice. In *Proceedings of the Academy of Management Annual Meeting,* August 8–13, Anaheim CA.

Villarroel, J. A., J. E. Taylor, and C. L. Tucci. 2010. Competitive advantage from knowledge brokering in distributed innovation. In *Proceedings of the Strategic Management Society International Conference*, September 12–15, Rome.

Villarroel, J. A., and F. Reis. 2010. Intra-corporate crowdsourcing (ICC): Leveraging upon rank and site marginality for innovation. In *Proceedings of the World's First Conference on the Future of Distributed Work* (CrowdConf-2010), October 4, San Francisco.

Villarroel, J. A., and Tucci, C. L., eds. 2007. Open source corporate strategy (OSCS): Reaching outside the firm's boundaries to tap upon global talent. Symposium. In *Proceedings of Academy of Management Annual Meeting*, August 6, Philadelphia.

von Hippel, E., and R. Katz. 2002. Shifting innovation to users via toolkits. *Management Science* 48 (7): 821–33.

III TRENDS IN OPEN INNOVATION

12 Educating Open Innovation Ambassadors

Anne-Katrin Neyer and Nizar Abdelkafi

Introduction

Tim, Paul, and Luisa, caricatured in figure 12.1, have just received their university degrees and are ready to start their first job. However, they are asking themselves: Are we well prepared? Do we have the skills to do a great job in an increasingly global, virtual, technology-mediated, work environment? Are we ready for what Lynda Gratton (2011) recently called "the shift," that is, the future of work? At the same time their potential employers are asking similar questions: Who can we hire with the ability to interact with others who have different backgrounds, functions, and interests (Neyer et al. 2009)? Who can be open enough to overcome long-recognized but still formidable barriers to innovation, such as the "not-invented-here" dilemma (Katz and Allen 1982) and group think (Janis 1982)?

We believe these pressing questions challenge higher education and that one promising response is to integrate an "open perspective" into universities. After getting their academic degrees many students will act as boundary spanners in increasingly open business environments. Educational institutions should do much more to prepare them for the challenges involved.

The first objective of this chapter is to summarize experience at a large German university aimed at helping students like Tim, Paul, and Luisa overcome the well-known, but still dominant barriers to innovation and to train them to develop an open innovation mindset. We propose that the use of well-designed teaching tools in class can allow students to become what we call "open innovation ambassadors." The analogy is to political ambassadors who represent their nations in foreign territories and work on protecting the values and interests of their home countries abroad. Open innovation ambassadors similarly have the mission to bring knowledge of open innovation principles to their employers and use them as they start working to advance the organization's interests.

Figure 12.1
Three students (potential employees)

Given the still relatively new phenomenon of open innovation and the needed skills of individuals working in such open organizations, we recognize an imbalance between what industry demands and what educational institutions offer. We propose that this may no longer only result from *what* is being taught but also *how* the content is delivered. The pressing issue thus is: What teaching methods can be used to support students in becoming open innovation ambassadors who recognize and value the benefits of spanning boundaries across different types of innovators?

The second objective of the chapter is to argue that educating students to become open innovation ambassadors requires that universities rethink their own approach to teaching and open themselves to a new generation of innovators. We term this ideal "open school" (Abdelkafi et al. 2010). Open school goes beyond existing concepts that focus on freely revealing teaching materials to the outside world, including but not limited to students themselves. Open school views educational institutions as open institutions in which students are considered as active university staff and knowledge producers.

Designing a Teaching Tool for Educating Open Innovation Ambassadors

Educating open innovation ambassadors means integrating lessons from innovation, technology, cooperation, and entrepreneurship into the classroom. This may imply, for instance, developing ambidextrous thinking (Tushman and O'Reilly 1996) that involves the left and right brains of students or introducing them to the world of cooperation and teamwork. In addition we argue that open innovation ambassadors could be educated through increased exposure to central skills well known from innovation management literature: critical thinking, cooperation, teamwork, and initiative-taking. Creating innovative-oriented mindsets in students also calls for the use of discontinuous models in teaching and adapting the content of courses to the learning process of learners.

The open innovation literature offers a variety of tools and methods, as described by Kathrin Möslein in chapter 5, which are designed to integrate different types of innovators into an organization's innovation process. While helping to design, apply, and evaluate some of these tools in business contexts, we became fascinated by the idea of whether innovation contests in particular could be of value in educating our students. Our experience-based proposition was that, by design, innovation contests are a tool that could help students learn how to cooperatively interact with each other while jointly developing innovative solutions.

This proposition is supported by the educational approach of action learning (Marquardt 1999). Action learning is typically applied in a group setting that aims at generating learning from human interaction, especially real-time work problems. There are six distinct interactive components of action learning (Marquardt 1999), which are reflected in the design of innovation contests:

1. *A problem:* A complex issue that one or more organizations are struggling with is selected as a learning objective. This corresponds to the task in innovation contests.

2. *The group:* The group comprises a limited number of individuals who meet to exchange ideas, to describe the problems they face, and to report on the progress they have made. This corresponds to the participants in an innovation contest.

3. *A questioning and reflective process:* This process builds on Revans's (1998) formula for learning in action: $L = P + Q$, where L stands for learning, P for programmed learning, and Q for questioning that aims to create insights into what individuals feel, see, or hear. We argue that this formula also applies to innovation contests that offer a community function, since individuals can comment and evaluate the ideas suggested by other participants.

4. *Commitment to taking action:* The focus of action learning is on implementation rather than on giving recommendations to others. In a typical innovation contest this crucial element of action learning can be supported by letting participants work on a real innovation task rather than telling or teaching them about innovation. Instead of learning theory about the inherent challenges of cooperation in an open environment, for example, they are required to design and implement a real solution for a particular innovation challenge, while working as a team.

5. *Commitment to learning:* Action learning goes beyond solving immediate problems, it aims to support an increase in the knowledge and capability to adapt to change. Commitment to learning in innovation contests can be emphasized by

enabling participants to reflect on what went well and what led to little or no success during the problem-solving process.

6. *The facilitator:* A facilitator or instructor can support a group in its learning process by taking on several roles: coordinator, catalyst, observer, climate setter, and communication enabler. In innovation contests, a moderator takes on these roles.

Case Study: University of Erlangen-Nuremberg

In the School of Business and Economics of the University of Erlangen-Nurnberg in Germany, each winter semester since the academic year 2007–2008, almost 1,200 first-year bachelor students are confronted with a demanding innovation contest in the class "Basics of e-Business." To set up this open innovation contest, the teaching staff uses HYVE AG's software, IDEANET, an open web-based platform for crowdsourcing which is described further in Chapter 14.

For example, in the 2009–10 winter semester, 1,198 students participated in the contest (49.8 percent male and 50.2 percent female). Study backgrounds were management (62.1 percent), international business (6.9 percent), information systems (6.7 percent), industrial engineering (11.2 percent), social economics (10.6 percent), and business education (2.5 percent). Students had to register on the platform to participate in the contest. They were randomly matched with a maximum of five colleagues to make a group. Relevant contact information of teammates was provided on the individual profile of each participant.

The task was to create and submit business concepts for service innovations based on smartphones. Each group was assigned to one of three contexts: (1) leisure and entertainment, (2) fitness and health care, or (3) education. The task of the innovation contest was to develop an innovative (business) concept for a service innovation in the assigned area that had the potential to solve an everyday problem. In total, 265 concepts were developed during six weeks (44 days). Additionally 810 comments (with 177 words on average) and 9,011 votes were given, resulting in an average of 3.06 comments and 37.86 votes per concept. Finally, the concepts were evaluated by experts in the field (faculty plus decision makers from corporate partners). The work on the innovation task followed four steps as summarized in figure 12.2.

Step 1: Search for Ideas

What would be an innovative solution? Do we have too many ideas? Which one should we choose? Do we all agree on the choice made? If so, how can we convince the "others," those outside of our group, that this is the most innovative solution?

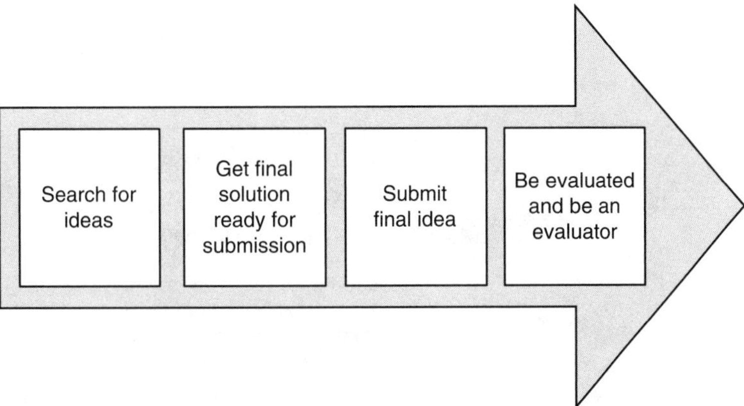

Figure 12.2
Four steps while working on the innovation task

Step 2: Get a Specific Solution Ready for Submission

What would be the best description of the business idea we have now chosen to work on? Have we clearly identified the value for the customer? Is it technically possible to implement the idea? What would be the best way to visualize our concept? Should we use flow charts, mock-ups, drawings, photo stories, or movies?

Step 3: Submit Final Idea

Do we have all information ready to fill in the predefined form for textual description on the innovation contest platform? Have we saved our concept in the right format to upload it on the platform? Will we collaboratively edit the concept on the platform, which is possible until the end of run-time?

Step 4: Be Evaluated and Become an Evaluator

How will the others evaluate our ideas? What comments do they write? How do we evaluate the ideas of the others? Thumbs up or down?

The winning team of the 2009–10 contest came up with the idea shown in figure 12.3. Imagine the following situation: You come back from holidays, the plane has been delayed, your luggage is lost, and even though you have asked the taxi driver to ignore all the red lights, your favorite grocery store has closed the minute before you arrive. Not to mention that the next day is a Sunday. To avoid stressful situation like this, the winning team developed the following business concept: Timeless Shopping. By using your smartphone, you can order your groceries whenever and wherever you

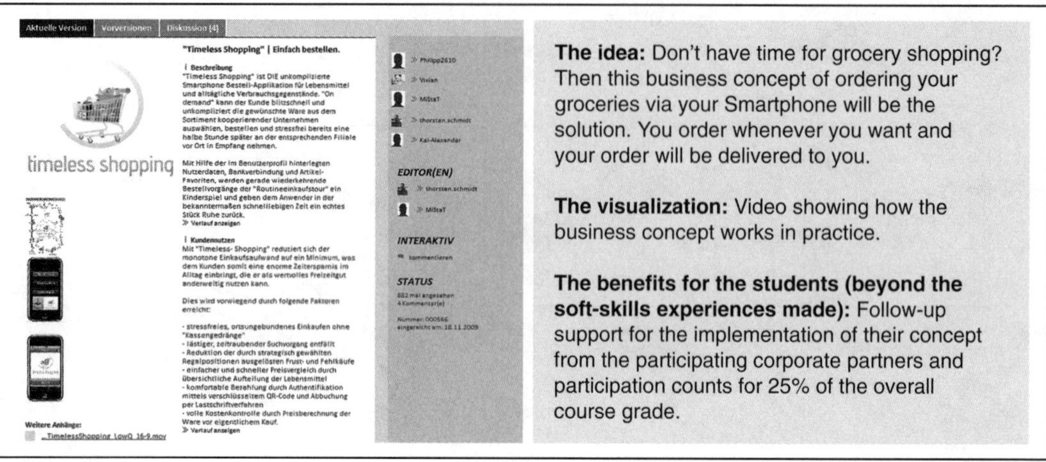

Figure 12.3
Winning idea: Timeless shopping

Table 12.1
What students experience while working on the innovation contest

Experience on the go	Experiences rooted in the design of the innovation contest
Cognitive experience	Parallel experience of becoming an innovator and engaging as a group worker
Emotional experience	Extent of motivation from being evaluated by peers and jury
Operational experience	Discrepancy between self-reflection and others' opinions of the group work

want, and your order will be delivered to you. By presenting their idea in form of a video, they convinced their peers and the jury of experts that they had a winning idea.

Data Collection and Analysis

In 2010 we collected students' reflections on their innovation contest experiences via questionnaire. We grouped their comments as shown in table 12.1. The first category deals with student experiences "on the go," while working on the innovation challenge. They reported three distinct types of experience: cognitive, emotional, and operational. The second category of reflections is rooted in the design of an innovation contest as a teaching method. Again, the data suggest three main types of learning: the double experience of becoming an innovator and engaging as a group worker, the extent of motivation due to the prospect of being evaluated by peers and jury, and the discrepancy between one's own and others' reflections on the group work.

Innovation Contests Lead to Cognitive, Emotional, and Operational Experiences

Let us assume that Tim, Paul, and Luisa had been involved in an innovation contest during their studies. What might they have learned? First, when asked about the extent of cooperation within their groups, students mentioned the problems that arise because of the differences in backgrounds of the group members. In particular, different levels of technical skills, education, and language backgrounds constitute major issues that need to be solved while working on the innovation task. Students similarly reported different understandings they had in their groups with regard to the ideas per se, and more specifically about the long discussions they had about how an innovative contribution should be visualized. However, even though they are struggling with agreeing on the optimal type of visualization, the cognitive process of discussing, negotiating, and visualizing their ideas helped them derive a shared mental model of options.

Second, while working in their groups, students noticed that they had to cooperate with people they had not previously known. Students reported the emotional feelings they had while working with "strangers" in their groups, especially with regard to two issues: the problem of unmotivated group partners and dogmatic behavior. Concerning the motivation problem, students reported on how difficult it is to cooperate with group members who pursue different goals. Those who were highly motivated at the beginning of the contest struggled with agreeing on how activities should be managed if students of the same group were less motivated than they were. No motivation was expressed in feelings such as "why should I participate, if there are others in the group who will do the work anyway?" These issues restricted the extent of cooperation among the students. With respect to dogmatic behavior, some students experienced the situation that some members of their groups pushed their own ideas forward, while completely ignoring those of the other group members.

Third, students not only reflected on cognitive and emotional experiences but also highlighted the issue of finding time to meet to work on the task. Because students had different time schedules and lived in different cities, cooperation was hindered, even if a high willingness to cooperate existed among all team members.

From these remarks, and those made by other classes, we concluded that the use of innovation contests as a teaching tool can lead to the achievement of five learning objectives. Clearly, these are rooted in the cognitive, emotional, and operational experience, which jointly support the education of open innovation ambassadors.

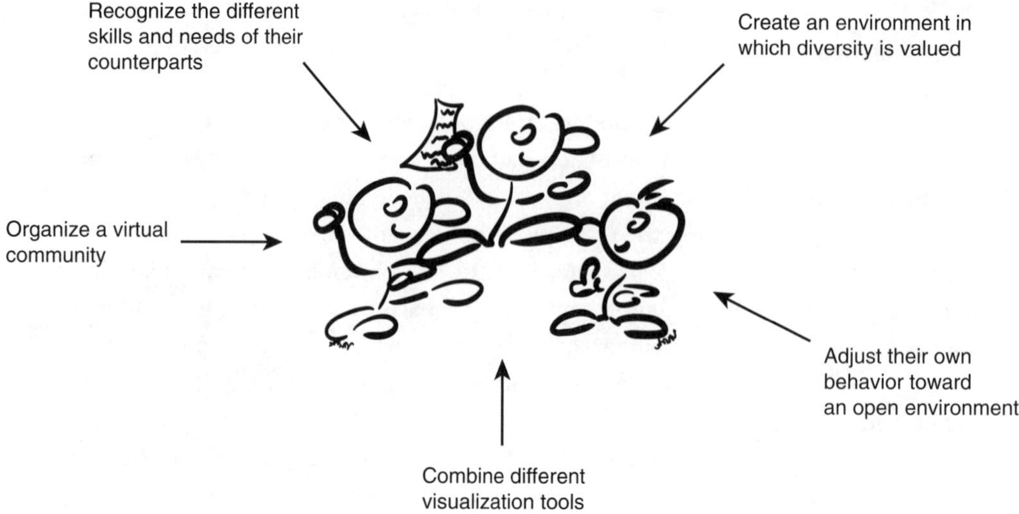

Figure 12.4
Five learning objectives rooted in the cognitive, emotional, and operation experiences

As illustrated in figure 12.4, by the end of the open innovation experience many students like Tim, Paul, and Luisa, were able to:

- recognize the different skills and needs of their counterparts,
- create an environment in which diversity is valued,
- adjust their own behavior toward an open environment,
- combine different visualization tools, and
- organize a virtual community.

Experiences Rooted in the Design of the Innovation Contest

What else makes it worthwhile to implement an innovation contest as a teaching tool? We find that students like Tim, Paul, and Luisa would not only profit from direct experience of open innovation but also from reflections rooted in the design of the innovation contests.

First, when students develop a solution to the innovation challenge, they can learn about themselves taking on the role of an innovator: How do I react to this challenge of coming up with something new? How do I deal with openly defined and unstructured tasks? Am I scared? Am I excited? Am I enjoying the work on the innovation contest platform? In addition to dealing with these questions, students had to become a group worker to get the task done. Thus they not only experience what being an innovator means but also what is expected of them as a group worker.

Second, students become more motivated by the prospect of evaluation. In addition to a large jury comprised of supervisors and external innovation experts, the peers evaluated their contributions. Knowing that their peers could comment on and criticize their innovations encouraged students to work cooperatively on the innovation challenge.

Third, the students' reflections suggest that even in the groups whose ideas were ranked among the top 10, students disagreed in their perceptions regarding the success and failure of group work. For instance, in some groups up to three members reported positive experiences whereas the remaining one or two reported negative experiences. Especially when students worked with group members they had not known before the class, they were confronted with a situation that can typically arise in business. They had to find solutions to the question of what to do if one or two of the group members were not willing to work the way the majority of the group does. From the students' reflections we found that they had to struggle between ignoring those group members and or expending time and energy to encourage them to participate.

Whereas we have already identified distinct learning objectives that are rooted in the cognitive, emotional, and operational experiences of students, the findings presented above also support a fourth learning objective rooted in the design of innovation contests, as summarized in figure 12.5. We found that by the end of the open innovation experience students like Tim, Paul and Luisa were able:

- to evaluate their own emotions, feelings, and behavior in an open innovation setting;
- to observe their own and others' reaction to socially undesirable behavior;
- to experience different forms of motivation; and
- to comprehend that tools such innovation contests are more than "tools for fun."

Implications for Innovation Contests as a Teaching Tool to Educate Open Innovation Ambassadors

When students are provided the opportunity to interact in an open environment, they can further develop the specific cognitive, emotional, and operational skills that enable them to become open innovation ambassadors. By understanding innovation contests as a teaching tool that supports action learning, students are able to experience an innovation environment with individuals they don't know, who come from different technical areas, and who might have different interests.

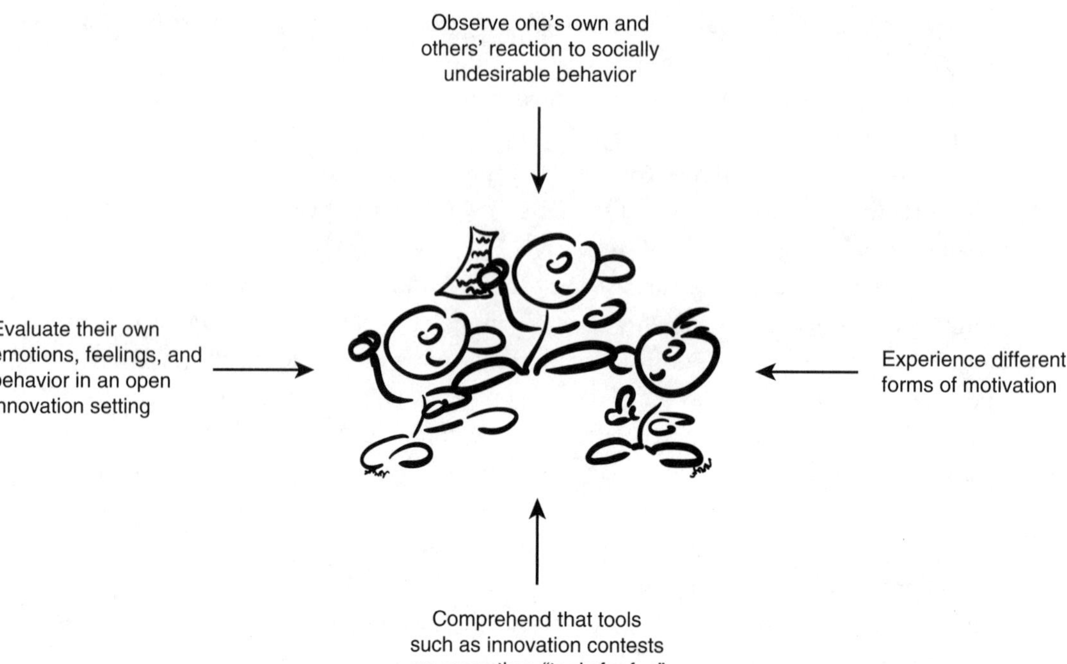

Figure 12.5
Four learning objectives rooted in the design of the innovation contest

Having thus argued that the learning objectives to be achieved depend on the design of the innovation contest, we discuss in the following paragraphs some of the design parameters that we found to be crucial.

1. Defining the Task

The innovation task should be carefully chosen and described in considerable detail. It should be achievable; otherwise, it is difficult to get the students motivated to participate in the innovation contest. But how specific should the task description be? Our experience shows that students may find it hard to make a contribution when the tasks are very specific. Very specific tasks may be more suitable for experts than students. Very general tasks, however, may trigger difficulties for students if they feel lost or without sufficient understanding of what they are asked to do. Therefore the task should balance appropriate degrees of specificity and generality.

In addition, students must feel that the task is feasible but challenging. They must feel that the task requires competencies and skills they have; at the same time the task should not be boring but present an intellectual puzzle. Besides the task description, students in our innovation challenges are asked to think about the technical and economical achievability of their new ideas. It seems useful to ask students to think of possible barriers, problems, and advantages of the innovation they propose.

In defining the task, one could predefine the methods and tools that students could use to reach their solutions. Specifically, they could be asked to use a variety of visualization tools, thereby encouraging them to try out new technologies they are not yet familiar with. If experimenting with different techniques is required, students may become open to new, unfamiliar, and nonconventional tools that go beyond familiar brainstorming for idea generation or PowerPoint slides for presenting solutions.

2. *Offering Trials before Official Start*

Before officially launching an innovation contest, it can be advantageous to provide students with some time to "play" and get comfortable with an open innovation platform. The main question that the instructor should ask is: "Is the Internet platform for ideation intuitive to use?" If the platform is easy to utilize, then trials are not necessary. If not, then it is wise to provide the students with a week or so to test the platform. Therefore it is up to the instructor to evaluate the degree of difficulty the platform presents and to decide whether it is appropriate to offer a trial phase.

3. *Motivating Participation*

When the innovation contest is an integral part of the curriculum, instructors can use grades to achieve 100 percent participation. Grades provide extrinsic motivation, like money rewards offered to solvers of an innovation contest organized by industry. It is relatively easy to similarly propose that the higher the activity level and the more innovative the ideas that a student comes up with, the better the grade. The literature on creativity (e.g., Amabile 1998) and open source innovation (e.g., von Hippel 2005), emphasizes the importance of intrinsic motivation. But what do instructors have to do to trigger intrinsic motivation engine?

Intrinsic motivation can be difficult to activate. Instructors need to find a way to relate the innovation contest objectives with the personal goals of students. They could explain to students that participation in innovation contests improves their problem-solving skills. We have also experimented with formulating tasks in terms of problems students are directly concerned about, such as an improvement in the university's daily business, like operating the student cafeteria more efficiently. If students are promised that the best ideas will be implemented, the level of intrinsic motivation seems to increase.

4. Evaluating Students' Performance

Students could be evaluated individually and as a group. The individual performance depends on a student's contribution to the group's activity; the higher the participation level and the quality of the contributions (e.g., ideas, comments, and files uploaded), the higher the student's individual performance mark.

When the overall team's performance is evaluated, all members of a team get the same grade. At the end of the innovation contest, the teams can be invited to present their ideas in a class session so that the instructor can assess the final result. The instructor can also involve other members of the class in the evaluation process. To ease the burden of evaluation, instructors could avoid giving individual grades and only assess the final group presentations. However, class presentations are only possible if the number of groups is of reasonable size. For instance, in our case study involving 1,200 students, there were so many teams that it was not possible to schedule a session for final presentations, so only the innovations developed by the top 10 teams are presented in the final classroom session.

5. Pre-defining Duration

From our experience an innovation contest should last six to eight weeks. The rationale behind this ample time period is to avoid time pressure, which can kill creativity (e.g., Goffin et al. 2009). Ideally contests should be over two weeks before examination periods begin. As students get busy preparing for their exams, they have less time to contribute to the innovation contest.

6. Use Moderators for Content- and Process-Related Feedback

Although, as our findings show, students benefit from the cognitive, emotional, and operational experiences acquired in working together on innovation tasks, they also need process-related support. How does the teaching staff ensure a smooth interaction between students during the innovation contest? They must define the rules of the game. It should be clear for students that they must treat each other equably, avoiding unnecessary negative comments. Of course, other conflicts can arise, such as when one group claims that its idea has been overtaken by another group, and these must be addressed on an ad hoc basis.

7. Integrate Readings on a Click

We suggest providing academic readings on the challenges of group work and working with new technology on the platform. By making these readings available on the platform, students can get immediate information if they are struggling with the task or team issues. We find that students are likely to consult the readings when they know that the information they get has a high chance of being immediately applicable.

Conclusion: Toward Open School

What needs to be done to provide students like Tim, Paul, and Luisa with an education that prepares them to work in an increasingly open work environment? Anchoring the education of open innovation ambassadors in universities requires more than the design and implementation of innovative teaching methods. As in private organizations, the organizational context needs to fit this change in teaching method. We argue that a new understanding of the contextual setting of universities is required. But what are the main characteristics of this change, and how can it improve higher education?

We propose a new idea, called the open school. An open school should produce a new mindset that goes beyond the use of open innovation methods in the classroom. An open school applies the principles of openness not just in a teaching environment but in all areas of the university. Consequently students have the opportunity to reinforce the skills needed to exercise their roles as open innovation ambassadors.

In an open school environment, the university should remove boundaries to enable closer connections to its students. For example, the university should provide a platform on which students can interact and work collaboratively to solve problems or carry out activities they feel are important. To make an open school happen, is an online platform supported by Internet technologies such as the one we used in the case study necessary?

In general, we believe there is no typical platform for the support of an open school; the platform can be online (web-based software) or offline (e.g., workshop spaces in which students make use of tools like pin boards and sticky notes to visualize their joint ideas). The main requirement of such platforms is that they are flexible and capable of involving students in different types of activities. It should be noted, however, that an online platform requires much less efforts than an offline workshop when setting up a new task. In addition students can work on tasks around the clock if they are submitted over an online platform. Therefore we recommend using web-based platforms to implement the open school concept. Information technology that supports open source development, online communities, creation of open contents, and innovation competitions facilitate an open school environment. For instance, in the case study presented above, HYVE's IDEANET web-based software for crowd sourcing supports a virtually unlimited and varied set of activities. They may range from simple tasks such as idea competitions aimed at improving university's life, to more complex tasks such as developing innovative learning materials or contributing to research projects.

Students can share their ideas, concepts, or drafts to help gradually develop solutions to the problems posted on the platform. These activities are not necessarily integrated with a curriculum but may be initiated anytime by students, the university's administration, or teaching and research staff. In line with the principles of Internet communities and open source innovation, members of the university community can work collaboratively to improve the ideas of other participants, and create new ideas. With open school, universities have improved access to intellectual resources that have been insufficiently exploited in the past. Their students are enabled to participate more as active staff members than passive consumers.

In theory, the idea of an open school seems achievable, but are there any difficulties that universities can encounter, if they decide to embark on such a project? We believe that the challenges of creating an open school are very similar to the challenges faced by those who wish to establish online communities. It is hard to predict whether a virtual community will be popular or if an open source project will be successful. A plethora of projects fail because they do not attract a critical mass of developers or contributors (e.g., Abdelkafi et al. 2009). Participation is therefore a crucial element for the success of these projects. In open source development, for instance, the level of participation depends on internal factors such as intrinsic motivation or altruism, and external rewards such as self-marketing or revenues (e.g., von Hippel 2005; Hars and Ou 2002). Consequently an open school project must attract a sufficient number of students who are willing to participate in such an initiative.

Being aware of its inherent challenges, an open school should have some specific features. First, students could be motivated to make contributions if they are directly affected by problems posted on the platform. If a problem is 'solved,' then the results should be obvious to everybody, in particular to the contributors, who personally profit from the improved situation. The analogy in open source software development, for example, is that users who have programming capabilities tend to be highly interested in advancing the software being worked on.

Second, the university should have control of important reward mechanisms; for example, student contributions can be linked to a course grade, if the activity is integrated in a curriculum. Third, the open school platform could be exploited to post problems coming from companies. The university's staff could serve as an important interface to industry. For example, it might be arranged that students with the best contributions to an industry project would have a chance to meet company representatives, which might lead to later employment.

In short, the open school concept constitutes a paradigm shift in higher education. Open schools also provide some answers to the question of how to rethink and modernize higher education at universities. In the digital age, students want more than traditional lectures and look for more flexibility in their studies (Tapscott and Williams 2010). The new possibilities of digital technology make it obvious that universities can play more of a role in industry innovations than they do today.

Today students can access online encyclopedias, they can watch the online lectures of instructors from the best universities worldwide, and they can be members of social networks and communities to exchange information. Therefore access to knowledge is no longer a problem, as knowledge is all around, a few clicks away. The value that lectures created for students in the past, before Web 2.0, have diminished, and this value diminution will continue, as the capabilities of the Internet improve.

The open school concept fills some gaps between what the university actually offers and what the students are looking for in the digital age. Open school engages students in real life projects, boosting their creativity and enabling them to enhance their learning. Universities are excellent in testing the intelligence and knowledge of students to solve problems for which a solution exists. But why does the university not involve its students in exercising their intelligence to solve problems for which we still have no solution? The innovation contests that have been carried out with students so far constitute a major step toward answering this question and drawing a picture of how universities might usefully change into open schools.

Idea for Innovative Leaders: Live What You Teach

The importance of educating students who are able to act as boundary spanners among different types of inside and outside innovators cannot be emphasized enough. Those who are responsible for educating open innovation ambassadors have to find innovative ways to do so. We have brought the argument forward that the time is right to experiment with tools that have worked well for open innovation in the business context. However, we also stress the need to act with caution in transferring innovation tools to an educational setting.

Leaders (i.e., instructors and policy makers) need to be aware that the implementation of innovation contests, for instance, requires a conscious re-designing of the university environment as well as a structured process and control of content. Thus they have to go beyond understanding innovation tools as mere add-ons in education.

Instead, they should think of these tools as important means to educate open innovation ambassadors.

We believe that the open school concept is the next obligatory step for universities that would like to educate their students to be able participants in a much more open global innovation environment. However, the open school concept requires much more openness of higher education institutions both inside and outside. It is a shift in the way we think of our universities, away from their hierarchical and pedantic foundations to a more dynamic and efficient institutions. We argue that leaders of universities should be aware that the university must change in the digital age, and this change means much more that the digitalization of materials that were once offline. The new media of the digital age open up a variety of new opportunities that were impossible in the past. Nevertheless, the opening of university boundaries is not an end in itself. It is a means that achieves a better integration of students into their universities. The open school engages students in creative ways and generates new ideas that have value. It is the right time to make a better use of students' intellectual capacities, enabling them at the same time to become open innovation ambassadors.

References and Further Reading

Abdelkafi, N., T. Blecker, and C. Raasch. 2009. From open source in the digital to the physical world: A smooth transfer? *Management Decision* 47 (10): 1610–32.

Abdelkafi, N., M. Bartl, J. Füller, C. Ihl, and M. Rieger. 2010. The open school vision—For more openness at universities. Informatik 2010: Service Science—Neue Perspektiven für die Informatik, September–October 2010, Leipzig. In K.-P. Fähnrich and B. Franczyk, eds., *Bonn Gesellschaft für Informatik e.V.* Bonn: Köllen, 949–55.

Amabile, T. M. 1998. How to kill creativity. *Harvard Business Review* 76 (5): 77–87.

Gratton, L. 2011. *The Shift: The Future of Work Is Already Here*. New York: Collins.

Goffin, K., C. Herstatt, and R. Mitchell. 2009. *Innovationsmanagement.* Munich: FinanzBuch Verlag.

Hars, A., and S. Ou. 2002. Working for free? Motivations for participating in open-source projects. *International Journal of Electronic Commerce* 6 (3): 23–37.

Janis, I. L. 1982. *Groupthink: Psychological Studies of Policy Decisions and Fiascoes*, 2nd ed. Boston: Houghton Mifflin.

Katz, R., and T. J. Allen. 1982. Investigating the not invented here (NIH) syndrome: A look at the performance, tenure, and communication patterns of 50 R&D project groups. *R&D Management* 12 (1): 7–20.

Marquardt, M. 1999. *Action Learning in Action: Transforming Problems and People for World-Class Organizational Learning*. Palo Alto: Davies-Black.

Neyer, A. K., A. C. Bullinger, and K. M. Möslein. 2009. Integrating inside and outside innovators: a sociotechnical systems perspective. *R&D Management* 39 (4): 410–19.

Revans, R. 1998. *ABC of Action Learning*. London: Lemos and Crane.

Tapscott, D., and A. D. Williams. 2010. *Macrowikinomics: Rebooting Business and the World*. New York: Portfolio.

Tushman, M. and C. O'Reilly. 1996. Ambidextrous organizations: Managing evolutionary and revolutionary change. *California Management Review* 38 (4): 8–30.

von Hippel, E. 2005. *Democratizing Innovation*. Cambridge: MIT Press.

13 Viral Marketing on Facebook for a New Open Innovation Platform

Catharina van Delden and Nancy Wünderlich

Introduction

Consumers are growing tired of traditional advertising and marketing campaigns (Phillips and Noble 2007). TV watchers often record their favorite shows so that they can leap over advertisements. Internet surfers use ad-blockers. Even those who prefer newspaper and magazine content have a tendency to read online—where advertisement blockers are installed. As traditional advertising thus seems to lose efficiency and coverage, more effective alternatives for reaching desired audiences have to be identified.

Ideas and messages about products and services spread the fastest when people talk about them and recommend their favorites to others (Goldenberg et al. 2001). Every company's marketing department dreams of this viral spread of its ideas (Rayport 1996). As Rosen (2005) notes, a successful virtual campaign is characterized by low budget requirements and high effectiveness in terms of number of people reached in comparison to traditional advertising.

Nowadays, viral marketing does not happen "over the garden fence" but increasingly and much more effectively in places where people meet online (Godes and Mayzlin 2004; Srinivasan et al. 2002; Trusov et al. 2009). Yet companies have much to learn about online marketing. The first thought of many managers regarding viral marketing is to post banners on social sites, just as they appear on Google and other search engines. But these advertisements support little or no viral action.

Social networks represent a much more attractive phenomenon in the world of online advertisement and communication. Companies are able to join social networks such as Facebook and thereby have the opportunity to be a part of online communities (Hanna et al. 2011). Within these communities a company can easily contact and interact with thousands of users and potential customers. And because these networks enjoy high user acceptance and frequent community interactions, they represent very attractive platforms for viral campaigns (Kaplan and Haenlein 2011).

However, in the social network environment new rules for marketing, advertising, and consumer communication seem to apply (Parent et al. 2011). Established marketing ideas often fail and the company with the highest budget and spending does not attract the most customers, instead success is more closely associated with consumer sympathy. Managers therefore have to formulate new approaches to designing and managing campaigns on social networks, especially if they hope for viral advertising.

In this chapter we derive a set of guidelines for those trying to conceptualize and implement viral marketing campaigns in social networks. The guidelines grow out of case study research at innosabi, a leading company on open innovation in Germany. We describe how innosabi successfully implemented results of research on advertising acceptance by virtual community members. Our research shows how the careful analysis of customer needs and behavior contributed to the invention of the open innovation platform unserAller (https://unseraller.de/home), which enables companies to run viral campaigns in social networks and collaboratively develop new products with consumers.

The Power of Social Media

Figure 13.1 illustrates the basic types of social media differentiated by Dan Zarella (2009). In the past few years social networks, shown at the bottom right, have become the fastest growing type of social media on the Internet as well as in companywide

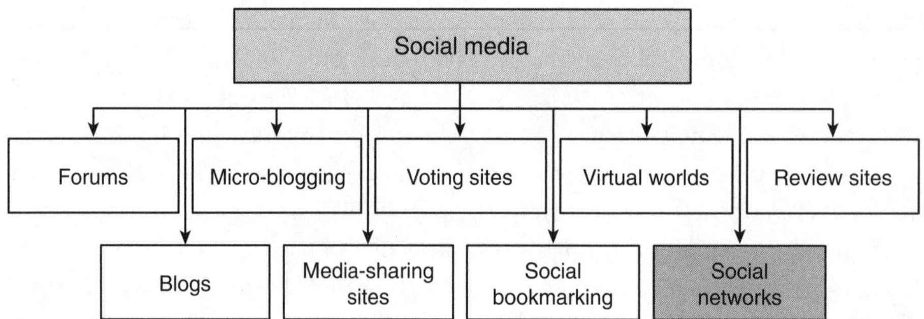

Figure 13.1
Overview over different forms of social media
Source: Zarella (2009)

intranets. By 2009, this form of interaction had overtaken the use of email, which had a reach of 65 percent of online users according to the Nielsen Company (2009). In March 2010, the social network Facebook even surpassed Google in viewed page impressions in the United States (Dougherty, 2010). Facebook alone claimed to have more than 500 million active users worldwide in November 2010. At that point half of the active users were logging in every day. In Germany the user base as of November 2010 was 12,743,900 people, with women and men equally distributed. This represented an increase of 240 percent in less than one year.

Not surprisingly, the amount of time spent in social networks has altered the way consumers conduct their normal daily lives and thus their purchasing behavior. As a consequence, according to a Nielsen (2009: 1) report, "the global media and advertising industries are faced with new challenges around the opportunities and risks this new consumer medium creates."

innosabi's Vision

innosabi enables companies to co-create products with consumers in order to lower the risk of market failure for new products. Managers of innosabi asked themselves two basic questions about making good use of social networks to help their customers communicate and advertise new products: What are the success factors for social network advertising campaigns? And more specifically: Does the motivation for general use of social networks influence the reaction to advertising campaigns?

Managers at innosabi have always been convinced, as Eric von Hippel (2005) says, that only the user of a product really knows what needs and requirements he or she has. They therefore developed the open innovation platform unserAller (German for "ours" or "all of us") to let customers collaboratively make decisions concerning new products. The idea is that these products initially have some market acceptance among those involved and are likely to find broader acceptance because users themselves make key product decisions. Because interaction on a social network can create brand messengers and buyers even before market entry, innosabi started unserAller as a Facebook application, as described in more detail below.

A campaign run for the yellow pages of New Zealand by the agency Colenso BBDO called "the taste of yellow" illustrates the kind of project we expected to be successful. In this campaign a chocolate that tasted "yellow" was developed using Facebook, a webpage, offline tools, and strong PR support. Thousands of users participated in the process (the Facebook fanpage alone reached more than 20,000 people). The chocolate was manufactured in a single run after "Josh," a brand ambassador selected through a video application process, toured the country conducting taste tests. Yellow chocolate became the fastest selling chocolate ever introduced in New Zealand. It was sold for NZ$1.99 (approximately €1.14 or US$1.52), which in New Zealand is a comparably high price for a chocolate. By the end of the campaign, more than 50 percent of the New Zealand population knew of the chocolate with its eye-catching label (van Delden 2011).

By developing unserAller, innosabi is standardizing a similar but expanded process of product development and making it accessible to companies with a consumer goods focus. The current unserAller site is designed to target a student audience in Germany, since students are often early adopters and a trend-setting group of people.

How Market Research Helped Design the Perfect Open Innovation Platform

innosabi conducted four empirical research studies in spring 2010 in order to develop the unserAller platform. The process is visualized in figure 13.2. innosabi first carried out an untargeted, qualitative survey to gain a general understanding of the use of social networks and their possibilities for viral spread. Then a second survey focused on quantifiable issues and targeted students in Germany. As a result of this study Facebook was identified as the social networking site used most by German students. In study three a field experiment featuring different Facebook advertising forms was

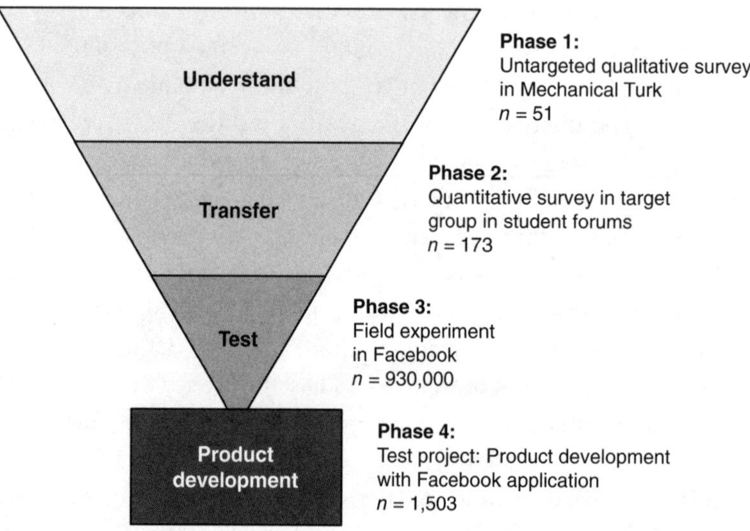

Figure 13.2
Four-phase study design

conducted in order to find an effective way of engaging this group. Based on the results of all three previous studies, the company then moved into phase four, developing the platform with a test project.

Study One: Qualitative Survey on the Nature of Social Networks

Study one was a pilot study intended to help find a starting point for subsequent research and company action. A short qualitative survey was listed on Amazon Mechanical Turk (https://www.mturk.com), an online collective work platform for accomplishing very small tasks. We accepted the work of all 51 participants who answered survey questions in the ten hours they were posted. Each participant received US$0.30 in credits on Amazon.com in return. The majority (37 people or 72.5 percent) came from the United States, while other participants came, in alphabetical order, from Barbados, Bangladesh, Belgium, Canada, China, Egypt, Italy, New Zealand, Pakistan, Portugal, and Romania. 55 percent of all participants were between 20 and 29 years old, 11.7 percent between 30 and 39, and 15.6 percent between 40 and 49.

Four questions were asked:

- *Question 1:* Please describe which networks you use (Facebook, LinkedIn, orkut, MySpace, etc.) . . . and how often you use each!
- *Question 2:* What do you use the networks for? What do you typically do there? Do you like those networks? If yes, what do you like best, and if no, what are you missing?
- *Question 3:* Please describe yourself in at least three sentences.
- *Question 4:* Did something interesting happen to you in those networks? We would be happy if you shared that story with us!"

Figure 13.3 provides a visual overview of the answers to these questions in the form of a tag cloud. The size of the individual words in the figure indicates the frequency with which they were mentioned in the answers. Since Amazon Mechanical Turk is a platform for performing online work, it can be assumed that the majority of participants have an affinity for computers, which implies a different view of marketing on social networks than marketing to less adept computer users. However, the words that dominate this figure seem applicable to a broad group of users, and are consistent with other studies. We still found it helpful to get our own view of the use of social networks. In fact, as these sites mature, we will continue to monitor responses to questions like the four we asked in this first study.

The self-descriptions of participants (requested in question 3) reveal a wide variety of personalities and backgrounds: Some respondents describe their job, some report other characteristics. The self-attributed characteristics vary from intelligent, creative,

Figure 13.3
Tagcloud of answers in study one

witty, and optimistic (Emmi: "I am probably the happiest person I know") to caring, sensitive, and honest, to quiet, reserved, and even anti-social (Pimpystick writes: "I'm a person who thinks 'things never go right for me'. . . and in a way they don't. I smoke too much and am a bit too chubby. Umm I'm boring.") An interesting observation is that many participants state they behave differently online than they do offline. For example, Clara from China says: "I do not have many friends and just stay at home most of the weekends. However, I am a very energetic person in the virtual space."

Further analysis with inductive category creation revealed the following results:

Motivations to use a social networking site (in alphabetical order): Find business partner, find new friends, find new job, find old friends, flirt, inform myself about companies, inform myself about products, let others participate in my life, play, stay in contact with friends, support good causes.

Activities on social networks (in alphabetical order): Join groups, look at pictures, look at profiles, moderate fanpage, open groups, play games, post news, read advertising, search for friends, upload pictures, write on fanpage.

Answers to the fourth question asked in the survey ("Did something interesting happen to you in those networks? We would be happy if you shared that story with us.") revealed the increasing importance of online social networks in peoples' lives. Respondents mainly report about the revival of old friendships. For example, Ferret, 21, writes: "I found a friend online who I hadn't met since elementary school and rekindled our friendship. It was amazing!" Others have even experienced life-changing events. Pancho, 22, says: "I met my current girlfriend and soon to be spouse"; and Cande, 31, writes: "I was able to update my child's birth as it happened."

Study one thus provided us with a first but fine-grained understanding of the nature of online social networks. Fourteen different social networks were mentioned, Facebook being the one used the most by far. Eleven different motivations to use social networks were identified as well as eleven different activities carried out on social networks. The results are very similar to the ones obtained by Brandtzaeg and Heim (2009) in their research on why people use social networking sites. Our study also reiterated that people use social networks as a very private space where they interact with friends, relatives, and acquaintances. By extension, it might be assumed that they may be reluctant to interact with companies or their products.

Study Two: Quantitative Survey on Usage Behavior in Social Networks

The survey conducted in study two had the goal of finding the online social network of choice among German students, especially in Bavaria. This group is unserAller's target group—we wanted to find out what social networks they use and the motivation behind that usage. This is important because we could not assume that this specific group of people has characteristics similar to the more diverse population of people who were sampled in the first study.

The survey, which consisted of ten questions, was sent to students across Germany. The first parts of the questionnaire tested knowledge and usage of 22 social networks extracted from the first study, augmented with commonly used German networks mentioned in the 2009 Nielsen report on "Social Networking's New Global Footprint." The second part of the questionnaire aimed at finding out how much time unserAller's target group spends in online social networks and their usage behavior. Again, the answering options were extracted using the categories "motivations" and "activities" describing results from the first study done on Mechanical Turk. The third part of the study asked demographic questions to check whether the desired target group was actually reached with the survey.

The questions were designed to be rather easy to answer in order to gain as many completed questionnaires as possible. In order to motivate participants, the request for participation was titled "5 minutes for you, a big step for my research." The following text explained the background of the study, especially that it was only one of four studies and therefore rather short: "That is why the whole thing with ten short and simple questions does not take longer than five minutes—promise!"

Unexpectedly, this wording sparked a spontaneous competition. Respondents started to compete on the amount of time needed to hand in a valid questionnaire. Some of their reactions revealed the playful character of the challenge: "Slow coaches! 60 seconds really are enough" or "Zack bum . . . That was really quick." The spontaneous competition might have led to lower quality data. However, a check revealed that no one clicked only one of the answering options throughout the questionnaire (e.g., always the first option) which would be one indicator of poor quality. The results also are consistent with general impressions of social network use as well as our own experience, so we assumed that data quality was not flawed.

The survey in study two was answered by a total of 173 people, 86.5 percent (154 people) from the target group. All data from this group were complete and thus none had to be excluded. Their answers showed that 50.6 percent of all participants spend at least one hour each week in social networks, 20.8 percent more than an hour per day, when surveyed in 2010.

Figure 13.4 shows the data for all networks that were known by more than 20 percent of all participants, scaled to 100 percent for better comparability. It shows that Facebook, XING, StudiVZ, and lokalisten are the four websites with the highest ranking (in the order mentioned). As shown, 98.9 percent of all survey participants know Facebook, 79.8 percent have a user account, 73 percent use it regularly, and 64.6 percent define it as most used. The second most used social network is XING, a German business network, with 15.7 percent, followed by StudiVZ (14.6 percent) and lokalisten (6.2 percent).

Perhaps the most important finding of this second study was the status of the social networking site Facebook for the unserAller's target group as the best-known and most used site. The dominance over the site StudiVZ is surprising, since this German network focuses exactly on the unserAller target group and it was expected that StudiVZ would be the dominant network. However, it is likely that the results shown in figure 13.4 would not have been so strong if the survey had been conducted even a couple of months earlier since Facebook experienced tremendous growth in Germany starting at the end of 2009.

Study two also reaffirmed that the use of social networking sites by the German students surveyed is primarily social in nature—keeping in touch with friends and communicating with friends, family, and acquaintances. This is an interesting finding

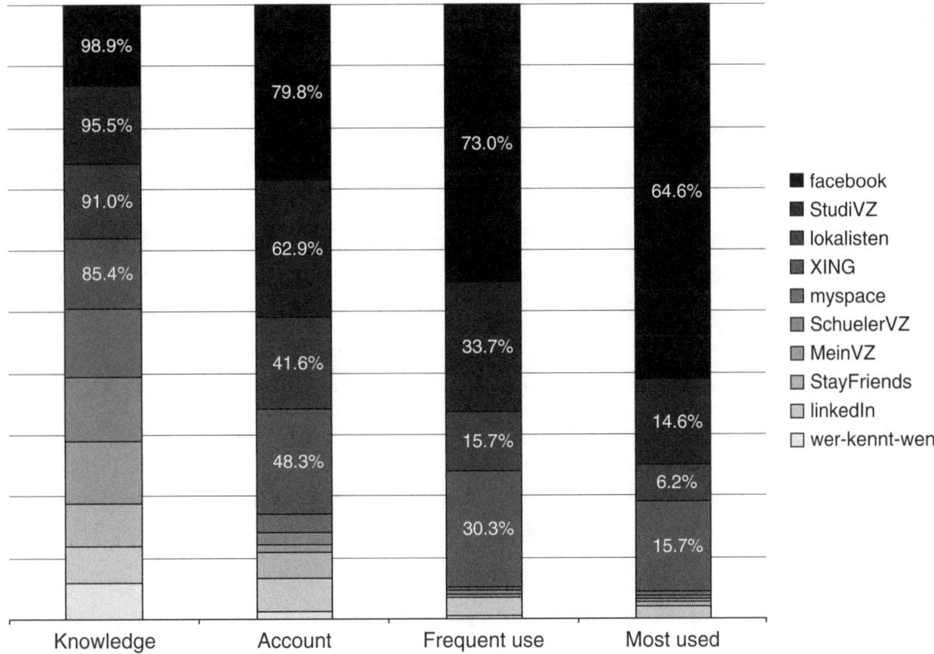

Figure 13.4
Usage of different social networking sites known by 20 percent or more survey participants

from two different points of view. First, we asked how could these motivations be utilized in social network advertising? Second, we asked how unserAller might provide an alternative to "classical" advertising forms on social networks? unserAller was founded to advertise and market new products in a way that is fun for the user, but also something to communicate about and thus create a viral effect. The findings from study two gave us confidence that unserAller could provide a good alternative to current advertising models for innosabi's clients, and thus we started to experiment.

Study Three: Field Experiment on Facebook

Given the importance of Facebook for the unserAller target group, it was chosen as the network for study three. Study three tested the results gained from studies one and two in a field experiment, defined by Witte (1997) as measuring the reactions to a stimulus in the natural environment.

At the time the study was run, unserAller was still in the development process and Facebook was only used as a blog-like site where friends and family of the founders were informed about the progress of unserAller. The stimulus in the experiment was to post different advertising texts linking to the unserAller Facebook fanpage. The campaigns were shown to male and female German members of Facebook in the age range of 18 to 35 years. That resulted in an estimated reach of 5,186,720 million people, a number that was provided by Facebook itself during the setup of the campaign.

In this kind of advertisement, the marketer has to first decide whether to pay Facebook per click on the advertisement or per 1,000 views. Once that decision is made, the advertiser is shown a range of what other advertisers are currently bidding to reach people in the selected target, the advertiser is then required to make their own bid. In a second step, Facebook asks for the maximum amount of money the advertiser is willing to spend per day, as well the duration of the campaign. For study three we set US$20 as the maximum bid per day for each campaign and the duration was set to one day.

The texts of the Facebook ad-campaigns were built upon the central motivations for using a social network found in studies one and two. The text addressed the Facebook user directly with a question or statement:

- *Campaign 1* *"Can you do it better?"* was aimed at the motives *socialize* (stay in contact with friends, find old friends, and let others participate in my life) and *play games.*
- *Campaign 2* *"Power for consumers!"* was aimed at the motive *support good causes.*
- *Campaign 3* *"Tangerine-mustard"* targeted the motive *play games.*
- *Campaign 4* *"Together you are strong!"* focused on the motive *socialize* and *support good causes.*

We had three hypotheses. First, that different Facebook advertising campaigns would lead to different results in terms of click-through rate and cost per fan/cost per click. Second, that referring a Facebook advertising campaign to the central motivations for using a social networking site would lead to a higher click-through rate and lower cost per click and per fan. The last hypothesis was that referring a Facebook advertising campaign to more than one central motivation for using a social networking site (campaigns 1 and 4) would lead to a higher click-through rate and lower cost per click and per fan than just referring to a single motivation for using a social networking site (campaigns 2 and 3).

These hypotheses involve eight key performance indicators, which are standards for online advertising in general and are enhanced by specific key performance indicators for Facebook (www.facebook.com/advertising):

1. *Impressions:* The number of instances of display of the advertisement at the side bar of the Facebook website toward non-unique users inside Facebook.

2. *Clicks:* The number of times a Facebook user clicked on the advertisement and therefore was directed to the fanpage.

3. *Fans:* The number of people who click on the advertisement link and then on the button "become fan."

4. *Click-through Rate (CTR):* The percentage of users who clicked on the advertisement (*CTR = number of clicks / number of impressions).*

5. *Click to Fan Conversion Rate (CtF):* The percentage of users who became fan in relationship to the number of clicks (*CtF = number of new fans / number of clicks).*

6. *Total Cost:* The amount spent on the analyzed campaign.

7. *Average Cost/Click:* The amount of money spent per click (*average cost per click = total cost / number of clicks).*

8. *Average Cost/Fan:* The amount of money spent per fan (*average cost per fan = total cost / number of fans).*

Tables 13.1 and 13.2 give an overview of each campaign as measured by these key performance indicators.

Table 13.1
Field experiment impact

Campaign name	Impressions	Clicks	Fans	CtF (%)	CTR (%)
Campaign 1: "Can you do it better?"	164,924	35	4	11.43	0.021
Campaign 2: "Power for consumers!"	236,189	33	3	9.09	0.014
Campaign 3: "Tangerine-Mustard"	278,334	41	3	7.32	0.015
Campaign 4: "Together you are strong!"	85,837	11	1	9.09	0.013
Total	765,284	120	11	9.17	0.016

Table 13.2
Cost of advertisement campaigns in field experiment

Campaign name	Average cost/ click (in US$)	Average cost/ fan (US$)	Total cost (US$)
Campaign 1: "Can you do it better?"	0.57	5.00	20.00
Campaign 2: "Power for consumers!"	0.77	8.44	25.32
Campaign 3: "Tangerine-Mustard"	0.76	10.36	31.09
Campaign 4: "Together you are strong!"	0.98	10.82	10.82
Total	0.81	7.93	87.23

As shown, the four campaigns differed in their effectiveness but only the first of the three hypotheses could be confirmed: different Facebook advertising campaigns did lead to different results in terms of click-through-rate and cost per fan/cost per click. While the impact on number of viewers was slight, the experiment linked to the unserAller fanpage, which at the time was solely directed toward the founders' friends and families. We thought the fanpage should be expected to be less interesting to people unknown to the founders. This fact might have led to a lower click to fan conversion rates but not to lower click rates since the first click is independent from the fanpage itself.

The four campaigns also varied in their outcome in terms of click-through rate and cost per fan/cost per click. The biggest difference is between campaign 1 and campaign 4 with a difference of 0.008 percent in CTR, US$0.41 in cost per click, and US$5.82 in cost per fan. These differences cannot be traced back to the central motivations to use a social networking site like finding old friends or keeping others up to date about one's own life. While we did not see as strong a result as we hoped from study three, the results were interesting enough that we decided to more actively investigate how we could use a social network advertising campaign.

Study Four: Test Project on the unserAller Facebook Application

Based on the results above, we designed unserAller as a pure Facebook application that provides users with a forum to collaboratively develop new consumer goods products the way they desire them rather than making unserAller a "stand-alone" site. More specifically, we wanted companies to be able to leverage our platform to create viral buzz for their new products.

All processes at unserAller were designed to be similar to Facebook's—for example, making a submission is as easy as posting news to one's profile and the process of rating ideas is very similar to the Facebook "like." This format is intended to lower users' inhibition threshold and increase the fun of participating. Users are incentivized for activity as well as the quality of their inputs, based on a peer-to-peer rating. They collect points that can be traded into discounts on co-developed products found at the unserAller online store or into small profit shares.

The launch of unserAller in June 2010 as an open innovation platform was carried out in cooperation with the Bavarian mustard producer Mari-Senf. Their mustard brand "Mari" was not yet widely known in Germany. The company functioned as the producer of the mustard and provided its expertise throughout the project. Their aim was to increase their knowledge of consumer needs and wants, bring three new mustard products to the market as line extensions, and increase awareness for their Mari brand.

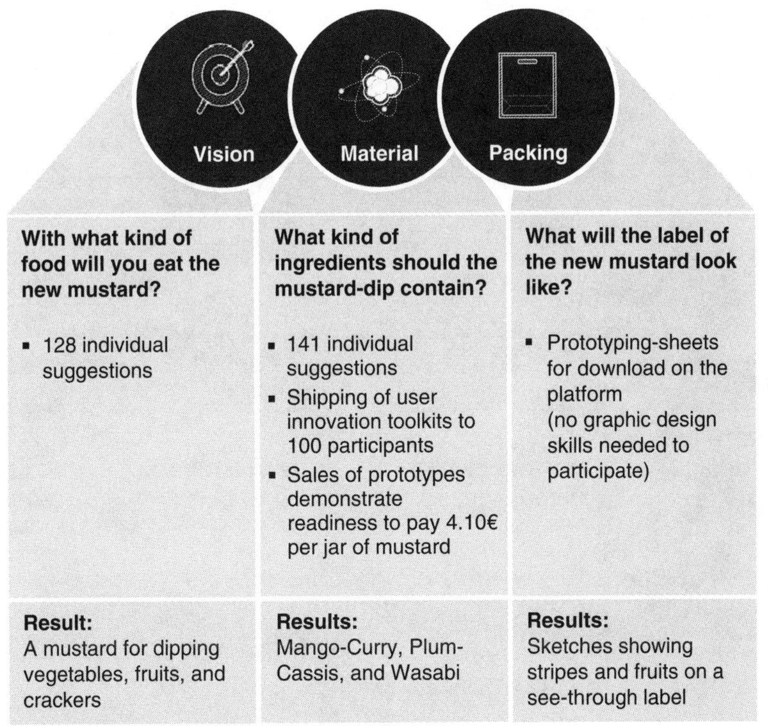

Figure 13.5
unserAller's product design process for mustard

The mustards were developed in a three-step approach, as shown in figure 13.5. First, the unserAller community decided on the "occasion to eat mustard" —a joint vision of the project—then they experimented with ingredients and, finally, packaging. An interesting aspect of the project was that innovation toolkits were sent to users, a strategy described in chapter 9 by Frank Piller, whose research affected our procedures. We used toolkits to establish a connection between the offline and online world and concluded at the end of the process that they increased the quality of submissions as well as the motivation of participants.

Two toolkits were developed, as shown in figure 13.6. The first involved recipe suggestions and provided raw ingredients. The second toolkit was in the form of downloadable patterns, so that customer co-developers could create labels using scissors and glue, which meant that participants did not have to be graphic professionals. In both cases professionals worked with the results so that community decisions were put into a producible and printable form.

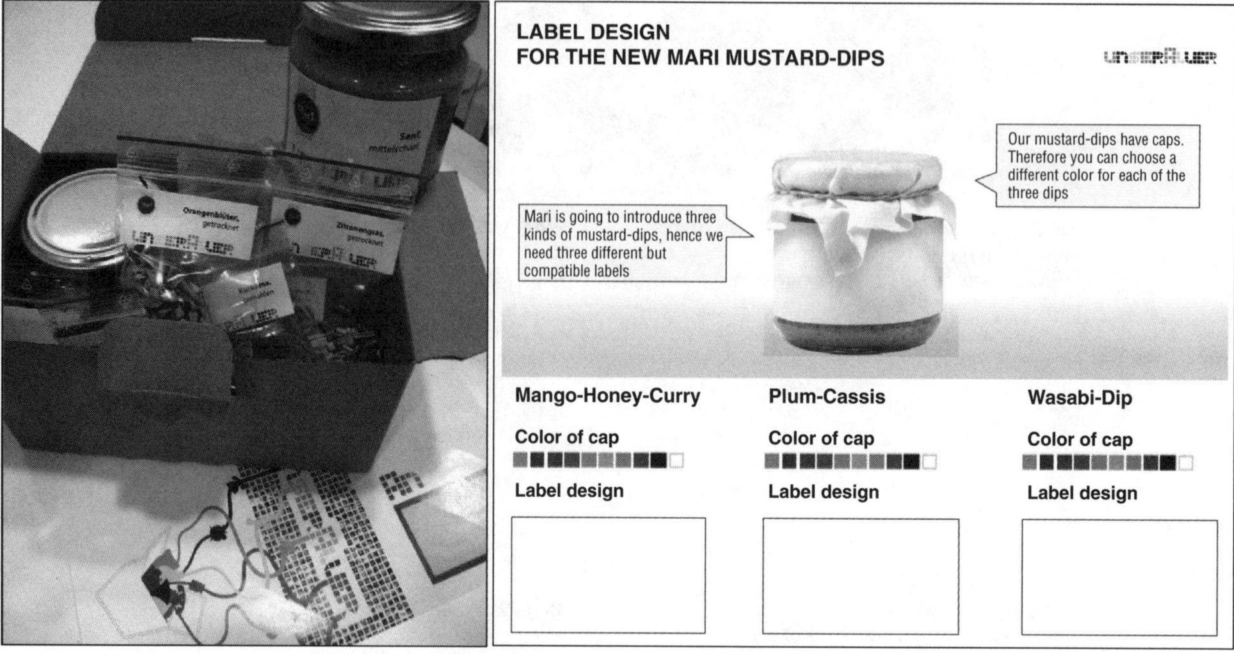

Toolkit 1: Material **Toolkit 2: Label design**

Figure 13.6
Picture of the two-user innovation toolkits: (toolkit 1) material; (toolkit 2) label design

The result of innosabi's first product development project on unserAller was three different mustard dips with the flavors wasabi, mango-curry-honey, and plum-cassis. The mustard is sold in the unserAller online store as well as in Bavarian food stores. In the first three months after the product launch, Mari-Senf was able to sell significantly more of this mustard via the unserAller Store than it sold of its other products in its own online store: This outcome is an important indication that the risk of market failure for a new product can be lowered by involving consumers in the process of product development. In addition the product had fans and ambassadors before market entry, which we believe increased its success.

Our first project attracted more than 1,500 participants (starting with no participant base at the launch of the site) and indirectly reached more than 11,000 Facebook users with a recommendation rate in the form of wall posts (messages that Facebook users post onto their profile for their friends to see) of 25.4 percent. This was accomplished completely without advertising or other media spending, solely through viral recommendations. Interesting, and opposed to our first assumptions, the viral message

Figure 13.7
Picture of the three collaboratively developed mustards

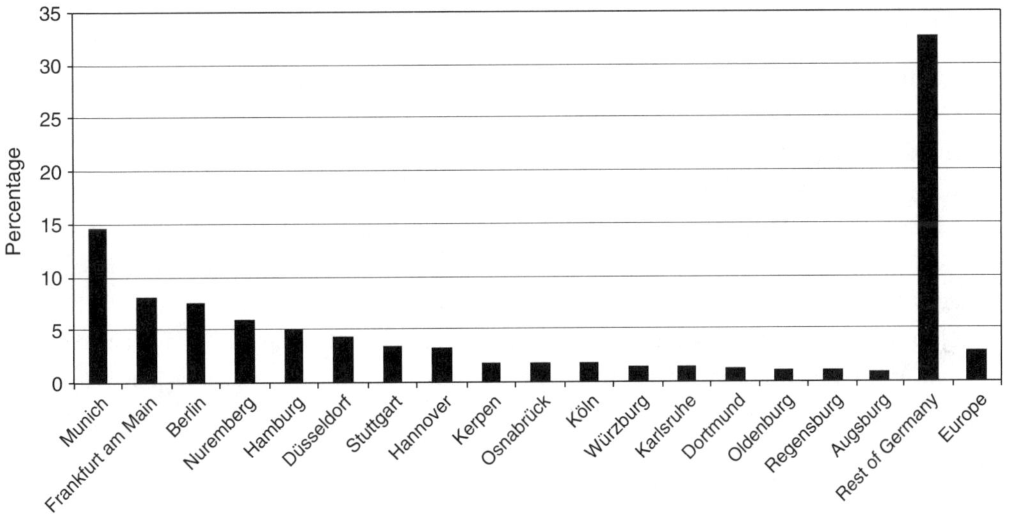

Figure 13.8
Mari-Senf project: Participants' spread

spread across the borders of Munich, where we started the campaign. Furthermore the campaign attracted mainly women between 25 and 35 years, spread throughout Germany. . Figure 13.8 shows the geographical spread of participants. Even though we only invited our friends and colleagues based in Munich to join, the original invitees spread the word over Facebook using functions such as "post on my wall" that recruited participants from all over Germany (and to a minor extent outside Germany).

Apart from attention in social networks, the mustard also received significant media attention from renowned German publications, including *Handelsblatt, Lebensmittelzeitung,* and *Absatzwirtschaft*, indicating that this approach is new and of interest to the general public. We could also see that mention in these publications led to increased sales in the unserAller online store, showing that the community-created products attracted nonparticipants as well. This is especially compelling because innosabi aimed at not only finding brand ambassadors in Web 2.0 for new products with unserAller but also generating new products that are more interesting to consumers because of their features.

Conclusion

In this chapter we show that Facebook advertising campaigns are relatively easy to set up and conduct. Therefore we recommend that practitioners run several campaigns using a low percentage of their total social media budget to discover what delivers the best results. Afterward the rest of the budget should be allocated to the most promising campaign. As there is little space in Facebook for campaign design, we also recommend working with a professional writer to develop creative text that appeals to as many people as possible.

Based on our research, we reluctantly concluded that advertisement campaigns in social networks are only viral to a limited extent due to their "official" character and lack of personal recommendation. However, they can provide a viral spread—albeit to a limited extend—when friends' connections to the advertised item are displayed.

After the success of our mustard product, innosabi used the unserAller platform to develop more products. These include a bubble bath, a salad dressing, a shower gel, a healthy snack, and summer accessories. These projects were conducted in collaboration with large German brands, such as Balea, a trade label from the drugstore Drogeriemarkt dm, and Görtz 17, a shoe retailer. The shower gel, which was developed through the unserAller-Community became available in all 2.403 drugstores in autumn 2011; the accessories were available in all of Görtz' 17 stores in spring 2012.

These were developed in a similar way to the mustard, using several steps in which the key characteristics of the products were defined by the community. In all projects innovation toolkits were sent out to the users, including downloadable templates and models. As a result of these efforts over 10,000 consumers are active on the unserAller platform within a year of the first research described in this chapter, with the next generation technology launched in summer 2011.

We learned that four factors lead to success in developing appealing products, on the one hand, and reaching many consumers through viral spread, on the other:

1. *Processes and standardization:* The consumer co-development process we used successfully covers all important characteristics of a consumer goods product and frames the activities on the platform.

2. *Values:* At unserAller, values such as transparency, openness, and honesty are the center of all activities. This is mirrored in the fact that there is no winner, but everybody contributes to the whole in small steps. Also the promise is given to manufacture the product that the community worked on.

3. *Communication:* Communication should be intuitive and fun; no effort should be needed to understand how the project works.

4. *Solution space:* For the partner company producing and selling the co-developed product, it is very important to define what decisions best involve the consumer and which competencies should still be with the company. This is how a high-quality product can be ensured as well as the "not-invented-here" problem avoided.

We also learned that students are not the only population who like being involved in product development, women between 25 and 35 have become especially engaged on the unserAller platform. It is still interesting that the decisions we made on the basis of asking students in our research proved to be successful with this second group of users.

Finally, we received considerable media attention in almost all major German publications and won several prizes, including the "most successful young company in communication-technologies in 2011" awarded by the German Federal Ministry of Economy and Technology. We are frequently invited to speak at conferences and symposia and receive many requests from companies that want their products to be talked about in the unserAller-Community.

Idea for Innovative Leaders: Engage Communication

We have argued that managers who decide to make social media a strong part of their marketing and advertising strategy must go beyond easily implemented advertising campaigns in order to set their campaign apart and make it recognizable. For stronger viral spread we recommend setting up individual campaigns that leverage the strengths of a company and provide users with interesting content that encourages discussion and recommendation. This was innosabi's intention in setting up the unserAller application for co-creation projects, and we believe viral campaigns will be increasingly important in the near future, given the strong growth and impact of socially motivated usage of the Internet.

Managers who want to leverage social networks to find and activate brand ambassadors should pay special attention to users' communication habits and incorporate those in their projects. It is crucial that participants have fun when collaborating in viral campaigns as well as feel that they and their ideas and recommendations are being taken seriously. In study two we asked for a favor, and we think that many people responded because of the lighthearted way the request was framed. The response rate grew as respondents tried to beat our time estimates. innosabi plans to use this and other ideas in the general communication on the unserAller platform to encourage more attention.

References and Further Reading

Brandtzaeg, P. B., and J. Heim. 2009. Why people use social networking sites. In A. A. Ozok and P. Zaphiris, eds., *Online Communities and Social Computing: Third International Conference*, San Diego. Berlin: Springer-Verlag, 143–52.

Dougherty, H. 2010. Facebook reaches top ranking in US (Web log comment). Available at: http://weblogs.hitwise.com/heather-dougherty/2010/03. Retrieved March 15, 2010.

Godes, D., and D. Mayzlin. 2004. Using online conversation to study word-of-mouth communication. *Marketing Science* 23 (4): 545–60.

Goldenberg, J., B. Libai, and E. Muller. 2001. Talk of the network: A complex systems look at the underlying process of word-of mouth. *Marketing Letters* 12 (3): 211–23.

Hanna, R., A. Rohm, and V. L. Crittenden. 2011. We're all connected: The power of the social media ecosystem. *Business Horizons* 54 (3): 265–73.

Kaplan, A. M., and M. Haenlein. 2011. Two hearts in three-quarter time: How to waltz the social media/viral marketing dance. *Business Horizons* 54 (3): 253–63.

Parent, M., K. Plangger, and A. Bal. 2011. The new WTP: Willingness to participate. *Business Horizons* 54 (3): 219–29.

Phillips, J., and S. M. Noble. 2007. Simply captivating: Understanding consumers' attitudes toward the cinema as an advertising medium. *Journal of Advertising* 36 (1): 81–94.

Rayport, J. 1996. The virus of marketing. *Fast Company*. Available at: http://www.fastcompany.com/magazine/06/virus.html.

Rogers, E. M. 2003. *Diffusion of Innovations*. New York: Free Press.

Rosen, E. 2005. *The Anatomy of Buzz: How to Create Word of Mouth Marketing*. New York: Broadway Business.

Srinivasan, S. S., R. Anderson, and K. Ponnavlou. 2002. Customer loyalty in e-Commerce: An exploration of its antecedents and consequences. *Journal of Retailing* 78 (1): 41–50.

Nielsen Company. 2009. *Global Faces and Networked Places*. A Nielsen report on social networking's new global footprint. New York: The Nielsen Company.

Trusov, M., R. E. Bucklin, and K. Pauwels. 2009. Effects of word-of-mouth versus traditional marketing: Findings from an Internet social networking site. *Journal of Marketing* 73 (5): 90–102.

Van Delden, C. 2010. Evaluation of social network advertising campaigns for a new open innovation platform in Germany targeting a student audience. Unpublished master thesis. Technische Universität München, Munich.

von Hippel, E. 2005. *Democratizing Innovation*. Cambridge: MIT Press.

Witte, E. 1997. Feldexperimente als Innovationstest—Die Pilotprojekte zu neuen Medien. *Zeitschrift für betriebswirtschaftliche. Forschung* 49 (5): 419–36.

Zarella, D. 2009. *The Social Media Marketing Book*. Sebastopol, CA: O'Reilly Media.

Web Addresses

Open Innovation platform unserAller: https://unseraller.de/homeOpen Innovation enabler innosabi: www.innosabi.com

Facebook-fanpage unserAller: http://www.facebook.com/unserAller

Facebook-fanpage yellow chocolate: http://www.facebook.com/tasteofyellow

Facebook advertising: www.facebook.com/advertising

Background information about yellow chocolate: www.stoppress.co.nz/news/2010/06/colenso-brings-home-a-pride-of-lions-to-its-auckland-den/

14 The Future of Crowdsourcing: From Idea Contests to MASSive Ideation

Johann Füller, Katja Hutter, and Julia Hautz

Introduction

No matter who you are, most of the smartest people work for someone else.
—Bill Joy, Sun Microsystems cofounder

Groups of people with highly diverse skills and professional backgrounds can often outperform an internal R&D department of a company in coming up with innovations (Tuomi 2003). Hence organizations are looking for ways to collaborate with employees from different departments and organizational backgrounds, as well as with customers, suppliers, and other partners outside the organization's boundaries. They are increasingly aware that they need to tap into both internal and external knowledge sources to accelerate innovation (Darroch 2005; Leonard-Barton 1995).

To connect several thousand innovative people scattered all over the planet, a number of methods and tools such as virtual customer integration (Dahan and Hauser 2002), netnography (Kozinets 1999), and toolkits (Piller and Walcher 2006; Thomke and von Hippel 2002) have been introduced. These tools mainly aim at actively integrating inventive users into the innovation process. Among the most popular and promising forms of open innovation are innovation competitions (Terwiesch and Xu 2008), ideagoras (Tapscott and Williams 2006), and problem-broadcasting platforms like InnoCentive (Lakhani and Jeppesen 2007).

Tournaments and competitions are another approach that in fact have played a major role in the economic growth of nations since the early stages of the industrial revolution (Fullerton et al. 1999). For example, in 1714 the British Parliament offered a prize of £20.000 (at today's value about £6 million) for a method to determine the longitude of a ship's location. The Longitude Prize was not only meant to lead to the invention of a superior piece of equipment but to grant the British Empire dominance at sea.[1] Similarly in the early 1900s the Orteig Prize of $25,000 was offered for achieving the first nonstop flight over the Atlantic Ocean. In 1927 Charles Lindbergh won by flying from New York to Paris in the single-seat, single-engine monoplane, *Spirit of St. Louis*.

More recently research tournaments and contests have been organized to create a variety of innovative products like high-tech fighter aircrafts for the military, digital televisions, and the first manned space mission to Mars[2] (Fullerton et al. 1999). These tournaments are proposed to a broad audience either by innovative corporations, governments, or nonprofit organizations. Organizations have also promoted their contests and prizes in channels where they believe they can reach experts.

Ever since the emergence of the Internet and other information and communication technologies, contests and competitions have been run using virtual platforms. These often address not only experts, scholars, and scientists; often anyone interested in the task or challenge can participate, create, locate, and share their ideas and thoughts. Open platforms like www.innovation-community.de, www.designboom.com, www.crowdspring.com, www.deviantARt.com, and www.newgrounds.com feature idea contests on a wide variety of subjects. These virtual platforms allow users not only to disclose their ideas but to interact with like-minded peers, build social networks, and establish a sense of community.

Companies use contests to invite interested users to consider a certain topic or product range, show their talent by uploading their creative content, and further discuss their insights with others. Participants can vote on the idea or design they like best, discuss various topics by leaving comments on other users' pin boards, and compete for prizes. Consumers' contributions vary according to the topic of the contest. They may relate to business or product ideas, design concepts, ad campaigns, slogans, or even user-generated content related to specific industries.

One Example of an Innovation Contest: The OSRAM Design Contest/LED Emotionalize Your Light

As mentioned in chapter 2, OSRAM, one of the top lighting manufacturers in the world, invited designers and customers from all over the world to engage in an online idea and design contest in 2009. The contest aimed at developing novel consumer-oriented LED light solutions. The contest was open for designers and engineers, as well as for all people with a general interest in LED technology, light solutions, and related topics. In phase 1, participants contributed a total of 541 ideas. In phase 2, participants could build on shortlisted ideas from phase 1 and develop them further. In both phases ideas were evaluated and openly discussed by the community as well as by experts from OSRAM. Altogether, participants made more than 1,890 evaluations and contributed 3,395 qualitative comments with an average length of 32 words. During the entire contest period (under 15 weeks), users spent 4,335 hours on the platform—submitting, exploring, reading, and discussing submissions.

In order to determine the winners, two independent committees were formed. One board, consisting of experts in light design and contest management, had the task of pre-selecting the best designs submitted in phase I and phase 2. The second committee was the final jury, which consisted of the company's CEO, four experts from OSRAM's engineering and marketing units, and one interior design expert. This jury decided on three winning designs from phase 1 and phase 2 that received monetary prizes. The most active community members with regard to evaluating and commenting also received attractive noncash prizes.

Difficulties and Hurdles Arising from Online Innovation Contests

Although online idea and design contests like the OSRAM's have become a popular tool in idea generation, they also have some difficulties that must be overcome in order to enrich an organization's product development process, as discussed below. While such contests ensure a large variety of submissions, the identification of the best and most promising entries often takes a large effort. Evaluation is even more difficult because submissions vary in their quality, maturity, and depth of elaboration. Contest formats, prize structures, number of calls, or entry barriers can create further difficulties.

Idea Overload

On the one hand, experience with idea contests shows that they collect an enormous number of idea and design submissions from individuals with diverse backgrounds, skills, and knowledge. Contributors from various cultures and disciplines promise a comprehensive view of problems and tasks. On the other hand, in the face of thousands of submissions the identification of the best and most promising ideas requires a large effort in time, money, and internal resources. For example, in the "Style Your Smart" design contest (www.smart-design-contest.com) initiated by the car manufacturer Daimler, participants from all over the world submitted 52,170 designs regarding the "skin" of the Smart car. Out of this overwhelming number of contributions, the company had to recognize and select the most promising submissions for further professional refinement and development. The process is shown in figure 14.1.

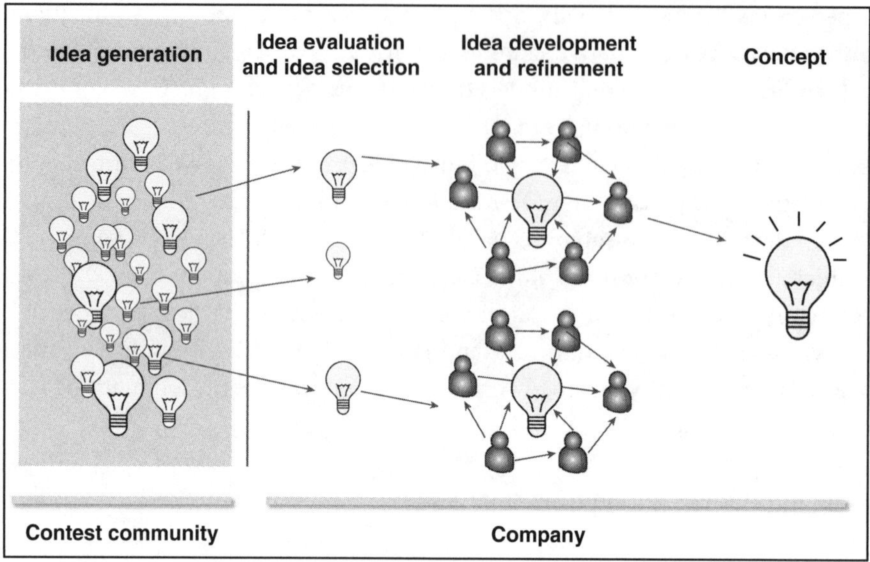

Figure 14.1
Open idea generation

Evaluation Overload

The demonstrated reality of contests like the one to design your own Smart "skin" is that Web 2.0 technologies can result in hundreds and often thousands of ideas generated by users, experts, or employees. The problem for organizations thus shifts from generating enough ideas to filtering and selecting ideas with the highest potential from a vast amount of submissions (Toubia and Florès 2007). The example of Google's project 10^100 further illustrates the problem. Asking for ideas for the health of humanity, Google received more than 154,000 external submissions. As a consequence they assigned 3,000 internal employees to the evaluation process (Siegler 2009), a resource intensive and not necessarily convincing evaluation endeavor.

In many cases a distinct gap exists in the quality of displayed submissions. A wide range of participants with different backgrounds and levels of skills and knowledge not only leads to the submission of ideas with diverse perspectives but also to proposals with varying degrees of quality, maturity, and depth of elaboration, which makes evaluation even more difficult. Some ideas and designs can be very original and innovative, but often a majority show little appreciation of innovative characteristics or are incomplete.

Organizations relying on idea and design contests have to be aware of these difficulties and must recognize that idea generation is only the first phase of the open inno-

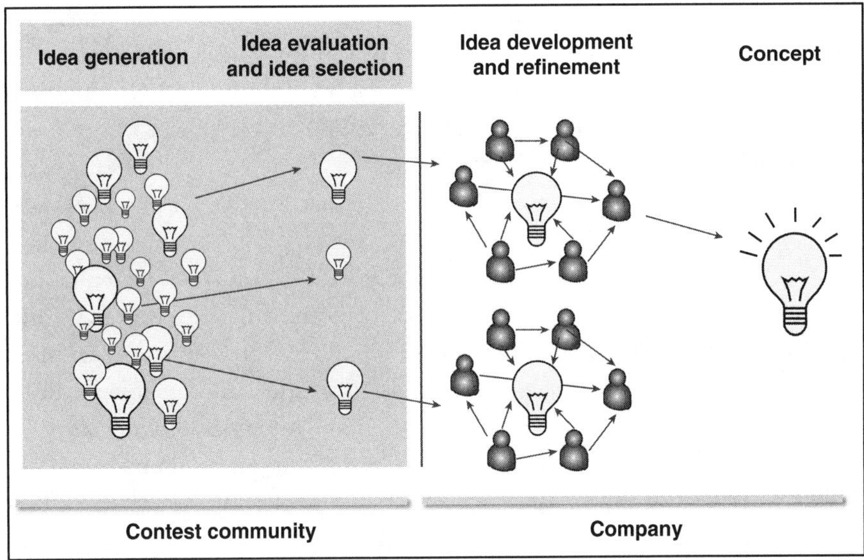

Figure 14.2
Open idea generation and selection

vation process. In other words, the availability of creative ideas is a necessary but insufficient condition for successful innovation. To identify genuinely creative ideas, the problem of evaluating and selecting the most promising designs has to be addressed. Yet the majority of idea and design contests only provide tools for idea generation and submission.

In our view contest designers have to ensure that participants not only engage in idea generation but also in evaluating and selecting ideas. Web 2.0 environments and social software technologies can integrate users' creative *and* judgment capacities, thereby utilizing the "wisdom of the crowd," as shown in figure 14.2. In other words, by embedding evaluation and selection mechanisms that are automated, efficient, and reliable, the contest community can also shortlist the most promising ideas. Hence organizations can focus their limited organizational resources only on the refinement and product development of high-potential ideas.

Further Elaboration: Joint Discussion and Development

Not only can the magnitude and varying quality of ideas generated by contests be overwhelming, most submitted ideas and designs cannot be simply transferred into market-ready ideas. Most submissions are rough ideas, drafts, or unfinished concepts that need further discussion and elaboration.

The development and enhancement of ideas is typically assigned to an organizations' R&D department. However, the tendency of R&D members to discount or ignore knowledge from external sources, defined as the not-invented-here (NIH) syndrome by Katz and Allen (1982), has been widely discussed in the literature. Legitimate questions about fit to the current organization's strategy or the absence of in-house competences to further elaborate and push ideas are other factors that lead to neglect of submitted concepts or ideas.

Previous studies have shown that collaboratively working on ideas in multidisciplinary teams significantly increases the chance of developing breakthroughs and high-value ideas (Fleming 2007). Although these initiatives helped generate ideas, they also revealed limitations in how most people recognize and build on others' ideas. Most online idea generation initiatives have shown that without moderators purposefully pushing toward consensus and collective action, conversations do not naturally move toward consensus. Good ideas are not automatically picked up by other participants in the contest, jointly discussed, and further developed.

The OSRAM LED contest demonstrates this kind of difficulty. Most ideas were not tagged and were not refined through continual dialogue. Few participants in fact built constructively on other's submissions. The contest was organized to capture a huge number of ideas, but it was purposely designed not to guide conversation toward a few really innovative light solutions. Instead, contest organizers asked a jury team consisting of several experts to subsequently evaluate the large number of ideas received. The selection processes required large effort without really increasing the chance of selecting the best suggestions or reducing the risk of relying on the wrong ones (Bjelland and Wood 2008).

One way to get contest participants to engage in joint development of previously suggested ideas is to transfer progressive development principles into an online setting in order to enhance elaboration without losing guidance and influence, as shown in figure 14.3. New information and communication technologies allow for real time interaction through different forms of communication channels such as chat, VoIP, and streaming videos or presentations. With these additions the online environment can become a collaborative platform where ideas and concepts can be further developed through joint interaction and dialogue, as it is in real life innovation workshops.

To provide a basis for further collaborative development when submitting an idea, users in this kind of contest are asked to add a description of ideas as well as an evaluation (e.g., regarding market potential or predicted volume of sales) and a risk assessment. Submitting users are also obliged to indicate estimated "time to market." For illustrative purposes, submitters also are able to upload attachments such as text files

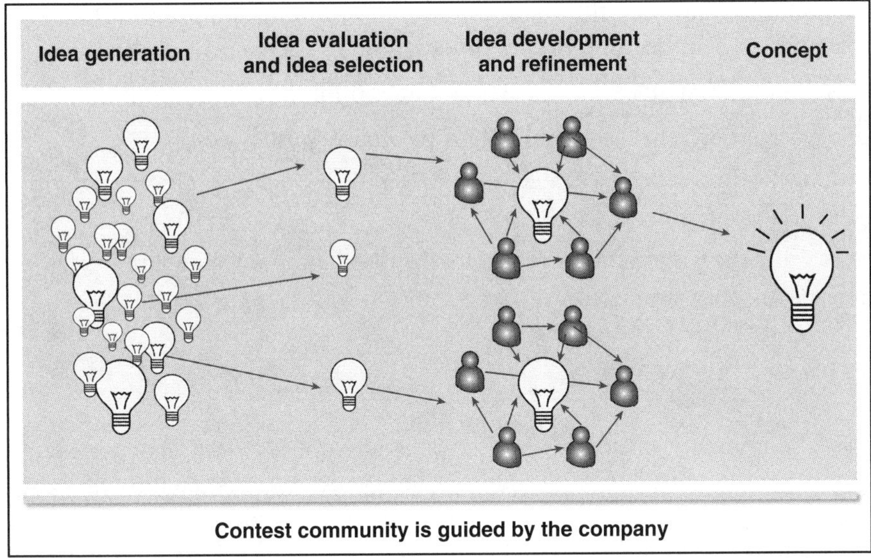

Figure 14.3
Idea development and refinement—Concept

or graphics. Then, as an open source setting, submitted ideas can be modified as well as extended by other users. The status of every idea also can be followed by community platform members, meaning that modifications and earlier versions can be tracked.

Further joint development can be fostered by establishing different contest phases. During the first phase everyone can engage in the generation and submission of new ideas. Subsequently all participants have the possibility of being inspired by selected ideas from phase 1. Participants are then restricted to building on selected ideas—developing, elaborating, and improving them in phase 2.

An appropriate reward structure may ensure participants' engagement in a variety of tasks and activities according to their skills and experience (Morgan and Wang 2010). In a winner-take-all tournament, only contestants who believe they have a chance to win will participate. When less experienced participants discover that they are competing with stronger contestants, their expectation of winning the prize will vastly diminish and they become discouraged about putting in greater effort.

In contrast, using a multiple prize structure energizes contestants who believe that they have workable ideas, contributions, or insights even though they might not be able to submit the winning idea (Morgan and Wang 2010). Incentives not only for the best idea but also for the most valid comments or the best concept elaboration in a multiple-round tournament thus help advance ideas and bring them closer to realization. In sum, weaknesses and hurdles of idea contests include:

- Generating a huge number of ideas that require significant effort to evaluate.
- Receiving suggestions that seldom build on previously posted ideas.
- Participants focusing on idea generation tasks rather than engaging in activities across the innovation process.
- Barrier to using the wisdom of the crowd for developing innovative solutions caused by homogeneous prize structures.

MASSive Ideation: A New Approach

To address the limitations of online idea and design contests listed above, we have developed the MASSive Ideation approach. This is a software-based method for carrying out idea contests that augments the advantages of virtual online interaction via idea contests with positive aspects of real-life innovation workshops. Basically MASSive Ideation supports an online innovation workshop with a "massive" number of participants. Our experience is that these work best with at least 100 participants—often many more. Idea contests allow the hosting organization to tap into the creativity of the crowd, while the structure and moderation of the workshop layout ensures that participants build on one another's ideas and engage in collaborative development activities as recommended by Julian Birkinshaw et al. (2011). This method has been developed in the course of a research project supported by the Peter Pribilla Foundation. The homepage of the platform is shown in figure 14.4

To ensure guidance and moderately intensive discussions, offline workshops are limited to a rather small number of participants. The aim of MASSive Ideation is to overcome the problems of structured offline workshop moderation while guiding collective selection, integration, and elaboration of ideas with hundreds or even thousands of participants. The approach goes beyond the generation and collection of a broad range of ideas and designs. It should ultimately result in highly elaborated concepts serving as a basis for future investment decisions. The MASSive Ideation process covers three main phases (idea generation, idea development, and concept elaboration) that allow the host organization to proceed beyond the "fuzzy front end" of merely collecting often premature ideas. The innovation funnel is thereby broken up into several consecutive innovation steps. Participants can engage in different individual and group tasks. The outcomes of these tasks are combined and integrated in several evaluation and clustering steps as they are consolidated into final concepts.

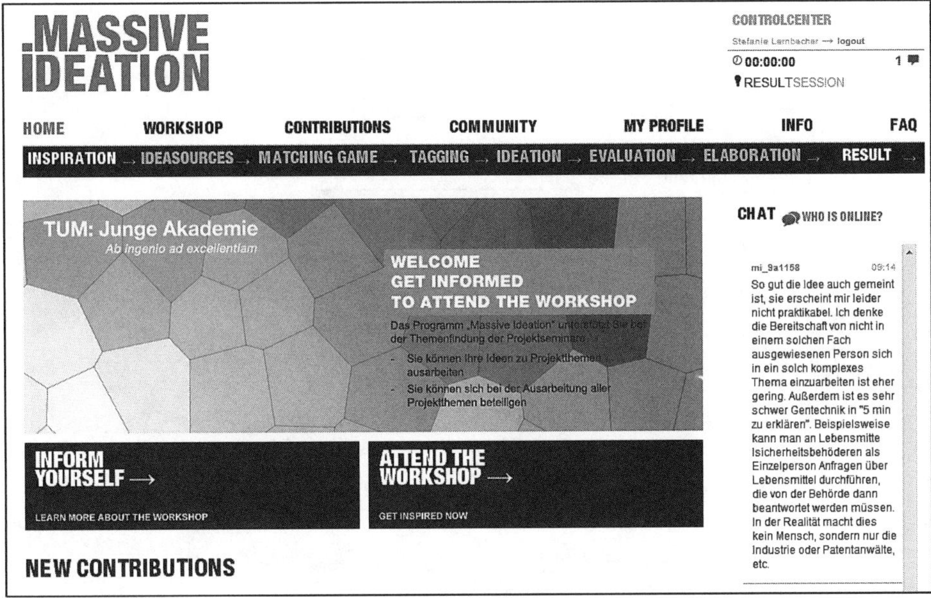

Figure 14.4
MASSive Ideation platform

Principles of MASSive Ideation

The MASSive Ideation approach is based on the following principles:

1. *Task distribution:* Participants may select and perform different tasks that fit together and contribute to a common concept. Participants not only generate ideas but also evaluate, cluster, and elaborate them in order to reduce management effort and to develop and integrate a large number of ideas into a few elaborated final concepts.

2. *Structure:* A well-structured process guides participants through various activities and navigates them toward the goal of detailed concepts.

3. *Computer intelligence and moderators:* Intelligent computer algorithms support moderators to steer and orchestrate the MASSive Ideation process. While decisions about available activities and are primarily assigned to the participants, moderators can initiate and spur interaction among participants.

4. *Human computing and gaming mechanisms:* Human computing and game mechanisms are applied to make tasks more enjoyable and playful.

5. *Single as well as group tasks:* As in real life, activities are handled both by individuals and by groups. The objective is to further elaborate ideas (utilizing individual knowledge and/or group diversity).

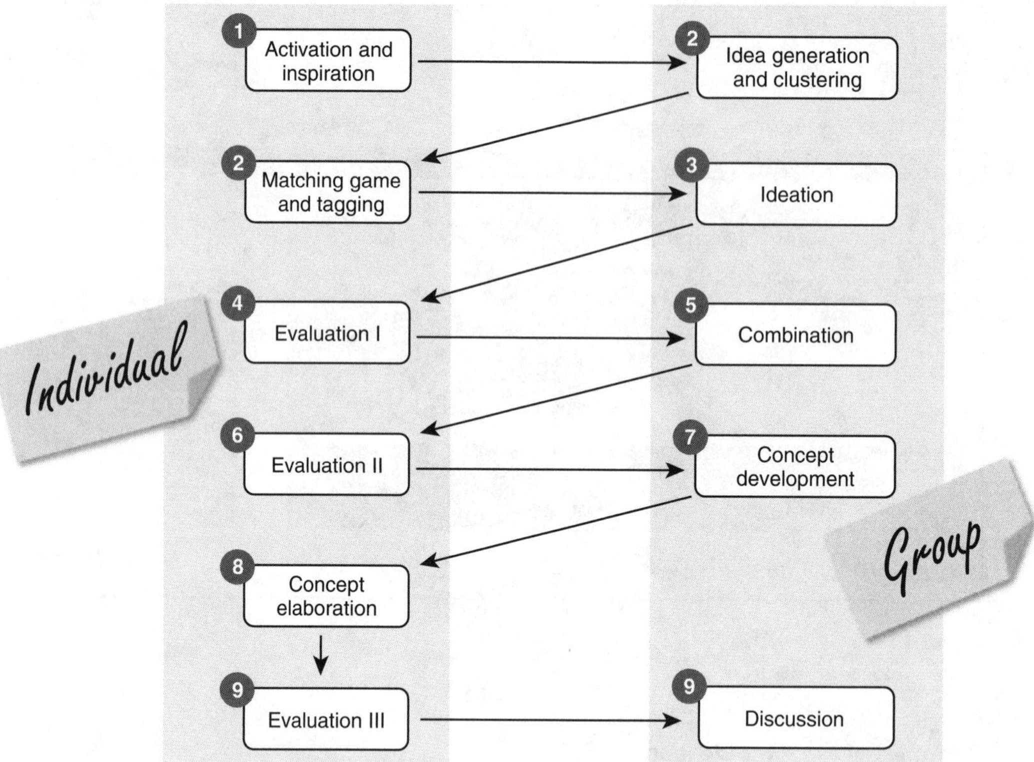

Figure 14.5
MASSive Ideation sessions

The MASSive Ideation Process

Analogous to live workshops, creative processes within the MASSive Ideation approach are divided into sessions, from the first inspiration to the final concept. Participants are led through the process, which is partly automated and partly self-guided. They have the opportunity to engage in all or just a few of the consecutive sessions according to their interests, skills, and knowledge (see figure 14.5). It is assumed that participants are distributed equally among sessions.

The rest of the chapter gives readers a feel for the process by showing screen shots from a recent pilot project conducted at Technische Universität München (TUM). Students who apply for the special "Junge Akademie" program of TUM have to run through the different phases of the Massive Ideation process and show their creativity and problem-solving competencies. In the process they come up with concepts that they then try to realize within the next year.

In total, more than 105 students joined the MASSive Ideation platform. Overall, 321 idea seeds were generated by this group and clustered into 117 categories. A matching game helped reduce the number of clusters from 117 to 55 by merging some categories. Out of these, 37 ideas were elaborated and 18 concepts developed. Finally, these 18 concepts were further elaborated (in total 421 evaluations were received), and after several refinement rounds, 10 concepts were selected. The MASSive Ideation application lasted around four weeks. The innovation project was conducted in German language, but basic aspects of the interface are translated into English for this chapter.

Session 1: Activation and Inspiration Session

The first session at the beginning of the online workshop attempts to engage participants in the project. They are introduced to the project topic by means of interactive games, presentation materials, videos, pictures, or audio files. For example, in the "Junge Akademie" contest participants could look at two posters referring to the topic of sustainability.

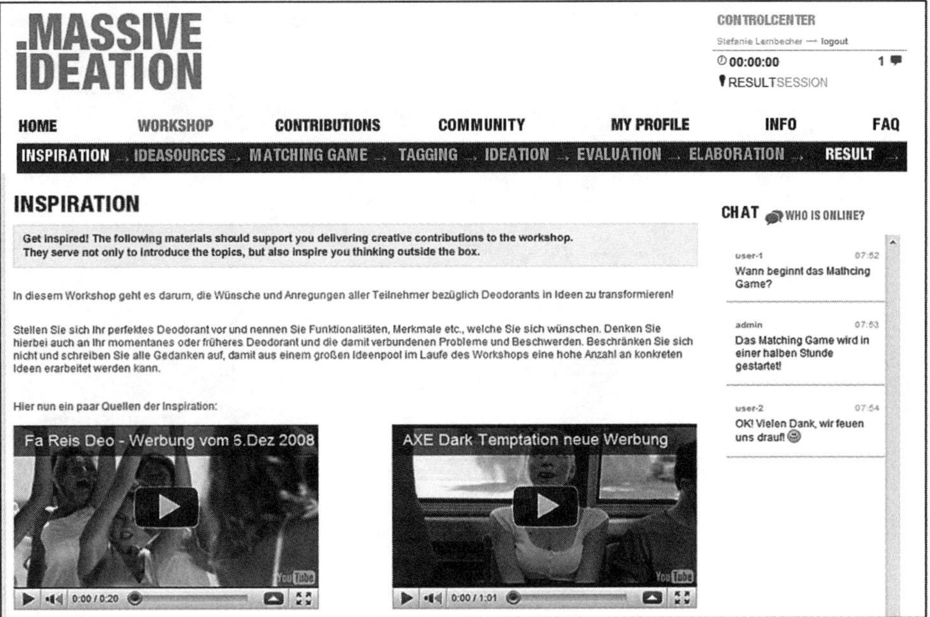

Figure 14.6
Activation and inspiration session

Session 2: Idea Generation and Clustering

In the second session participants are randomly assigned to groups. Within these groups as many "idea seeds" as possible are generated regarding the introduced topic with the help of different creativity and brainstorming techniques. All idea seeds generated within a particular group are simultaneously visible on a whiteboard for every group participant, thereby stimulating the generation of additional idea seeds. Thereafter, participants can cluster similar "idea seeds" submitted by individual participants. When a certain number of idea seeds are reached or no more seeds are submitted by the group members, the session is closed.

The "seed and breed" phase of the second session starts with the goal to combining and integrating developed seed clusters across groups. A mechanism called "matching game" is applied to make categorization and clustering more enjoyable and interesting.

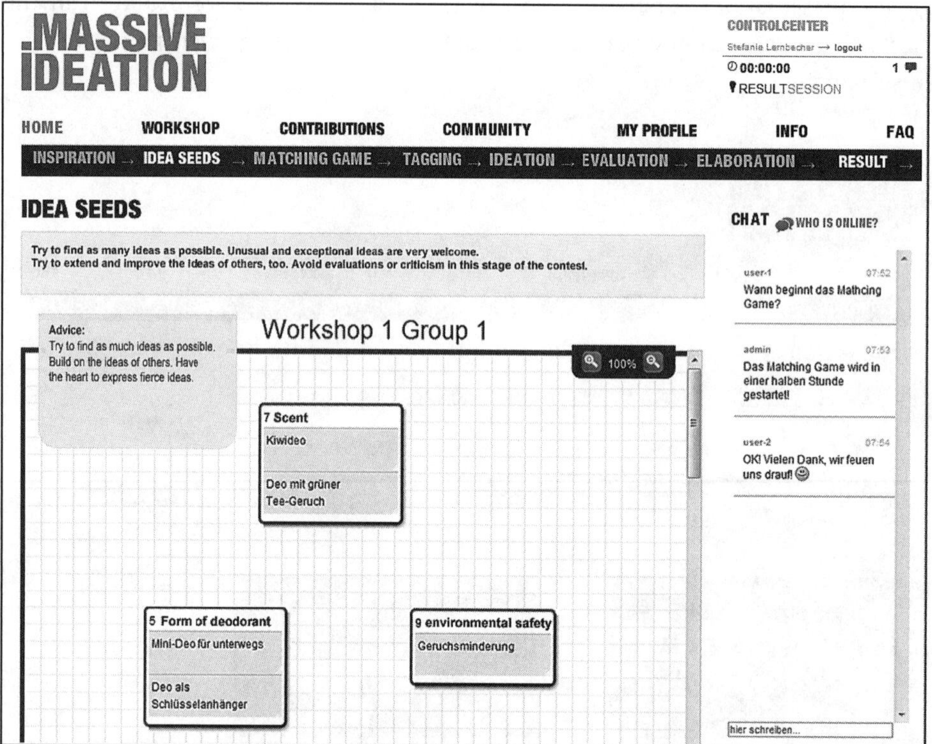

Figure 14.7
Idea seeds

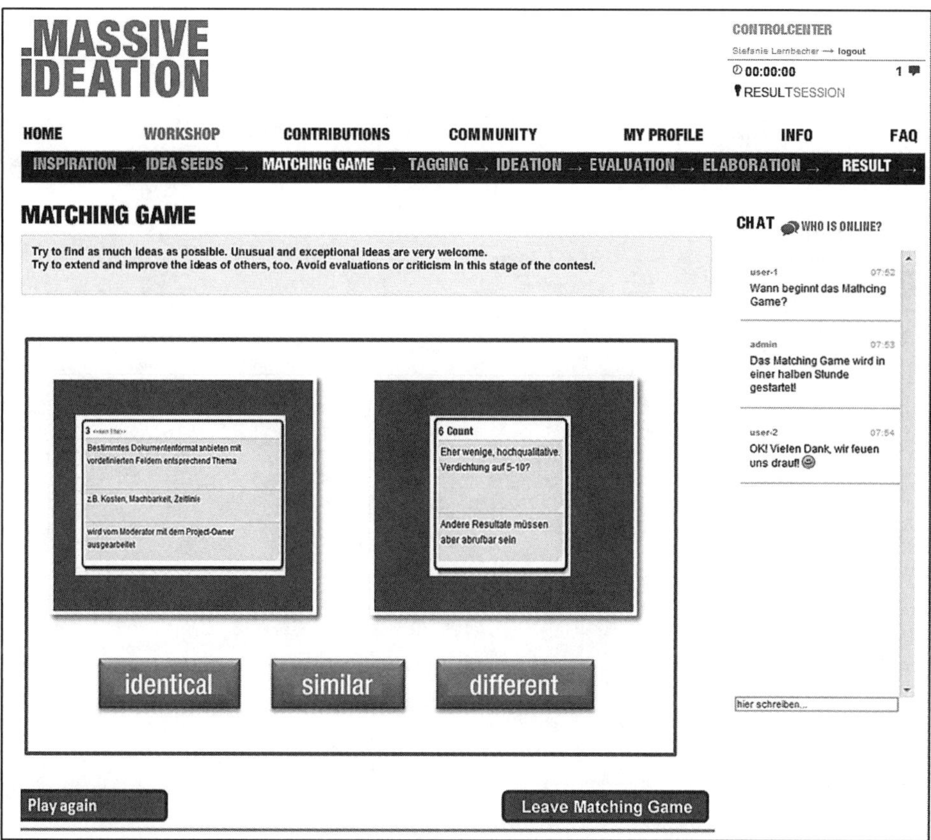

Figure 14.8
Matching game

The matching game is a two-player game where one player is randomly matched with another participant. These two participants play several rounds where each player is asked to evaluate the similarity of two seed clusters based on a three-category scale (identical, similar, and different) as shown in figure 14.8. Based on an algorithm behind this matching game, it is decided whether or not seed clusters generated by different groups can be combined and integrated into "clusters of ideas."

After the matching game has generated idea clusters, these are assigned to individual participants who are asked to tag idea clusters based on a list of key terms. This tagging allows further linkage and structuring of initial idea clusters, as shown in figure 14.9.

Figure 14.9
Tagging

Session 3: Ideation

In the third phase, the ideation session, participants can build on the previously integrated clusters of ideas and can further develop and elaborate these idea clusters into more specific ideas. Participants browse the idea clusters with the help of different search functions. If a participant especially likes an idea cluster, he or she can further develop it. The options include adding a detailed description of the idea or contributing ideas for the idea cluster's realization. Idea clusters can also be chosen and further discussed and elaborated upon by groups of participants with the first who has chosen the idea functioning as the group leader. Chat functions allow synchronous elaboration within the group, as shown in figure 14.10.

Sessions 4, 5, and 6: Evaluation and Combination

The goal of the next three sessions is to evaluate and further combine existing ideas. The objective of these sessions is that participants become familiar with as many ideas

Figure 14.10
Ideation

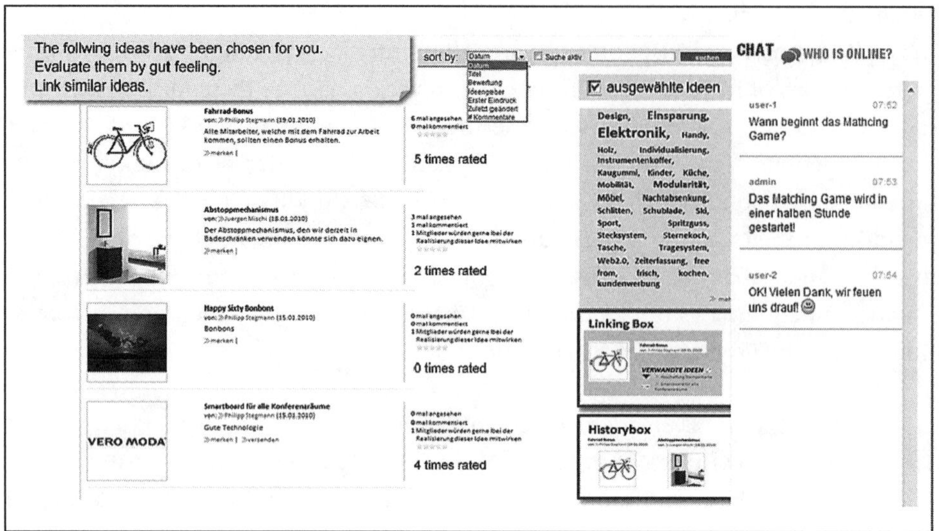

Figure 14.11
Evaluation and combination

as possible; therefore three sessions are devoted to evaluation and combination. Participants browse through submitted ideas and evaluate them along certain criteria. They can simultaneously combine and link ideas if further similarities are recognized, as suggested in figure 14.11.

Sessions 7 and 8: Concept Development and Elaboration

The goal of the next two sessions is to further develop ideas that receive the highest evaluation scores based on defined criteria and then arrive at one or more concepts that are the most promising. Again, groups are created and assigned specific tasks, as shown in figure 14.12. For example, members may be asked to describe the specific functionality of a suggested product, suggest an appropriate customer segment to target, conduct Internet research, or develop a business plan for the selected idea. In the elaboration phase groups also can initiate activities. For example, they might conduct a market survey or interview experts to check the feasibility of an idea. Participants can also discuss an idea, as shown in the chat box to the right of figure 14.12.

Session 9: Evaluation and Discussion

In the last session evaluation of final concepts takes place. The goal is to decide which concept(s) will be realized. Every participant is asked to evaluate all developed concepts and vote for or against further realization, as outlined in figure 14.13.

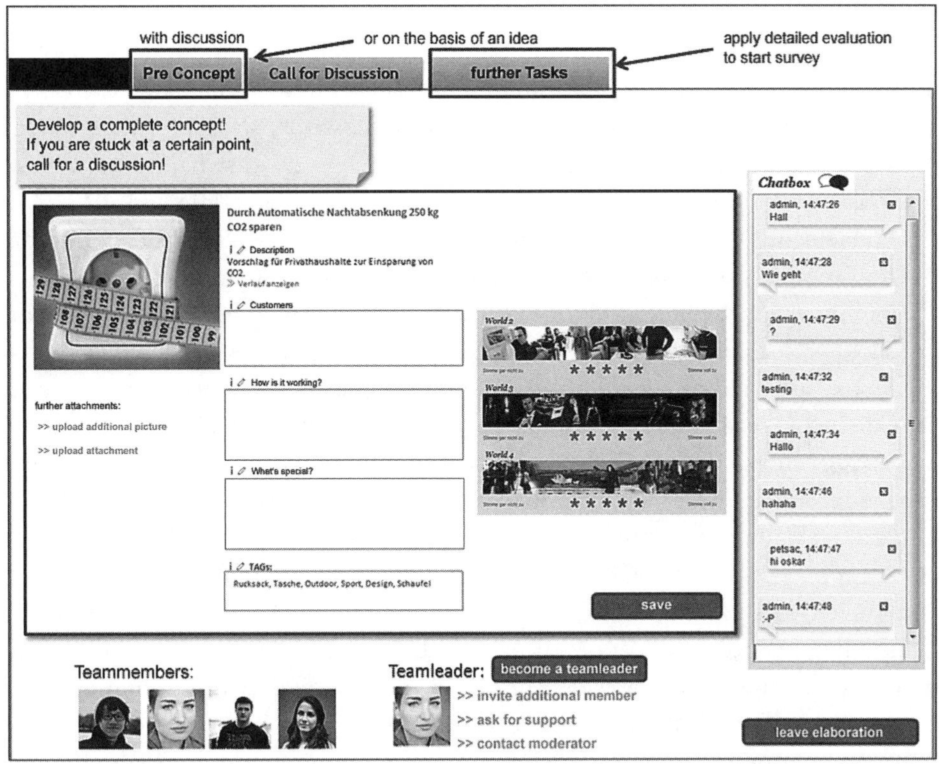

Figure 14.12
Concept development

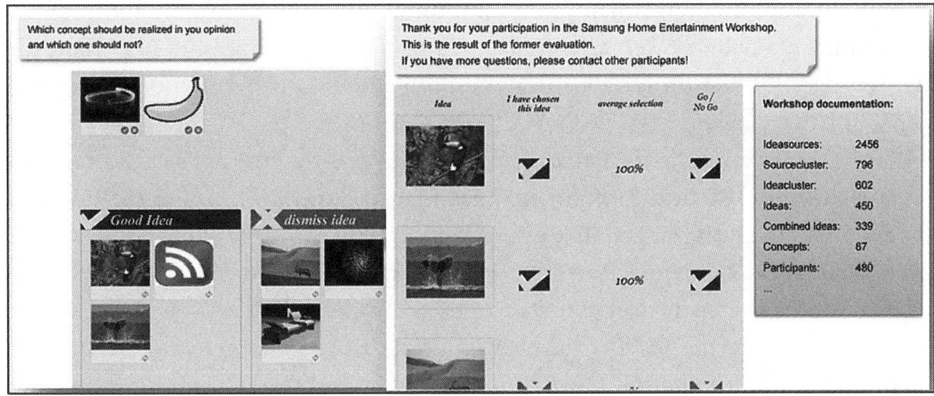

Figure 14.13
Vote for final concepts

Discussion/Conclusion

In the future, more and more companies may consider using the enormous creative potential of crowds to enrich their innovation processes. Instead of setting up an innovation contest and collecting a multiplicity of ideas, in this chapter we suggest that organizations can implement crowdsourcing activities for additional R&D activities including idea generation, idea development, and concept elaboration, allowing the host organization to proceed beyond mere collection of often premature ideas.

Typically, the best solution for an organizational problem is not the achievement of a single person, but the result of a collaborative effort. More specifically, crowdsourcing projects that allow intensive collaboration among users with diverse backgrounds are expected to lead to more ideas and also more variance. Users of similar products or services, external experts, or customers may be engaged in various innovation tasks, depending on required inputs. MASSive Ideation sets up precisely defined work flows in the innovation process, the opportunity to gradually learn according to the trial and error principle, while participating according to acquired know-how, expertise, and interest. As shown in the summary of the MASSive Ideation approach shown in figure 14.14, a process that defines the overall structure and the range of action is still necessary. But the work flow is dependent on the task, project description, and, of course, the particular interests of the users involved.

MASSive Ideation captures the advantages of two forms of creative collaboration—real life innovation workshops and virtual online interaction via idea contests—to ensure knowledge exchange and collaboration. Certain principles critical for the MASSive Ideation, including task distribution, a structured process, single as well as group tasks, self-selection, human computing elements, game mechanics, moderation, and facilitation skills, as well as computing intelligence, are not only important for MASSive Ideation but for collaboration within innovation communities and crowdsourcing more generally.

Whether physician, mathematician, painter, musician or chess player, no one can achieve their creative peak performance unless they intrinsically enjoy the task and approach it with an almost childlike enthusiasm. Playful experiences have been shown to be important not only in leisure time, but also in working life; they especially make a difference in the context of innovation tasks. "Games with a purpose" have the effect of increasing the playfulness of innovation activities (von Ahn and Dabbish 2008). Many tasks can be solved without conscious effort when playing a game. The matching game was developed for the MASSive Ideation approach with this idea in mind.

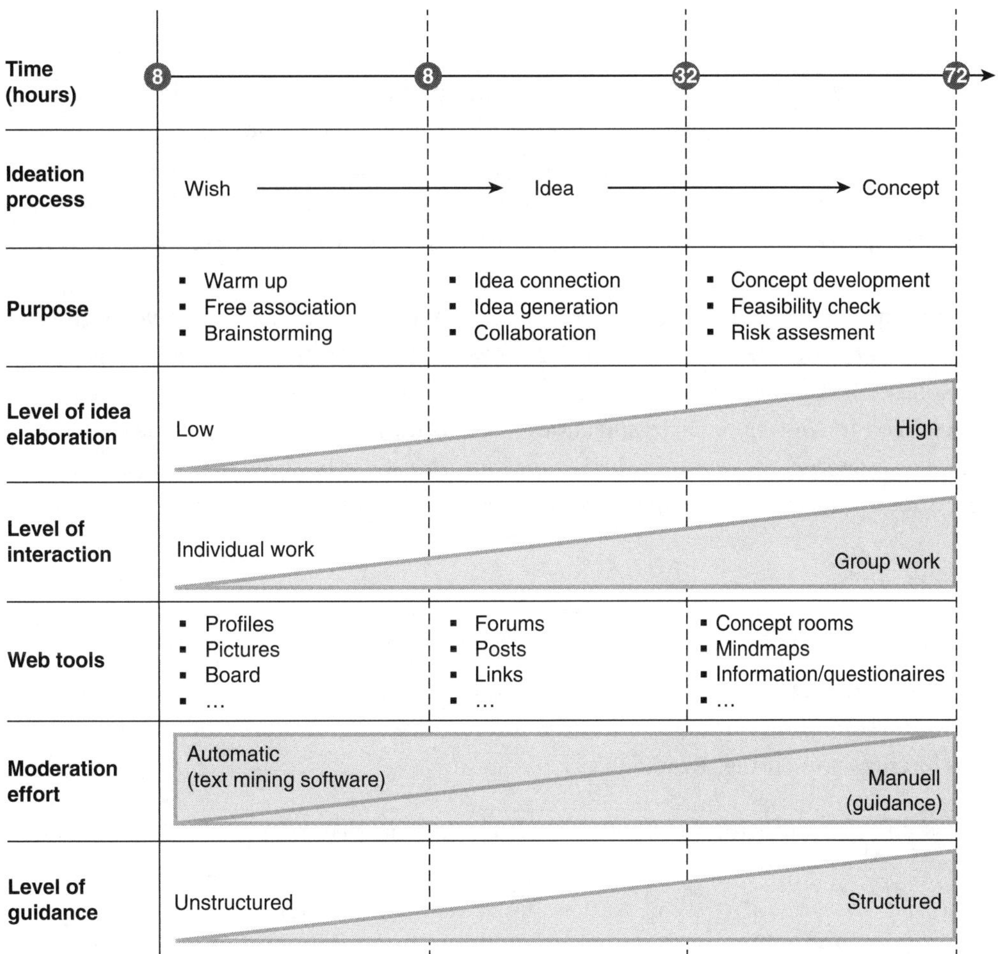

Figure 14.14
Key dimensions of the MASSive Ideation approach

However, organization and process structures also need to be able to support development in dynamic networks and need to align with participant interests. Organizers of idea contests therefore need to interact with participants and develop processes to effectively integrate elaborated concepts as much as possible. Although some concepts and ideas may be promising, often there is a "not-invented-here" attitude (Katz and Allen 1982) even in an idea contest. That attitude prevents further development. We know that this tendency to reject ideas from is dominant in many companies, especially toward external input.

In order to ensure the success of crowdsourcing initiatives such as MASSive Ideation and benefit from the creativity of the crowd, we believe that the way companies manage their innovation processes may have to evolve according to principles described in this chapter. Organizations need to learn to treat external ideas in the same way as internal ideas. Innovation managers must not be afraid to realize concepts introduced and even developed from outside the company.

Notes

1. For additional background information on the British Longitude Prize, see Sobel (1996).
2. For additional information, see Zubrin (1996).

References and Further Reading

Birkinshaw, J., C. Bouquet, and J. L. Barsoux. 2011. The 5 myths of innovation. *MIT Sloan Management Review* 52 (2): 43–50.

Bjelland, O. M., and R. C. Wood. 2008. An inside view of IBM's "innovation jam." *MIT Sloan Management Review* 50 (1): 32–40.

Dahan, E., and J. Hauser. 2002. The virtual customer. *Journal of Product Innovation Management* 19 (5): 332–53.

Darroch, J. 2005. Knowledge management, innovation and firm performance. *Journal of Knowledge Management* 9 (3): 101–15.

Fleming, L. 2007. Breakthroughs and the "long tail" of innovation. *MIT Sloan Management Review* 49 (1): 69–74.

Fullerton, R., B. G. Linster, M. McKee, and S. Slate. 1999. An experimental investigation of research tournaments. *Economic Inquiry* 37 (4): 624–36.

Katz, R., and T. J. Allen. 1982. Investigating the not invented here (NIH) syndrome: A look at the performance, tenure, and communication patterns of 50 R&D-project groups. *R&D Management* 12 (1): 7–19.

Kozinets, R. 1999. E-Tribalized marketing?: The strategic implications of virtual communities of consumption. *European Management Journal* 17 (3): 252–64.

Lakhani, K. R., and L. B. Jeppesen. 2007. Getting unusual suspects to solve R&D puzzles. *Harvard Business Review* 85 (5): 30–32.

Leonard-Barton, D. 1995. *Wellsprings of Knowledge: Building and Sustaining the Sources of Information*. Boston: Harvard Business School Press.

Morgan, J., and R. Wang. 2010. Tournaments for Ideas. *California Management Review* 52 (2): 77–97.

Piller, F. T., and D. Walcher. 2006. Toolkits for idea competitions: A novel method to integrate users in new product development. *R&D Management* 36 (3): 307–18.

Siegler, M. G. 2009. One year later, Google's project 10^100 lives! But overwhelmed Google needs your help. TechCrunch. Available at: http://techcrunch.com/2009/09/24/one-year-later-googles-10100-project-lives-but-overwhelmed-google-needs-your-help/. Accessed September 24, 2009.

Sobel, D. 1996. *Longitude: The True Story of a Lone Genius Who Solved the Greatest Scientific Problem of His Time*. New York: Penguin Group.

Tapscott, D., and A. D. Williams. 2006. *Wikinomics—How Mass Collaboration Changes Everything*. London: Portfolio.

Terwiesch, C., and Y. Xu. 2008. Innovation contests, open innovation, and multiagent problem solving. *Management Science* 54 (9): 1529–43.

Thomke, S. H., and E. von Hippel. 2002. Customers as innovators: A new way to create value. *Harvard Business Review* 80 (4): 74–81.

Toubia, O., and L. Florès. 2007. Adaptive idea screening using consumers. *Marketing Science* 26 (3): 342–60.

Tuomi, I. 2003. *Networks of Innovation: Change and Meaning in the Age of the Internet*. Oxford: Oxford University Press.

von Ahn, L., and L. Dabbish. 2008. Designing games with a purpose. *Communications of the ACM* 51 (8): 58–67.

Zubrin, R. 1996. Mars on a shoestring. *Technology Review* 99 (8): 20–31.

15 Open Manufacturing

Mitchell M. Tseng

Introduction

In recent years open innovation has been accepted as a concept not only among academics but also among those in business and industry. It embodies the free flow of ideas for innovation across boundaries that were considered insurmountable in the past. Scaling down these boundaries, be they organizational, functional, cultural, political, or social, has unleashed significant new human capabilities and transcended nonproductive barriers for greater wealth of the economy at large.

The questions addressed in this chapter are about extension of openness to a comprehensive context that includes not just ideas but also physical materials involved in producing tangible goods. Can open innovation be extended to simultaneously include material movement with wider participation of contributors who bring in higher value added than others? There are immediate operational questions that need to be addressed, such as: Will transportation costs dominate transactions? How will different players be coordinated? Will the entry barriers (technological, capital, skill, etc.) become prohibitive hurdles for openness? Will additional widespread manufacturing capability destroy the sustainability of our environment? Last, will open manufacturing exacerbate or moderate the growing issues of social and economic sustainability in employment? Although it is not possible to address many more academic and practical questions in this short chapter, I will make the case that the idea is worth further consideration from several different points of view.

Following the manufacturing value chain popularized by Michael Porter (1980), the flow of materials can be seen as playing the central role in manufacturing. Producers need inbound logistics and outbound logistics to move materials while manufacturing "operations" transform materials to the form, fit, and function that customers want. The flow of ideas from product concept to sales and marketing through human resources and information technology are in the background to support the enterprise as infrastructures.

In the innovation value chain Hansen and Julian Birkinshaw (2007) identify idea generation, idea conversion, and idea diffusion as key elements for transformation. The challenge is then how to synchronize the movement of materials and movement of ideas in such a way that innovation is not confined to the idea but is well integrated with material flows. In essence, a well-orchestrated flow of materials and ideas not only creates new ideas, it converts them into well thought out actions, orchestrates difficult decisions, and diffuses them to products. It is also well connected with reality by minimizing inventory, avoiding shortages, and producing profit.

However, the complexity of simultaneously orchestrating both idea flows and material flows can be daunting in reality. A simple but often accepted practice is to decouple these two flows. Companies like Nike, Cisco, and Liz Claiborne outsource the majority of activities related to material flow and then focus on idea flow.

Conceptually, we can see manufacturing as a network of nodes where value-added activities occur. Activities at these nodes can be done by whoever is the most valuable contributor, namely most capable in providing the results with the lowest cost subtracting transaction cost. The nature of these value contributions can be acquisition, conversion, or diffusion of either ideas or materials, or both. If entry barriers are relatively low, the possibility of participating in the network can be determined by the economic value provided, namely by the value of capabilities offered, instead of factors such as relationships, market domination, or alliances.

If we extrapolate on this idea, one day we may have a dispersed environment. The expertise of manufacturing can then be everywhere regardless of geographic location. The elements of capabilities will then participate in different forms of business proposition by self-assembly in order to achieve different missions and be rewarded according to each manufacturer's value contributions.

A number of examples of open manufacturing are emerging. A notable one is the "Shanzhai cell phone" (Lee et al. 2010), which is the result of several thousand small companies organized in an ad hoc supply chain to design, produce, and market cell phones. The product design and production system of these phones embodies a blend of Chinese-style social networks, profit-driven entrepreneurship, fearless experimentation, single-minded determination, and flexible interpretation of rules. At first glance, this might seem unlikely—the cell phone requires sophisticated product technology, capital-intensive design, and manufacturing processes, as well as compliance with a variety of international communications regulations. However, in this example open participation of various designers, component suppliers, electronic module producers, assemblers, product marketers, and sale forces makes the contribution and receives the reward. A group of companies, each of which consists of a small number of employees—most of them only have 5 to 10 people working for them—was able to churn out about 110 million cell phones a year in 2007, roughly 18 percent of worlwide cell phone outputs. By 2009 they were estimated to be close to one-third of the market.[1]

An Example of Open Manufacturing: Shanzhai Cell Phones

The key enabler of open manufacturing is to move ideas as well as materials in a cohesive manner so that the value added by each participating entity will not be overburdened with cost—cost related not only to transactions but also to material movement, direct or indirect.

Shanzhai companies form ad hoc networks to pursue business opportunities. The opportunities can be an underserved niche market or a customer base with desires currently not served by the market. The term "Shanzhai" originated in a Chinese classic book, *Shui Hu Zhuan* (水滸傳), commonly translated as *Water Margin* or *Outlaws of the Marsh*. The story is derived from a collection of folklore legends about events that happened in China around the twelfth century. One hundred and eight men and women connected with small units of the oppressed masses on a marsh-girt mountain. These seemingly independent groups were able to work together to become an outlaw army of thousands who fought bravely and resourcefully against well-equipped but heartless tyrants. Their activities have been a popular theme of storytellers and enjoyable readings directed at all ages in China for generations.

To understand Shanzhai phone manufacturing, let's start with a short introduction to the Chinese market for cell phones. In 2003 we had around 200 million people who could afford to buy Nokia, Sony Ericson, and similar international branded phones, along with some rather expensive local brands. Yet there were about one *billion* people who needed this modern convenience but could not afford to buy name brands with fancy features. To this kind of buyer, price is a very important decision factor.

Recognizing that every segment of the population has different needs, Shanzhai cell phone companies positioned themselves to fill this gap. These companies worked together to offer customers very different phones, a few of which are shown in figure 15.1. Some are especially designed for children. Some are novelties in the shape of sports cars or a package of cigarettes. Some are for farmers who work in all kinds of weather, far from service and transmitter towers. At harvest time these farmers cannot get to electricity locales for several days. That means that they cannot recharge their batteries. Shanzhai companies responded to their needs by producing phones that go

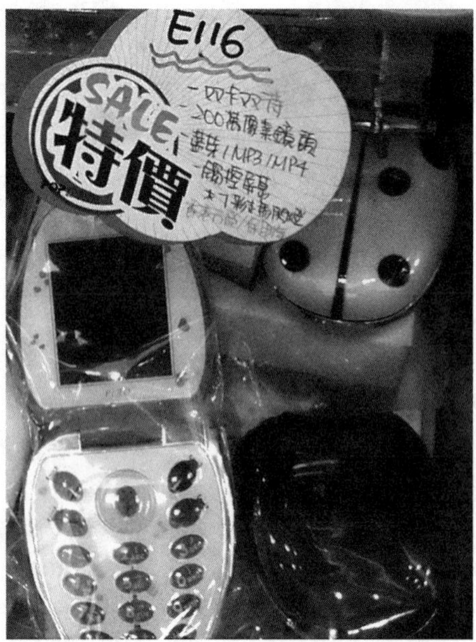

Figure 15.1
Shanzhai cell phones

from seven days up to about one month without recharging. Other phones are designed for people who work in very noisy places. It has six speakers so that users can hear more clearly.

The prices of these phones range between 100 RMB and 1000 RMB. That's about 100 euros at the high end, which is a very, very low price for making a connection with the world. Even farmers and poor people can afford to buy one of these phones. And Shanzhai manufacturing has a huge market. They now export to countries in Africa, to the Middle East, as well as to India and Pakistan, among others.

Often we believe that flexibility has to be a trade-off with additional cost. The magic of Shanzhai manufacturing is its ability to be responsive to the market and simultaneously achieve very tight cost control. How can they do it? To crank out phones in less than two weeks, Shanzhai cell phone companies rely on suppliers that are symbiotically connected with each other's capabilities. Even the most complicated designs seldom take up to two months.

Technically, most Shanzhai phones are built on top of chip sets made in Taiwan that power primary cell phone functions; these chip manufacturers help Shanzhai companies by providing an expected platform. In the meantime Shanzhai phone manufacturers outsource most other activities to a network of suppliers. As a whole the group works together to configure the cell phone's case, user interface, battery, speakers, and so forth. There is an appropriate trade-off in terms of cost and delivery schedules.

These companies not only achieve low cost, they work with a very small amount of capital and cash flow, typically somewhere around 100,000 RMBs, or 10,000 euros. With this amount of capital, they cannot afford to have very nice facilities, the latest machines, a lot of inventory, test equipment, or many human resources. They have to be very focused on their value contribution and make sure they are well connected to customer needs, suppliers' capability, and use of resources.

Value Chain Differences

It is interesting to contrast Shanzhai cell phone producers with manufacturing of only a few decades ago, shown in figure 15.2, as first presented by Michael Porter from the Harvard Business School. In this widespread view of the firm producers need inbound logistics, outbound logistics, "operations" (which primarily means manufacturing), technologies, human resources, IT infrastructures—they need all kinds of different capabilities. In the end, hopefully, the manufacturer makes money when final goods are delivered.

Manufacturers of today's traditional cell phone brands have significantly departed from this model. Conventional companies often rely on an in-house marketing department to find market needs. They do their own product definition and development,

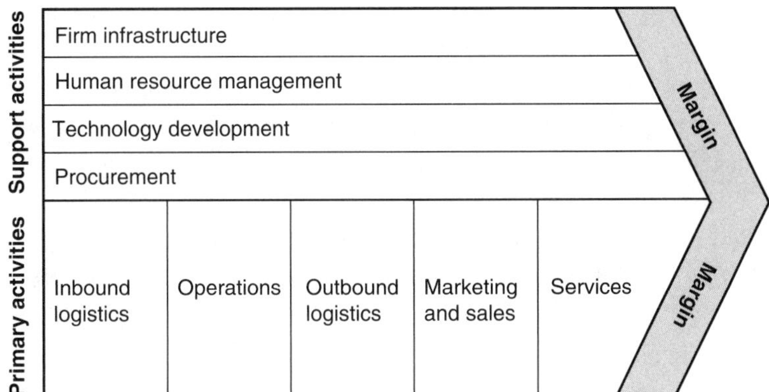

Figure 15.2
Manufacturing value chain

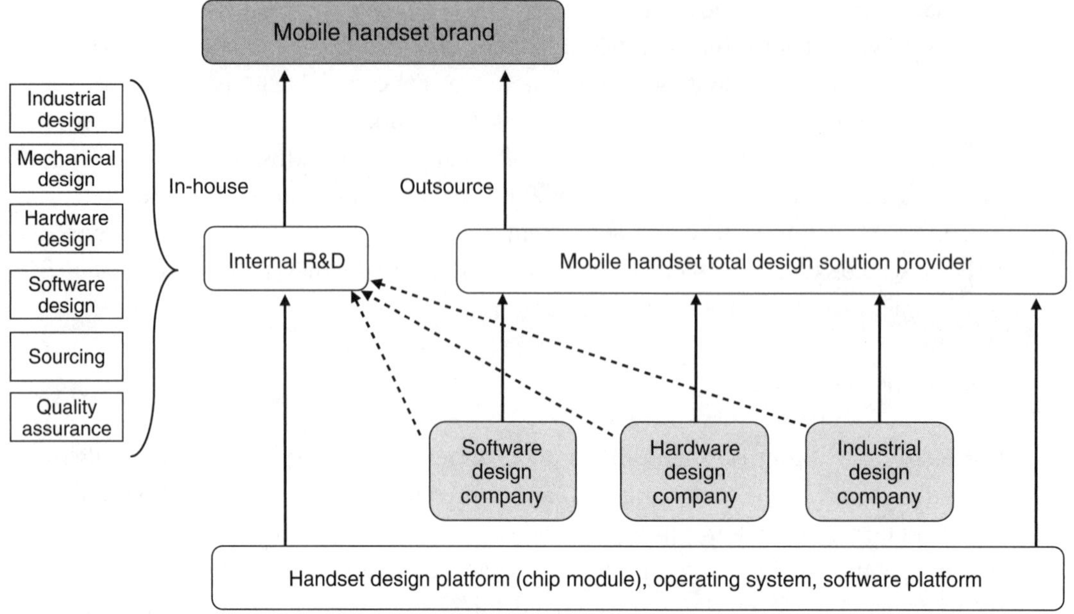

Figure 15.3
Traditional handset product development

produce prototypes, verify requirements, arrange production in anticipated large quantity, and then use their marketing force to get order commitments. This scheme of things is shown in figure 15.3.

The Shanzhai manufacturer works in a very different way, as shown in figure 15.4. First, they sell the phone before they manufacture it. The purchase includes the number of units, specifications, industrial designs (perhaps to look like model xyz of a certain brand), usage, displays, special applications, and so forth. Based on these inputs, similar products or prototypes may be shown to customers to determine the final selections.

Because the business is run with a very thin margin, everything has to be done with tight cost control. In particular, the small company in charge of the customer interface and doing the selling has to make the selection of other players—specifying who will be in charge of making the phone case, who will make the printed circuit board, where to buy other components, who will assemble, and so on. The company arranging the deal has to be responsible for quality, delivery, and overall cost control. All this is done very quickly. Normally customers expect delivery within weeks and final payment will not be made until products are delivered.

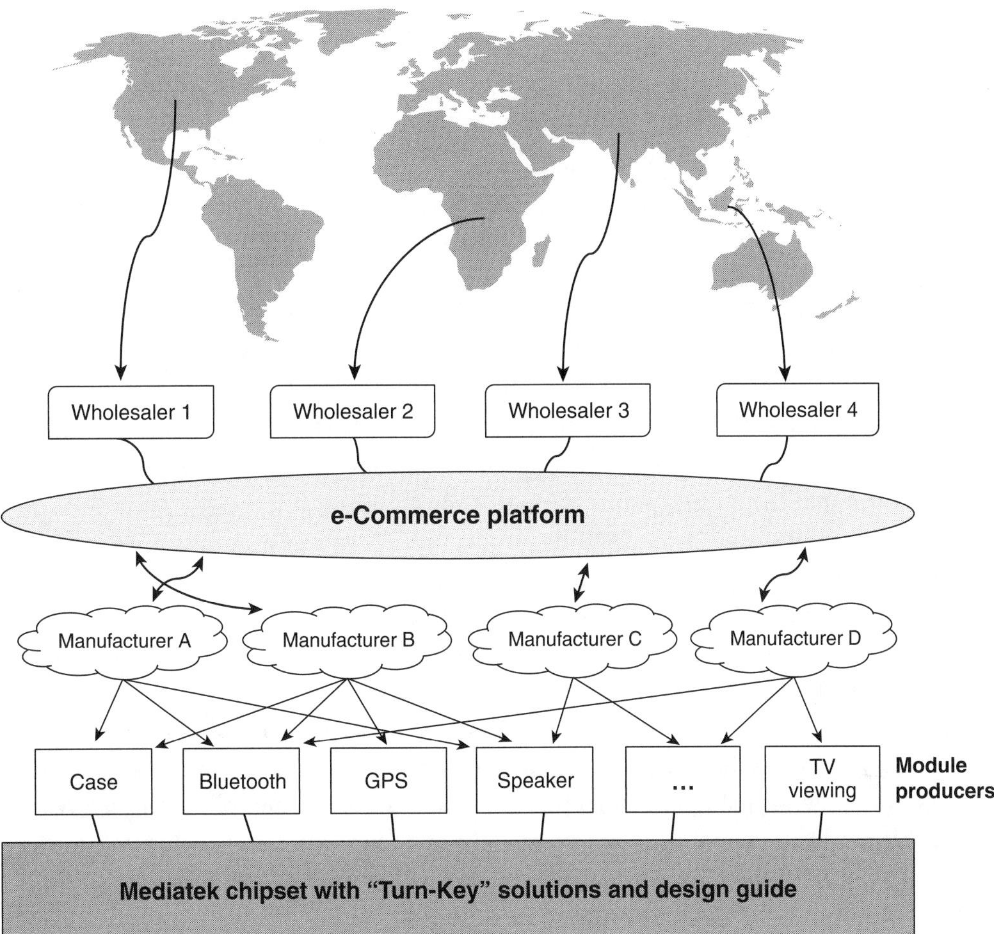

Figure 15.4
Shanzhai cell phone value chain

These companies are becoming increasingly formidable competitors in the global cell phone market. The word "Shanzhai" can be translated as "bandits." Shanzhai companies are like a swarm of bandits engaging in a type of guerrilla warfare.

Quality and Innovation

Although they take a lot of shortcuts, at the end Shanzhai manufacturers have to deliver "good enough" quality. Typically, the performance of their products is quite reasonable. This is not because most Shanzhai groups retain people with testing expertise. Coordinators rely on information about which companies are very good at making circuit boards, who writes good software, who is good at injection molding to make the outside case, where to find good batteries, speakers at a good price, and so on. Weaker players do not last long.

Quality is also the result of customers specifying products based on similarity to existing phones. When someone wants a phone, their idea may be based on a Nokia Model 2100. Since they can specify their needs and wants, typically the customer group wants some capabilities of existing brands but does not care about others. It is important to note that shanzhai companies walk away from untenable requests. They are motivated to cut less desired features to keep their costs down. This is not a personalized product. Shanzhai orders have to be large enough to justify costs. Another saving is that companies do not have to worry about long-term customer relationships in the way that the big cell phone companies do.

A key point, however, is that Shanzhai negotiation to reach a product is very different from what the name brands do—companies that normally take the position of "take it or leave it." In some ways Shanzhai are closer to customers than the big brands with their market surveys because Shanzhai have to be more aware of the variance in demand.

Interestingly, a key player in "normal manufacturing" is missing. Typically distributors of name brand phones buy a substantial number of a certain model, often thousands—the number depends on price and volume negotiation. These middle men are responsible for selling the units they purchase. If they cannot sell them in a reasonable period of time, they have to take a loss and sell them at fire sale prices. Shanzhai do not need these intermediaries because they do not start manufacturing until they know how many phones of a certain kind to produce.

Users of these phones are concerned about value, but they are not interested in paying for brand names. And normally Shanzhai manufacturers do not provide after sale service. Since branding is not emphasized, and the configuration of players changes rapidly, service would be difficult to carry out anyway. But obviously word of mouth is important among those who are consolidating demand and making commitments on orders. Don't forget there are hundreds of players in China involved in the Shanzhai manufacturing of cell phones. Reputation matters. If a company is not doing a good job, they are likely to be dropped from the next value chain, either as integrators or as capability suppliers.

Given the emphasis of this book, it is important and interesting to think about the role of innovation in this setting. Openness here means there is a lower entry barrier for a vast number of potential buyer–supplier relationships than in traditional manufacturing. These relationships involve not only component suppliers but also things like assembly and distribution. That perhaps means unexpected opportunity. Think, for example, of an inventor with a solution for extending battery life; it might be cheaper or it might last longer. Luckily the market for a new battery is not limited to a few big companies. There are a lot of small companies that are willing to try new components in order to be more competitive. An inventor who is tuned to market demand is therefore likely to find a buyer in the world I have just described.

Other Examples of Open Manufacturing

Another open manufacturing example is Threadless, the company that runs design competitions on an online social network. As described by Frank Pillar and Christoph Ihl in chapter 9, members of the network submit hundreds of ideas for T-shirts each week—and then they and the larger community vote on which ones they like best. Hundreds of thousands of people are using the site as a kind of community center, where they blog, chat about designs, socialize with their fellow enthusiasts—and buy a ton of shirts at $15 each.

Revenue has been growing 500 percent a year, despite the fact that the company has never advertised, employs no professional designers, uses no modeling agency or fashion photographers, has no sales force, and enjoys no retail distribution (Orgawa and Piller 2006). As a result costs are low, margins are above 30 percent, and—because community members tell them precisely which shirts to make—every product eventually sells out. In this example, designers both professional and amateur make contributions and let the market make selections.

Another case involves a company providing living space design. Many people who buy a house or an apartment want to hire an interior designer. Most designers are very creative, but many are not very good implementers. The innovator in this second case study is working with interior designers but then turning around and lining up a bunch of component sources for curtains, lights, chairs, and so on. Customers can go to the middleman's website and select what they want, working with an interior designer to decorate their house.

The third example of open manufacturing involves even more customization. If you have an idea for a very beautiful desk, it is now possible to contact a new kind of customizer that can cut the wood for you and you can assemble it yourself. Alternatively, the customizer could cut and assemble it for you. In my case study a designer provided by the customizing manufacturer comes up with CAD drawings of desired furniture; these are then given to a satellite fabricator.

Another effort is called builditwith.me. The focus of this company is on web development, but the "build" logic is very compatible with what I have been talking about. Their website says:

> Build It With Me is a tool that connects design & development entrepreneurs. It exists to make creating apps easier by connecting you with like-minded designers & developers with the same goal: create cool & useful apps.
>
> Getting funding for your app idea is hard and often unrealistic. Most of the time you may just need to connect with a partner who has a skill set you lack to finish off your app. This is where Build It With Me comes in, connecting you to those people.
>
> Skip the funding. Build It With Me will help you bootstrap your ideas into actual apps.[2]

What is interesting about these examples is that they are based on a very simple business idea: connection. The interior designers already exist. The desk designers already exist. The companies that transform raw materials into products exist. Entrepreneurs have always existed and are increasing in number around the world. What has happened recently is that new, open interfaces are becoming available to connect these and other players with much larger groups of customers than they could reach before.

It is more accurate to say that "more open" interfaces are becoming available. Few companies are targeting every user. They are targeting users who have specific capabilities. In my third case the desk designer has to use CAD software to create new solutions. Today there are more and more players with this skill. The reason is that in the last few years it has become possible to access manufacturing platforms that allow people to directly realize new ideas that were much harder, if not impossible, to finalize in the past.

The underlying economic force propelling open manufacturing is important. In conventional manufacturing, the cost of equipment and setup, commonly called a fixed cost, often is the dominating factor in decision making. The advent of modern manufacturing is known for its flexibility, adaptable machines, better-educated workforce, and advanced information systems such as Enterprise Resource Planning. All of these forces have drastically reduced the variable cost and the marginal cost of producing one additional unit. Perhaps the future role of manufacturing is to be a simple copy machine. If you can follow the manufacturers' formats, you can create a product virtually, transmit the specifications, and then download to a machine to get the physical reality you desire.

Labor Participation in Open Manufacturing: New Employment

In the past three decades technology advancements, improvements of management, competitive market forces, and better-educated workforces have accelerated productivity in almost every sector of economic activity. Productivity increases have been particularly high in the manufacturing sector, where high transferable outputs and the force of global competition have substantially driven down the costs of production. Productivity gains have largely been achieved through improvements in manufacturing technologies, automation, and quality improvement, which have led the world to produce more output with less human involvement.

The rapid increase in labor participation from emerging economies, in the form of low labor cost, has substantially increased the size of the productive labor pool, thus further compounding job shortages as more workers compete for a diminishing number of manufacturing jobs. On the one hand, we are enjoying the unprecedented abundance of material goods. On the other hand, the continuing de-humanization of manufacturing reduces employment opportunities. The total manufacturing employment worldwide has not increased in the last decade, even though outputs have steadily increased (United Nations 2010).

For a while, the issue was camouflaged with the intense promotion of consumerism. Increased consumption of manufactured products tended to conceal the shortage of employment before the beginning of this millennium. With our recent awareness of environmental issues, however, it becomes apparent that we cannot continue to step up our consumption in order to create more jobs in our endless pursuit of higher productivity.

Because of the stagnant and diminishing pool of manufacturing job opportunities, the issue of manufacturing employment has long been considered a zero-sum game on a global basis. Most discussions are confined to the competitive industrial strengths of different countries, regions, or other entities. The consequences are similar to those of the arms race during the cold war era. Each country or region has been trying to "win" with a more productive workforce and/or business environment, but always at the expense of another country or region, leading those "losing" regions to suffer prolonged unemployment. In fact, a lack of employment opportunities for certain age groups in some geographic regions has become a longstanding social problem and cultivated other social ills such as crime, unrest, and riots. There are few conventional remedies beyond buying out the unemployed with unemployment insurance and/or redoubling efforts to achieve competitive productivity.

While recent developments in manufacturing technology, intelligent flexible systems, and information technology have significantly reduced technical barriers for participation in manufacturing, other technology developments, particularly automation, are lowering human participation in manufacturing. Reduced opportunities can dislocate the labor force and create substantial social cost. Although unemployment insurance alleviates some financial issues for the unemployed, it fails to address a fundamental relationship between humans and manufacturing.

Yearning to produce something meaningful, find opportunities for learning, networking, and recognition are all natural human needs that cannot be ignored. True human needs go beyond material gratification. We cannot see humans as mere operators, organizers, or users of the output of manufacturing systems. Rather, humans are an essential part of the manufacturing ecosystem. The connection between humans and work is more than a means for measuring output for distributing the wealth generated by manufacturing systems. Work provides other soft values. It fulfills a human capacity to contribute, and it provides other psychological and physiological gains for participants.

With open manufacturing the individual needs of customers can be more accurately presented, and thus reduce the waste of producing something that does not satisfy real needs. Indeed lower entry barriers enable wider participation of the workforce. Every corner of the world could experience increased job and learning opportunities, and therefore essential aspects of developing human capacity could be realized. If economic forces can be shaped in an open environment and participants are assured they can join the value chain for the fulfillment of their needs, open manufacturing may bring the dynamism needed for a new era of manufacturing.

Conclusion: Coordination as the Center of Open Manufacturing

Discussions about open innovation focus on three players:

- Who has the problem?
- Who provides the solutions?
- Who operates the market?

The players in open manufacturing are very similar. You have a vast number of customers who have needs to be fulfilled. There are a vast number of manufacturers and suppliers who can provide solutions, and then a vast number of operators who are willing and eager to compete to operate the market.

The difference between open innovation and open manufacturing appears to be in organizing and operating the flows of ideas and materials. The complexity involved cannot be handled with the traditional hierarchy of provider–customer relationships because of the vast choices that are now available, constraints on time, and limits on costs. In the Shanzhai case a common platform, a critical mass of players, and a very strong entrepreneurial spirit quickly organize and reconfigure to overcome complexity and potential transaction costs to make it all work.

The key question seems to be who selects players. In true openness we can imagine that almost anyone could be the coordinator of open manufacturing. Whoever I am, wherever I am, whatever role I played in the past does not matter much if I have done a good job. What matters is that a critical mass of other players is convinced that I will bring the best value to the network. Therefore, if my capability is coordination and orchestrating, and I have ambition, someday I may become a market coordinator.

If the coordinator is not doing a good job, the customer is going to get out. If the coordinator is seen as making too much money, controlling too much, the customer and other players may get out. However, these market dynamics of open manufacturing may not be easily understood. More research is needed on how the invisible hand in the market is played out as players in a node are selected, organized, coordinated, and then goods are delivered to a market.

The coordinator making these moves is playing a new role that is critical to the entire value chain in open manufacturing. What functions and responsibilities do effective market coordinators need to provide? How do they conduct transactions so that players feel they are treated fairly? How do they divide the profit with other players? These are all very interesting questions about the emerging world of open manufacturing for both research and practice.

Ideas for Innovative Leaders: Enable Open Manufacturing by Orchestrating Idea Flows and Material Flows

From the Shanzhai case study and other examples of open manufacturing we have some interesting insights. In delivering value to customers, innovative leaders cannot be confined to only the generation, transformation, or diffusion of ideas. The reason is very simple. Value is often embodied in material substances. By extending the scope of open innovation to include open manufacturing, innovative leaders can take up challenges that bring innovations, people, processes, and products together to create new value and build new business advantages. To this end there are at least three enabling factors that are important, if not critical, to the smooth running of open manufacturing.

Product Identification and Traceability

In order to facilitate accountability, there needs to be some means of tracking products, players, and other attributes of manufacturing such as time and place of activities. For open manufacturing to move forward, systems are needed to facilitate tracking in very fluid relationships so that who is doing what can be well connected with quality, cost, schedule, and other important performance indicators. The recent development of RFID technology has potential as an important element to facilitate open manufacturing.

Common Language Standard

Free flow of communication is the bedrock for coordination and exchange of ideas and materials in open manufacturing. Common language is the essential element in order for participating parties to interact. Additionally standards are needed and include product specification, business protocols, and basic processes. All are important to move ideas and connect them with the status of material flows. For instance, specifying a cell phone so that there are no misunderstandings among various players requires a well-established set of standards.

Product Platforms

Open manufacturing requires an environment that ensures that participants treat each other fairly, proper accounts of rights and responsibilities, and a fair market mechanism for contracting. All these factors can make or break the smooth operations of open manufacturing environment. Obviously no single company can pull all these requirements together alone. Like open innovation, open manufacturing can be a force to achieve responsiveness and efficiency simultaneously with self-regulating behavior. The system involves self-selection, self-organizing, and self-motivation with relatively little central control and less contracting. A very different framework than used by traditional manufacturing is needed to insure that work is shared and learning accumulated.

Notes

1. See http://www.chinastakes.com/2009/11/multinationals-trying-to-stem-expansion-by-chinas-shanzhai-cell-phone-makers.html, accessed April 26, 2010.

2. See http://builditwith.me/about/, accessed June 10, 2011.

References and Further Reading

Chafkin, M. 2008. The customer is the company. *Inc. Magazine*. Available at: http://www.inc.com/magazine/20080601/the-customer-is-the-company.html. Accessed June 1, 2008.

Economist. 2011. Print me a Stradivarius: How a new manufacturing technology will change the world. *The Economist*. Available at: http://www.economist.com/node/18114327. Accessed February 10, 2011.

Hansen, M. T., and J. Birkinshaw. 2007. The innovation value chain. *Harvard Business Review* 85 (6): 121–30.

Lee, H., M. Tseng, P. Siu, and D. Hoyt. 2010. Shanzhai ("bandit") mobile phone companies: The guerrilla warfare of product development and supply chain management. Case study, product GS-75 DATE: 2/10/10. Stanford Graduate School of Business and Hong Kong University of Science and Technology.

Orgawa, S., and F. T. Piller. 2006. Reducing risks in new product management. *Sloan Management Review* 47 (2): 65–71.

Porter, M. E. 1980. *Competitive Strategy: Techniques for Analyzing Industries and Competitors*. New York: Free Press.

United Nations. 2010. *International Yearbook of Industrial Statistics 2010*. Vienna: United Nations Industrial Development Organization.

Epilogue: Learning to be More Competitive, More Cooperative, and More Innovative

Anne Sigismund Huff, Yves Doz, and Karim R. Lakhani

In this concluding conversation we suggest that the definition of strategy is changing and that learning how to innovate helps organizations move away from formulaic behaviors. Innovation is often hampered by what people think they know, by purely competitive behavior, hoarding knowledge, resisting ideas that are "not invented here," continuing to do what worked in the past, and putting managers at the center of information collection and analysis. New ways of working can be found in the world's largest and most successful organizations but also in organizations pressed to invent by economic necessity. Managers are trying to find balance, especially between competition and cooperation in organizational ecosystems.

How Open Innovation Fits into Organizational Strategy

Anne: I speak for the co-editors of this volume in thanking the two of you for your contributions to the Peter Pribilla network, including this conversation. Let me begin, Yves, by asking if you find that the concepts of open innovation described in this volume are compatible with ideas about agility you present in chapter 3?

Yves: Absolutely. Open innovation is one element or component of strategic agility. The basis of our strategy sensitivity argument is that organizations need to be more open to the outside world—they need to be better able to pick up innovative ideas, wherever they are. Some ideas will be technical or product innovations and some will be based on market and customer understanding. Some innovations will be about business systems or concepts or models.

A second important point about agility involves opening the strategy process, which again is almost analogous to open innovation. Agility is about creating a more participative process internally and also about becoming more externally connected. So yes, absolutely, the two ideas are consistent and complementary.

Karim: I completely agree. Open innovation is one of a portfolio of strategies to pursue innovation. It is a way to get access to distributed knowledge. The key requirement is recognizing that knowledge is broadly available inside and outside the organization. The challenge then becomes how we find ways to access this knowledge. Open innovations, or open source practices, require that companies broadcast information to the outside world that they once thought was proprietary, inviting the outside world to participate in further development.

Consider how open innovation has revolutionized ideas about who should be involved in software development. This revolutionary concept has changed the structure of competition between Microsoft and its competitors. It lets companies like Google get involved because they use open source ideas. We are seeing similar open innovation approaches by various nonprofit organizations, like the Institute for One-World Health.[1] This company's organizers believe they can out-innovate big pharmas that have tight models of how to organize innovation. To develop new medicines to fight infectious diseases, they are pushing for much more collaboration, much more transparency among scientists across fields.

Yet, as we see the open source model take over and produce outstanding results in many different fields, a next question is are we educating leaders and managers to look outside? So much of our curriculum is still focused on control and protection instead of engagement.

Unlearning Competitive Habits

Yves: New ideas about open innovation and agility mean that managers have to unlearn. When I give a seminar on alliances, for example, the unlearning needed is actually more difficult and more important than the learning needed. It is especially important to unlearn taken-for-granted implicit assumptions and behavioral heuristics that assume competitive and uncollaborative environments.

Anne: That is definitely important. Too many managers still think "I cannot be competitive if I am not king."

Karim: The switch to being competitive *and* cooperative involves tapping new ideas inside as much as outside. There are at least as many people hoarding knowledge and not sharing it on the inside as on the outside.

Anne: Another critical area of needed change involves behavior around "not invented here." It is not just that people hoard their own knowledge; they genuinely do not see the good ideas that others have.

Karim: The whole apparatus of unlearning and learning is pretty huge, but it takes time and effort. I think that most people inherently understand that collaboration with varied participants leads to good outcomes, but we need to provide more evidence. There is some nice economic modeling that shows the rewards of collaboration and I hope to provide other kinds of evidence as well. We need to show that working with others is good in practice. A lot of that will come by showing real life examples of organizations and firms that have excelled in different sectors. Their stories will show in a compelling way that there are new ways to organize that can provide competitive advantage. This volume makes a good start on that agenda.

Anne: I agree that the detailed stories you and others provide are helpful, yet I worry that we often "preach to the choir." The purpose of this book is to engage a broad audience, where current evidence may not be convincing enough to change behavior. I've been working on the idea of framing for a long time. A group of academics and practitioners at the FrameWorks Institute suggest that contrary evidence often does not change opinion when people have a strongly rooted way of thinking about a situation.[2] The reformer has to find some (often weak) signals in the way people are thinking now that can serve as a bridge to something new.

Karim: It may be that destruction of the old is required, and then typically you have to wait for the old guard to die. But it could also be that change is the result of a message from the market. This is what I think Microsoft is experiencing. As I say in chapter 10, people in Microsoft are beginning to think in new ways and the impetus for this new framing comes from the market.

Examples of New Ways of Thinking and Working

Anne: Yves, you have been working with Nokia and other large companies for some time. Can you point to firms that are becoming more agile because of messages from the market?

Yves: Some companies definitely are thinking about these issues. In some way Nokia has always been open source; there always was a platform to bring in new innovation and applications. SAP has shifted quite a bit and so has IBM. HP has not had much choice, their market is shifting.

But we have to be careful to distinguish true open source innovation, where companies post problems in areas of interest and call for solutions or proposals about research or application, from collaborative innovation. The latter is often more strategically central to firms, but not open; in fact it operates more like a closed club. IBM develops semiconductor core technologies in a collaborative way with a broad network of partners, but it's not open innovation. When it comes to application areas, from supercomputers to game consoles, then IBM's strategic alliances are focused and exclusive.

Intel is moving more than ever toward open innovation around application areas. They tried a little earlier, but now they are investing heavily in two things. One is trying to anticipate usage models, trying to understand how MBM, their motherboard monitor, and other new technologies might dramatically change the ability of people to use information technology. Their second strong investment is in ecosystems. They are trying to understand the logic of ecosystem development and how a company can get ecosystem players to participate in a process on their own terms and with their own benefits—but in a highly cooperative way.

Back to your point, Karim, Intel is a good example of how it is possible to be both competitive and collaborative. They are very keenly interested in how ecosystems develop and what they need to do to make it happen. They are basically saying "here are the various players with whom we want to be involved, but each will have to participate with their own business system in their own way. Please play by the same rules. We won't make side payments. It's your surface. We will create value collectively, and we will make our best individual effort to capture our share of that value."

Learning to Be Part of a Cooperative/Competitive Ecosystem

Anne: What are you doing to help companies that do not know how to be part of an ecosystem?

Yves: There are two or three keys. Thinking about middle managers, the first thing is making sure they understand complex open business models. That means moving away from ideas like "I make something and then I sell it" or "I buy something as cheap as I can and then I do something with it." It means moving away from a vertical view of transaction to an ecosystem view of value creation. It means moving away from looking for a direct link between market performance and financial performance in the organization's subunits to think through measurements and interdependencies in a more thoughtful and deliberate way than they have in the past. In other words, the analytics and the intellectual issues are important. These points support my comment about unlearning: we need to help managers unlearn the reflexes or almost intuitive behavior of high competition.

Even more important are the behavioral or the emotional issues. We also need to guard ourselves against our human DNA. We tend to make a very quick judgment in a few seconds about friend or foe. When humankind was organized as small tribes that was probably important. Now we need to move away from friend or foe polarities to recognizing friend AND foe at the same time. It is a question of how we can generate some connection, be empathic to another person, without necessarily losing our sense of self-interest. Faced with ambiguity and uncertainty and lack of understanding, can we learn to say "I will find out more before I move backward or forward"? In the face of uncertainty or ambiguity, we should not let our emotions and possible discomfort drive us.

Karim: It's interesting that evolutionary biologists have shown that cooperation is also an important mechanism in evolution. We know that competition among species, within species, and across species is one evolution mechanism, but cooperation at all levels is also part of evolution.

Anne: Right. Cooperation can be seen at other scales too, beginning, so the biologists tell us, with the molecular. We often talk about bees and ants as social beings, but at the human level cooperation can be seen in many things, starting perhaps with raising children and making music.

Karim: Yes, scientists are coming to recognize that in fact cooperation may be deeply embedded. Yet, when we run our organizations, we've been doing the competition bit but not the cooperation bit.

Yves: In management we can build on some of the work by Woody Powell or Bruce Kogut, both of whom have written about networks and knowledge. They help us understand collaboration as a selection mechanism in the context of corporate interactions. The ability to play a useful role in a network further reinforces the position of a firm in that network, making it an increasingly valued partner. Of course other participants might grow worried that a firm's centrality in the network leads to too much power and look for other partners. Conversely, inability to play a useful role also leads to marginalization and exclusion.

Anne: You are saying at the corporate level exactly what Lynda Gratton says at the individual level in chapter 7: the people who make the best contributions to groups have broad contacts and know how to cooperate. The ideas of working to be a valuable partner, and trying to find valuable partners, are themes throughout this volume.

Karim: I would add the notion that communities and markets are actually intertwined. Markets have always emerged out of communities—whether it's a product community or a village, there's always a market there. The result is a system of collaboration and competition at the same time. But how do we understand an ecosystem as both a set of cooperative communities and a set of marketplaces with their competition? I don't think we have it sorted out yet. First, how do we even think about it and, then, how do we enable people to cooperate more effectively at one level while competing at another?

It is instructive to look at SAP. They have set up a software development network of over a million people. Participants pose questions to help solve their problems. At the same time some participants systematically compete against each other. The uncertainty members have to live with is "we are collaborating, and then we are also competing, but if I answer a question from Accenture, which is it?"

I think that good practice like this network is leading theory, but academics can also make a contribution here by exploring how the nexus of communities and markets can be put together. These are complicated situations.

Anne: What would you suggest to people from a company that has not been doing much about ecosystems but want to learn?

Karim: I say start by looking outside the firm's boundary. Look at what users are doing. Look at communities that have formed even without your knowing about them. For example, I was talking at a major food company. People there said "there are no real communities around food." I responded by saying "let's pick a boring, boring food product; let's pick granola as a product." Within half a day we found 300 communities discussing granola, inventing and changing combinations. The food company didn't know about any of them!

So the first thing that people in companies can do is just look outside. Usually there is an iceberg—there's a lot beneath the water, it's just not visible. Then the question becomes when and how do we participate with external communities? Do we embrace them or do we resist them? The initial reaction that I have most often seen is "I don't want to hear about it." But, of course, that's not the right way.

A better reaction by those who want to think about an ecosystem is "do we create our own communities or do we participate in theirs?" That's a strategic choice that you need to think about. People in companies tend to immediately think "how do we engage them in our next generation of products and services? And how do they help us define better what we do?" They also worry that external groups perhaps won't work on strategy in an appropriate way. My advice is to look outside first, and then decide how to participate.

Learning from Lean Environments

Yves: Another idea for helping people learn to be more open or agile is to send them to a real but almost physically threatening environment, or to a highly constrained environment. In the case of business innovations especially, it is necessary to go to places where things are done very differently in order to get information and gain insights. Often the difference in business concept is based on necessity. That's C. K. Prahalad's argument about the bottom of the pyramid: economic necessity becomes a source of invention. For me this is very important.

I sometimes ask "can we take people in this company to a virtual world?" Second Life[3] is the best-known example, but there are many environments that are less constrained than the real physical environment. These are places where it becomes very difficult to make a mark unless you are tremendously innovative; you have to have a completely different concept of how you can do things.

There are also very different real world environments. For example, at a hospital in Bangalore popularly known as the Heart Temple,[4] a visionary MD, Doctor Devi Shetty, created a completely different concept of how to deliver heart surgery, mostly to babies but also to adults. They do so at approximately 10 percent of the cost required in western Europe or in the United States.

If you send people to a setting like this and say "let's understand how this place works," you will find amazing things. For instance, the Heart Temple hires teenage girls from poor villages and turns them into technicians who read images. The basic argument is twofold. First, these are people who are not much involved with the written word, so they are likely to be much better at looking at pictures and images and making sense of them. The second point is that they take very smart but poor girls who might otherwise be tending cows all of their lives and turn them into technicians in striking new medical facilities. For them, it's the chance of their life.

Karim: There is a similar example from the Barefoot College[5] in India. It was founded by social entrepreneur Bunker Roy in 1972, before the world was thinking much about social entrepreneurs. The college trains people (mostly women) from India and a number of other countries to be solar technicians. These are illiterate women, speaking many different languages, of varied ages—from teenagers to grandmothers. Instruction is primarily by example, given the variety of spoken languages, yet within a few days students begin to learn how to electrify their homes and villages. They end up knowing how to install these systems, check circuits, fix problems, and perhaps work on a solar cooker as well. All of a sudden they are doing fairly high-tech jobs.

Anne: I love hearing about these examples, but it also makes sense to look in our backyards. I was driving through a relatively poor Los Angeles community a couple of weeks ago and saw several guys working on a car at the side of the street. It looked like they were doing a major repair—replacing a transmission or something like that! They didn't have a garage, or any other support, but the work was underway. It is very interesting that even in my more "developed" country there are groups of people who are figuring out ways to get things done without the infrastructure most of us take for granted.

Yves: I would love for us to be more innovative. To be honest, I'm not sure that what we do now is that innovative. But what we do at INSEAD and other people do at many other places is this: we organize all kinds of learning expeditions. Often the greatest learning is not anything intellectual or anything to do with a workshop-like context. I remember years ago taking a bunch of people from Nokia to Japan. The most useful experience came from pairing each of the senior people with a young local employee and sending them for an afternoon in an electronic market. The point was partly for senior executives and their guides to better understand the market. Even more important, we wanted the executives to hear one on one what Nokia was doing that was wrong or right in Japan—things that would never have surfaced otherwise, at least not at a senior level.

Actually this is an example of something I think we do fairly well around the world. We understand a lot about basic group leadership training. We often get people to lower some of their defensive mechanisms and come closer to others. Whether it is working as a team, or interacting with a partner, or thinking about innovation as an open and shared process, we succeed when we help people think of strategy as more participative—internally and externally.

Advice to Newcomers

Anne: What would you say to new employees who want to learn how to work in these new ways? What kind of experiences lead to becoming a good manager in a changing world? How would you help your children begin their careers?

Karim: Look at settings where authority does not come from position. Observe how people motivate others in these settings. It is important to learn how to organize people when you don't have authority over them. Some organizations are still very authoritarian, start by looking for a job in other places.

Yves: I would say when you are on a project, you have to evolve into the project. There will be people who are much more senior than you are, whose time and attention are relatively scarce and precious, so you basically have to learn to negotiate.

Anne: It is also important to note that there are many opportunities in the world of open innovation. Younger contributors are more likely to be sought out for their fresh ideas and their contacts with emerging consumer groups. Newcomers should be prepared to offer their opinions, though, of course, they should know that many others are also being contacted for inputs.

Yves: Then it is important to think in terms of varied rewards. While most companies tend to over-rely on a very simplified, mechanistic view of extrinsic reward, if you look at NGOs and similar organizations, you will see they offer some extrinsic compensation, maybe recognition in the community, but there also is a lot of intrinsic motivation—which is important for the world and for the worker.

Karim: Motivation is a huge, important point. A recurring theme in this volume is that intrinsic satisfaction accounts for most of the variance in success. When we ask people why they participate in open innovation projects, extrinsic reward comes through. But the intrinsic part is often the driver of performance, as I describe in more detail in chapter 10. People say "I get involved for fun, for enjoyment, for the internal reward, for the connection."

The Changing Definition of Strategy

Anne: Do you think that improving agility in these and other ways is the next generic strategy, Yves? Do you, Karim, put your bets on open innovation? Is there some other theme—maybe cooperation—that shows where strategy is going as a practice and a field of inquiry?

Yves: If you are referring to Michael Porter's definition, I would say, speaking for myself and my own work, that strategic agility is not a generic strategy. The work I'm doing is around the quality of internal processes, around sense-making, around issue framing, around effective internal dialogue, the quality of internal resource allocation processes, and the mechanisms that allow effective resource allocation. For me, agility is the organizational capability to be more responsive to strategic opportunities, or perhaps a kind of meta-capability, as I explain in chapter 3. It is not linked to any type of substantive generic strategy. In fact it may be a way to transcend and go beyond the categorizations and polarities assumed in generic strategies

It may be that good old generic strategies still apply in some situations, but I think that strategy is a little more random. Go back to history and ask how military breakthroughs happened. When the Russians wanted to defeat the Germans in Stalingrad, they found a spot between Romanian and other Axis units and then aimed their forces at that spot. It was a classic strategic maneuver: they were able to cut supply lines to the Germans fighting in the city. That success is often seen as the true turning point of World War II, and it has been widely studied.

But when you ask generals today how most breakthroughs happen, you tend to get a different answer, pointing to a partly random process. Today's generals will say "well, we probe and probe and probe and when we find a weak spot, we go out with everything we have as fast as we can."

So part of strategic agility is probing for a weak spot and then allocating resources very swiftly. The capacity to do that is an organizational capability. I am more interested in learning how an organization can pour all that they have into a breakthrough once it has been discovered, than in examining the thinking process that precedes that discovery. But whether they discover it intellectually or experimentally, or not at all, does not actually matter unless the ability to mobilize and commit resources is there too.

Of course, opportunities are not always random. There has to be some sense of purpose. Strategists have to know what to do and they have to do it rather than something else. Still, for me, it is more important to have the organizational capability to quickly react to opportunities than to follow some generic idea that tends to become too easily a recipe or an assumption.

Karim: There is a well-established view of strategy as planning—being able to forecast or to predict how things turn out. You are saying in contrast, Yves, that once you see an opportunity, strategy is knowing how to go after it.

Yves: Probing is not exactly random, but strategy is an art of data analysis and probability assessment, and some of that is intuitive, judgmental, and collective.

Karim: But you want to add some randomness, some variety, into your probing strategies?

Yves: You see exactly the point about more open strategy. Agile, open companies are able to probe across a wider front, get more signals of weakness and opportunity. That is difficult for companies to do because people tend to focus. People want to concentrate on what they do best in areas they know well. As we said at the beginning of this conversation, people want to feel comfortable and tend to concentrate on what has made them successful in the past.

Karim: Let me give an example. I just finished a case on the use of prediction markets within Google. Prediction markets are one way to gain access to knowledge distributed inside of the firm. In Google anybody can propose a market if there is a decision or an outcome they care about. For instance, they can ask how many people will be using product X within the next six months. If they get an accurate answer, it helps capacity planning, and so on.

Our research shows that the mechanism works extremely well. It aggregates knowledge and is highly decisive. But managers at Google, a company that is widely praised for being innovative, just do not want to use predictive markets. Because all of a sudden there is a mechanism that is helping make decisions—which is the managers' role. Most managers think "I have to be at the hub of information to manage. I have to be able to say exactly what is going on." If there is an amorphous mass of people in the company (someone in China, someone in India, someone in Palo Alto, etc.) providing weak signals that are aggregated to provide an answer that may be contrary to what you think as a manager, how do you reconcile that? Many managers are saying "it's my job to be the one who collects all information, since I make decisions about it, and present it to the executive with my perspective. If that is taken away from me, what is my job?"

We found tremendous resistance to using this very elegant aggregation device. So we are back to this: within an organization there is a great distribution of knowledge, but the people who are in charge are afraid to access it.

Yves: My experience suggests that people also fear open innovation and open strategizing because they do not know when and how to open up without running too much risk. They get into a fear mode. To put it another way, there is a risk from good ideas because of their originality, so democratizing innovation requires bravery.

Karim: And if brave leaders do say "let's try opening up," their lawyers often say "no, don't do it!"

Anne: Given these problems, what is the end of your Google case about prediction markets, Karim?

Karim: We leave it as an introduction to aggregating knowledge. We hope people talk about the real tension prediction markets create. This volume presents some new technologies or approaches—they are not really new, but they are available in new ways—that challenge traditional means of organizing. The question becomes what should intelligent managers do? How should they engage with new technologies for accessing distributed knowledge? My answer is to embrace them, try them out, and learn from them.

Future Absorption of Open Innovation?

Anne: We have neatly come back to open innovation. At an early meeting of the Peter Pribilla network members agreed that open innovation is important because it expands the solution space for innovation. Over time we have concluded that open innovation does even more. The immediate purpose may be new and more varied products, services, and experiences, delivered more quickly, but the larger positive effect is opening organizational mindsets, processes, and structures. When that happens, open innovation can make a significant contribution to increased organizational agility—your very powerful word, Yves.

However, our conversation today suggests to me that open innovation may have a limited life span as a separate topic for strategists. Today's world clearly requires more contributors from inside and outside organizations who can work in more encompassing ways. We have been saying that the next questions are about balance. When to be open and when to protect? What to unlearn so that new learning can take place? How to be both cooperative and competitive? Is it better to dip quickly into a broad ecosystem for new ideas or to build a smaller number of more enduring relationships over time? Organizations need experience with open innovation to answer these and other questions, but perhaps these experiences are best seen as the first rungs on a new ladder—once managers climb them, open innovation will not need much separate attention.

Notes

1. http://www.oneworldhealth.org/ (accessed May 1, 2010).

2. See, for example, the Framing 101 toolkit available at http://www.frameworksinstitute.org/assets/files/PDF/FramingPublicIssuesfinal.pdf (accessed May 1, 2010).

3. http://secondlife.com/?v=1.1 (accessed May 1, 2010).

4. http://www.indiahospitaltour.com/narayana-hrudayalaya-heart-hospital-bangalore.htm (accessed May 1, 2010).

5. http://www.barefootcollege.org/ (accessed May 1, 2010).

References and Further Reading

Coles, P. A., K. R. Lakhani, and A. P. McAfee. 2008. Prediction markets at Google. Case 607–088. Harvard Business School.

Doz, Y. L., and M. Kosonen. 2008. The dynamics of strategic agility: Nokia's rollercoaster experience. *California Management Review* 50 (3): 95–118.

Doz, Y. L., and G. Hamel. 1998. *Alliance Advantage: The Art of Creating Value through Partnering*. Boston: Harvard Business School Press.

Doz, Y. L. 1996. The evolution of cooperation in strategic alliances: Initial conditions or learning processes? *Strategic Management Journal* 17: 55–83.

Feller, J., B. Fitzgerald, S. Hissam, and K. R. Lakhani, eds. 2005. *Perspectives on Free and Open Source Software*. Cambridge: MIT Press.

Huff, A. S., and K. Möslein. 2004. An agenda for understanding individual leadership in corporate leadership systems. In C. Cooper, ed., *Leadership and Management in the 21st Century: Business Challenges of the Future*. Oxford: Oxford University Press, 248–70.

Huff, A., D. Tranfield, and J. van Aken. 2006. Management as a design science, mindful of art and surprise: A conversation between Anne Huff, David Tranfield and Joan van Aken. *Journal of Management Inquiry* 15 (4): 413–24.

Kogut, B. 2008. *Knowledge, Options, and Institutions*. Oxford: Oxford University Press.

Lakhani, K. R., and L. B. Jeppesen. 2007. Getting unusual suspects to solve R&D puzzles. *Harvard Business Review* 8 (5): 30–32.

Lakhani, K. R., and A. P. McAfee 2007. *Wikipedia (A)*. Multimedia/video case 607–712. Harvard Business School.

Porter, M. 1980. Generic competitive strategies. In *Competitive Strategy: Techniques for Analyzing Industries and Competitors*. New York: Free Press, 34–46.

Powell, W. W., D. R. White, K. W. Koput, and J. Owen-Smith. 2005. Network dynamics and field evolution: The growth of interorganizational collaboration in the life sciences. *American Journal of Sociology* 110 (4): 1132–1205.

Powell, W. 1990. Neither market nor hierarchy: Network forms of organization. *Research in Organizational Behavior* 12: 295–336.

Powell, W. W., K. Koput, and L. Smith-Doerr. 1996. Technological change and the locus of innovation: Networks of learning in biotechnology. *Administrative Science Quarterly* 41: 116–45.

Prahalad, C. K. 2005. *The Fortune at the Bottom of the Pyramid*. Upper Saddle River, NJ: Pearson (Wharton School Publishing).

Peter and Hannelore Pribilla's Vision for Practical Research

Ralf Reichwald

We collaborate in a worldwide network of knowledge and learning. Our corporate culture is shaped by its diversity of people, cultures, open dialogue, mutual respect, defined goals, and decisive leadership.
—Peter Pribilla, 2003

The Peter Pribilla Foundation was founded in July 2005 by Hannelore Pribilla as part of the corporate body of the Technische Universität München (TUM). The foundation supports research and teaching in the fields of innovation and leadership.

Peter Pribilla was born on the 11th of June, 1941. He studied Communications Engineering at the Technische Universität München (TUM). After graduating with a Masters of Engineering degree in 1968, he joined the engineering conglomerate Siemens. After working in several different Siemens units, he became president of the subsidiary Rolm Communications in Santa Clara, California from 1993 to 1996, then a member of the Executive Management Board of Siemens in 1997.

Peter Pribilla was also one of TUM's most influential corporate partners. In addition to numerous guest lectures, he taught courses on innovation and leadership for a number of years. In recognition of his many contributions in research, teaching, and

administrative advice, he became an honorary TUM professor in 1997. We were just completing a joint study on corporate leadership at the time of his untimely death in August 2003.

The activities of the foundation in his honor are based on the content and style of Peter Pribilla's very fruitful interactions with TUM. We are fostering personal connections among business people and academics to advance understanding of the leadership of innovation—a critical subject in today's globalizing economy.

Hannelore Pribilla was born on the 26th of May, 1942, in Dresden. After studies in mathematics, she began to work as a member of the pioneer research and development group at the IT department in Siemens AG. From 1997 Hannelore Pribilla was a member of the research group at the Institute for Information, Organization and Management at TUM. As a member of the academic family she was interested in the research works of our doctoral students, advised doctoral theses, and supported the team in uncertain times.

One of Hannelore Pribilla's main research fields involved human relations and the computer. In this and other areas she established contacts between scientists at Siemens AG and researchers at different universities. In the 1980s she was involved in numerous projects on the "future of work in a computerized world." In the 1990s at the TUM, Hannelore Pribilla was one of the founders of the "forum of telecooperation" together with Kathrin Möslein and Johann Schlichter. In 1992 she initiated an important research project in cooperation with her husband, Peter Pribilla, in the field of top management communications. This empirical research project focused on the "application of new media in telecommunications and their effects on the working environment of top level management." One output of this project was the book authored by Peter Pribilla, Ralf Reichwald, and Robert Goecke: *Telecommunication in Management—Strategies for a Global Competition,* published by Schäffer-Poeschel in 1996.

We are very pleased to follow the pioneering footsteps of two individuals who successfully contributed to both practice and academic study in this book.

Contributors

Anne Sigismund Huff is Visiting Professor and Director of Research Development at the National University of Ireland Maynooth and an academic director of the Center for Leading Innovation and Cooperation (CLIC) at HHL–Leipzig Graduate School of Management. She was founding director of the Advanced Institute of Management Research (AIM) at the London Business School, with prior appointments at the Technical University of Munich and the Universities of Colorado, Illinois, and UCLA. She held various leadership positions at the Academy of Management, an association of management researchers with 19,500 members from 110 nations, and was president in 1998–99. She was awarded an honorary doctorate from Jönköping University, Sweden in 2008. Her research interests focus on open innovation, strategic change, and the processes of academic research and publication.

Kathrin M. Möslein is Professor of Information Systems at the School of Business and Economics at the University of Erlangen-Nuremberg and Professor of Management and member of the team of directors at the Center for Leading Innovation and Cooperation (CLIC) at HHL–Leipzig Graduate School of Management. She held prior appointments as Associate Director of the Advanced Institute of Management Research (AIM) at the London Business School from 2003 to 2005, Vice President of the European Academy of Management (EURAM) from 2006 to 2012, and Research Dean at the University of Erlangen-Nuremberg from 2007 to 2012. Currently Kathrin serves as member of the Business School Panel for the UK REF 2014 as well as member of the advisory boards of the Peter Pribilla Foundation at the Technische Universität München (TUM), the Fraunhofer IIS-SCS, Erlangen, and the Cambridge Service Alliance (CSA) at the University of Cambridge. Her current research focuses on innovation, cooperation, and leadership systems.

Ralf Reichwald is Professor of Organization, Innovation, and Management at HHL–Leipzig Graduate School of Management and Academic Director of HHL's Center for Leading Innovation and Cooperation (CLIC). From 1990 to 2009 he has been head of the Institute for Information, Organization, and Management at the Technische Universität München (TUM), from 2002 to 2005 Dean of the new founded TUM–School of Management, and from 2005 to 2009 Academic Director of the TUM–Executive Program.

Furthermore from 1991 to 1993 he was Founding Dean of the Faculty of Business Administration at the Technische Universität–Bergakademie Freiberg, Saxony. The university awarded him an honorary doctorate in 1994. Since 1998 he has been teaching as permanent Visiting Professor at the University of Tunis EI Manar, École Nationale d'Ingénieurs de Tunis (ENIT). In 2006 the University of Tunis EI Manat awarded him with the honorary degree, "Professeur honoris causa." In 2009 the Technische Universtät München awarded him with the honorary title, "Emeritus of Excellence."

Nizar Abdelkafi is a Senior Researcher and Head of the unit "Business Models and Services" at the Fraunhofer Center for Central and Eastern Europe (MOEZ) and lecturer at the University of Leipzig. He received his PhD in business administration from Hamburg University of Technology. He has also been a lecturer at MIP, the School of Management of Politecnico di Milano, Italy, and at the National Engineering School of Tunis. His main research interests include the study of business model innovation, service management, and the application of new methods and tools in higher education. He has published his research in two books, six journal articles, and many conference papers and book chapters.

John Bessant holds the Chair in Innovation and Entrepreneurship at the University of Exeter Business School. He has advised a number of companies, various national governments, and several international bodies—including the United Nations, the World Bank, and the OECD. Four recent books summarize key aspects of his research for academics, practicing managers, and students: *Managing Innovation,* now in its fourth edition (Wiley, 2009), and *Innovation and Entrepreneurship* (second edition, Wiley, 2011), both with Joe Tidd, *Innovation* (Dorling Kindersley, 2009), and *Creating Wealth with Knowledge*, with Tim Venables (Edward Elgar, 2008). Other details can be found at http://business-school.exeter.ac.uk/about/whoswho.

Yves Doz is the Solvay Chaired Professor of Technological Innovation and Professor of Business Strategy at INSEAD. His teaching and consulting focus on strategic alliances, innovation and corporate entrepreneurship, and on the design and implementation of competitive revitalization programs. His research on the strategy and organization of multinational companies in high-technology industries has led to numerous books and articles, most recently *Fast Strategy: How Strategic Agility Will Help You Stay Ahead of the Game* (Wharton School Publishing, 2008). His co-author, Dr. Mikko Kosonen, is currently head of the Finish National Fund for Innovation, and until recently the chief strategy officer at Nokia.

Johann Füller (johann.fueller@hyve.de) is CEO of HYVE AG, an innovation and community company, and lecturer at the Innsbruck University School of Management, Austria. In line with his research focus, he regularly gives guest lectures about open innovation, community based innovation, virtual co-creation, and user generated brands. Johann has published more than 60 articles in journals such as *Journal of Product Innovation Management, Journal of Business Research, MIS Quarterly, Harvard Business Manager,* and *Technovation.* As CEO of HYVE AG, Johann consults for top corporations on the development of customer focused innovations.

Lynda Gratton is a Professor of Management Practice at London Business School and founder of the Hot Spots Movement. She has written six books and numerous academic articles and is considered one of the world's authorities on people in organizations. In 2007 she was ranked by *The Times* as one of the top 20 Business Thinkers in the world, and in 2008 *The Financial Times* selected her as the business thinker most likely to make a real difference over the next decade. She was also in the top two of the *Human Resources Magazine*'s "HR Top 100: Most Influential" poll and actively advises companies across the world.

Rudolf Gröger was from 2001 to 2006 the CEO of O_2, the fourth and initially the smallest mobile phone service in the German market. Open information was a key aspect of turning O_2 around and he won many awards for the effort. In 2006 the year O_2 was acquired in the largest all-cash takeover ever experienced in the telecommunications industry, the company was listed as one of the top 100 places to work in Europe. A member of several scientific and advisory boards in Bavaria, he was awarded an honorary doctorate from the Technical University of Munich in 2006. In December 2009 Dr. Gröger became the president of the Munich Business School.

Julia Hautz is an Assistant Professor at the Department of Strategic Management, Marketing and Tourism at the Innsbruck University School of Management, Austria. She received her doctoral degree in Social and Economic Sciences from the University of Innsbruck. In her research she focuses on investigating online innovation communities and on user innovation from a social network perspective.

Katja Hutter is an Assistant Professor at the Department of Strategic Management, Marketing and Tourism at the Innsbruck University School of Management, Austria. She holds a doctoral degree in Social and Economic Sciences from the University of Innsbruck. Her research focus is on innovation management, online innovation communities, co-creation, and user-generated content.

Christoph Ihl is an Assistant Professor at the Technology and Innovation Management Group of RWTH Aachen University, Germany. He holds a doctoral degree in Business Administration from the Technical University of Munich. His research focus is on firms' organizing for innovation, technology transfer and commercialization, and user innovation and co-creation.

Thomas Lackner is Head of the Open Innovation Program at the Chief Technology Office of Siemens. He has spent more than twenty years at Siemens in various management positions such as Vice President Transport Telematics at the headquarter of Siemens One, CEO and founder of the Siemens Technology Accelerator GmbH (STA) in Munich, and head of several departments within Siemens Corporate Technology, Siemens Traffic Control Systems, and Siemens Information and Communication Networks. Before joining Siemens he worked for Philips and for the Ministry for Science and Research in Vienna, Austria. In 1982 he was awarded the postdoctoral fellowship of the Max Kade Foundation, which enabled him to work as a postdoctoral fellow at MIT in Cambridge. Dr. Lackner is a frequent speaker within Siemens and to outside groups on innovation-related subjects.

Karim R. Lakhani is an Associate Professor in the Technology and Operations Management Unit at Harvard Business School. His scholarly work focuses on the management of technological innovation and product development in firms and communities, with special attention given to the emergence of open source software communities and their unique innovation and product development strategies. He is co-editor of *Perspectives on Free and Open Source Software* (MIT Press, 2005) and cofounder of the MIT-based Open Source research community and web portal. Professor Lakhani has been recently quoted in *Business Week*, the *New York Times*, *Inc.*, *Fast Company*, *Science*, and the *Washington Post* in articles that address the movement of innovation to the edges of organizations. The word identifying his blog, http://spoudaiospaizen.net/, can be translated as "serious play."

Anne-Katrin Neyer is Head of the Strategy and Organization Research group at the Fraunhofer MOEZ (Leipzig). She received her PhD in International Management from the WU Wien and her venia legendi (Habilitation) from the University of Erlangen-Nuremberg. She was a postdoctoral research fellow at the UK's Advanced Institute of Management Research at London Business School. Dr. Neyer is Research Fellow at the Center for Leading Innovation and Cooperation (CLIC) at HHL–Leipzig Graduate

School of Management and German National Representative in the board of the European Academy of Management. Her major research interests are to understand the "heart" of social interactions (e.g., knowledge dynamics, sense-making processes) and, normatively, how to manage, organize, and lead social interactions in newly emerging organizational forms.

Frank Piller is Professor of Management and Director of the Technology and Innovation Management Group of RWTH Aachen University, Germany. He also is a Co-director of the MIT Smart Customization Group at the MIT Design Lab. He has a worldwide reputation for research on strategies of customer-centric value creation, including investigation of mass customization, personalization, user innovation, and customer co-creation. As an expert in these areas he is frequently quoted in the *New York Times*, *The Economist*, CNN, and other media. His blog, http://mass-customization.blogs.com, is a major source of information on mass customization and customer driven value creation. He consults and provides executive workshops to large and small companies interested in serving their customers better by using customer-centric strategies. Additional information can be found at http://tim.rwth-aachen.de/piller

Mitchell M. Tseng is the founding Department Head of Industrial Engineering at Hong Kong University of Science and Technology and Director of both the Advanced Manufacturing Institute and the Zhejiang Advanced Manufacturing Institute at UST. He is also Adjunct Professor of the MIT–Zaragoza International Logistics Program. He started his career in industry as a manufacturing engineer and progressed through several senior management positions at Xerox and Digital Equipment Corporation before holding faculty positions in the United States at the University of Illinois at Champaign-Urbana and MIT. His research interests focus on technology for mass customization and personalization, systems integration, design, and manufacturing automation. Further details can be found at http://www.ielm.ust.hk/dfaculty/tseng/.

Catharina van Delden is an entrepreneur and co-founder of the leading open innovation enabler innosabi GmbH, a company that develops methodologies and platforms for companies interested in open innovation. The company's co-creation projects on Facebook are based in part on the research reported in this book. The company's social network platform, unserAller, which means "all of us" in German, facilitates the development of new consumer products.

Eric von Hippel is Professor of Technological Innovation in the MIT Sloan School of Management, and also a Professor in MIT's Engineering Systems Division. He specializes in research related to the nature and economics of distributed and open innovation. He also develops and teaches about practical methods that individuals, open user communities, and firms can apply to improve their product and service development processes. An influential review of this work can be found in *Democratizing Innovation*, published by the MIT Press in 2005, which is also available as a free pdf download from MITPress.com and other websites under a Creative Commons license. References to academic articles and other resources can be found at http://web.mit.edu/evhippel/.

Bettina von Stamm is founder of the Innovation Leadership Forum, co-founder of the Discontinuous Innovation Lab, a frequent lecturer in advanced degree programs around the world, and a consultant to major corporations and public organizations. Her PhD from London Business School on complexity in new product development was followed by several publications and three books: *The Innovation Wave: Meeting the Corporate Challenge* (Wiley, 2002), *Managing Innovation, Design and Creativity*, now in its second edition (Wiley 2008), and *The Future of Innovation*, with Anna Trifilova (Gower, 2009). More information about the Innovation Leadership Forum and its activities can be found at http://www.innovationleadershipforum.org.

Andrei Villarroel held appointments as Assistant Professor at Católica-Lisbon School of Business and Economics, Research Affiliate at the MIT Center for Collective Intelligence, and Visiting Faculty at the University of Pennsylvania Organizational Dynamics at the time of this writing. He was also appointed International Faculty Fellow at MIT Sloan School of Management and Visiting Scholar at the MIT Center for Collective Intelligence. His research focuses on the organization of open and distributed approaches to work and innovation beyond the formal boundaries of the firm, also referred to as "strategic crowdsourcing." He was recognized with two consecutive Best Paper Awards, in 2006 and 2007, from the North American Association for Computational Social and Organizational Science (NAACSOS), and in 2008, he was awarded a postdoctoral fellowship from the Swiss National Science Foundation. He holds a PhD in management of technology and entrepreneurship from the Swiss Federal Institute of Technology (EPFL) and a master of science from Carnegie Mellon University (CMU).

Nancy Wünderlich is a Professor of Service Management at the University of Paderborn, Germany. She received her doctorate from TU München and during her studies also was a visiting PhD scholar in the department of marketing at Arizona State University. Her research focuses on innovation marketing, technology-based services, and customer collaboration. Her dissertation about the perception and acceptance of technology-mediated remote services received awards from the American Marketing Association, the Academy of Marketing Science, the Society of Marketing Advances, and the German Ministry of Research and Education.

Index